D0504909

A Democratic Audit of the European Union

One Europe or Several?

Series Editor: **Helen Wallace**

The One Europe or Several? series examines contemporary processes of political, security, economic, social and cultural change across the European continent, as well as issues of convergence/divergence and prospects for integration and fragmentation. Many of the books in the series are cross-country comparisons; others evaluate the European institutions, in particular the European Union and NATO, in the context of eastern enlargement.

Titles include:

Sarah Birch
ELECTORAL SYSTEMS AND POLITICAL TRANSFORMATION IN POST-COMMUNIST EUROPE

Sarah Birch, Frances Millard, Marina Popescu and Kieran Williams
EMBODYING DEMOCRACY
Electoral System Design in Post-Communist Europe

Andrew Cottey, Timothy Edmunds and Anthony Forster (*editors*)
DEMOCRATIC CONTROL OF THE MILITARY IN POSTCOMMUNIST EUROPE
Guarding the Guards

Anthony Forster, Timothy Edmunds and Andrew Cottey (*editors*)
THE CHALLENGE OF MILITARY REFORM IN POSTCOMMUNIST EUROPE
Building Professional Armed Forces

Anthony Forster, Timothy Edmunds and Andrew Cottey (*editors*)
SOLDIERS AND SOCIETIES IN POSTCOMMUNIST EUROPE
Legitimacy and Change

Andrew Jordan
THE EUROPEANIZATION OF BRITISH ENVIRONMENTAL POLICY
A Departmental Perspective

Christopher Lord
A DEMOCRACTIC AUDIT OF THE EUROPEAN UNION

Valsamis Mitsilegas, Jorg Monar and Wyn Rees
THE EUROPEAN UNION AND INTERNAL SECURITY
Guardian of the People?

Helen Wallace (*editor*)
INTERLOCKING DIMENSIONS OF EUROPEAN INTEGRATION

One Europe or Several?
Series Standing Order ISBN 0–333–94630–8
(*outside North America only*)

You can receive future titles in this series as they are published by placing a standing order. Please contact your bookseller or, in case of difficulty, write to us at the address below with your name and address, the title of the series and the ISBN quoted above.

Customer Services Department, Macmillan Distribution Ltd, Houndmills, Basingstoke, Hampshire RG21 6XS, England

---

A Democratic Audit of the European Union

Christopher Lord
Jean Monnet Professor of European Politics,
University of Leeds, UK

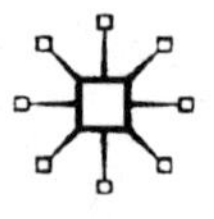

First published 2004 by
PALGRAVE MACMILLAN
Houndmills, Basingstoke, Hampshire RG21 6XS and
175 Fifth Avenue, New York, N.Y. 10010
Companies and representatives throughout the world

PALGRAVE MACMILLAN is the global academic imprint of the Palgrave Macmillan division of St. Martin's Press, LLC and of Palgrave Macmillan Ltd. Macmillan® is a registered trademark in the United States, United Kingdom and other countries. Palgrave is a registered trademark in the European Union and other countries.

ISBN 0–333–99282–2

This book is printed on paper suitable for recycling and made from fully managed and sustained forest sources.

A catalogue record for this book is available from the British Library.

Library of Congress Cataloging-in-Publication Data
Lord, Christopher
A Democratic Audit of the European Union / Christopher Lord.
p. cm. – (One Europe or Several?)
Includes bibliographical references and index.
ISBN 0–333–99282–2 (cloth)
1. European Union. 2. Democracy. I. Title. II. Series.

JN40.L67 2004
341.242′2—dc22 2003062316

10 9 8 7 6 5 4 3 2 1
13 12 11 10 09 08 07 06 05 04

Printed and bound in Great Britain by
Antony Rowe Ltd, Chippenham and Eastbourne

Contents

List of Tables and Figures

Tables

Figures

List of Abbreviations

AEM	Association of Mountainous Regions
AEBR	Assembly of European Border Regions
AFSJ	Area of Freedom, Security and Justice
ARUP	Assembly of the Outermost Regions
CALRE	Conference of European Legislative Assemblies
CAP	Common Agricultural Policy
CEMR	Conference of Peripheral Mountainous Regions of Europe
CFSP	Common Foreign and Security Policy
CoR	Committee of the Regions
COREPER	Committee of Permanent Representatives
COSAC	Conference of the Parliaments of the EU (European and national)
CPRM	Conference of Peripheral Coastal Regions
DG	Directorates-General of the European Commission
EAC	European Affairs Committees (of National Parliaments)
ECB	European Central Bank
ECHR	European Convention on Human Rights (Council of Europe)
ECJ	European Court of Justice
EDD	Europe of Democracies and Diversities
EFA	European Free Alliance (Regionalist Parties)
EFGP	European Federation of Green Parties
ELDR	European Liberal Democratic and Reform Party
EMU	Economic and Monetary Union
EP	European Parliament
EPP	European People's Party
ESDP	European Security and Defence Policy
EUL	European United Left
Eurojust	European Authority for Criminal Justice Adjudication
Europol	European Police Office
IGC	Intergovernmental Conference
INTEREG	Inter-regional Agreements
JHA	Justice and Home Affairs
MEPs	Members of European Parliament
OECD	Organisation for Economic Co-operation and Development
OJ	Official Journal of the European Union

PES	Party of European Socialists
REGLEG	Co-ordination of Regions with Legislative Powers
QMV	Qualified Majority Voting
TEU	Treaty on European Union
UEN	Union for a Europe of Nations

1
What is a Democratic Audit?

Introduction

It is commonly remarked that the European Union (EU) is a political system in democratic deficit. But what is the nature of that deficit? Is it offset by any democratic achievements? Do any democratic qualities or deficiencies pertain to the EU's political system as a whole, or to some parts of it more than others? Does the Union perform worse or better in relation to some attributes of democratic rule than others? Does it even make much sense to debate the presence or absence of a democratic deficit at all? Do answers to these questions vary with which model of democracy is used, and, if so, does that mean those who ask 'how democratic is the EU?' need also to have some clear idea of why they believe the EU ought to be democratic in the first place?

Questions such as these are asked with increasing frequency in a Union that touches ordinary lives, demands sacrifices, allocates values and struggles for legitimation. The argument of this book is that the attempts to answer them can be significantly improved by a particular approach to the assessment of the democratic qualities of political systems known as democratic auditing. Democratic auditing was first developed by David Beetham and Stuart Weir in their study (Weir and Beetham, 1999) *Political Power and Democratic Control in Britain: The Democratic Audit of the United Kingdom*. It has since been used to assess democracy in other political systems as diverse as Bangladesh, El Salvador, Italy, Kenya, Malawi, New Zealand and South Korea (Beetham *et al.*, 2002).

This book is, however, the first to attempt to apply democratic auditing to the EU, or, indeed, to any process of governance beyond the state. This chapter begins by identifying what might reasonably be expected of any method for assessing democracy in the EU and ends by introducing democratic auditing as a possible solution. Chapter 2 then considers how a Democratic Audit should proceed in the case of the EU. The rest of the book undertakes an illustrative Audit of the Union against each of the following attributes of democratic rule: citizenship, rights and participation (Chapter 3) consent (Chapter 4) representation (Chapter 5); accountability (Chapters 6–7) and constitutionalism (Chapter 8). In other words the assessment undertaken here will be 'norm-driven' rather than 'institution-driven', though, it is hoped, students of the intricacies of EU decision-making will also find much to satisfy that particular peccadillo, since, for reasons that will be explained, this book defends an 'input' over an 'output' orientated approach to democracy assessment.

Why undertake a Democratic Audit of the EU?

The goal of undertaking a Democratic Audit of the EU implies that it is important to have a reliable means of assessing democracy in the EU and that current methods are not quite up to the job. This section seeks to vindicate these claims.

One reason for wanting to develop methods of assessing its democratic performance is that the Union is the best case study available to us in a debate of central importance to how we think about democracy in its contemporary international setting. On one side of the debate in question are those who hold that democracy can only prosper within the state. On the other are those, like David Held (1997), who, ask whether the nation state can retain its place at the 'centre of democratic thought' under conditions where it no longer corresponds to 'communities of fate', or, in other words, to many of the processes and institutions that shape the 'life chances' of ordinary citizens. The EU is a good case study in the difficulties that rule beyond the state create democracy and, conversely, in any original ways by which democracy might be delivered from such a setting. It also prompts reflection on whether different meanings and expectations ought to attach to democracy inside and outside the state (Schmitter, 2001).

If such enquiries into the lessons that the Union holds for democracy beyond the state are to be open-ended and even-handed, they require tools of analysis that are as capable of analysing the presence as the absence of democracy from the EU. It is, therefore, reassuring that recent research has moved beyond a mere lamentation of democratic deficits. One (normative) literature has considered which model of democracy should be used in the case of the EU. As will be explained in Chapter 2, a number of pair-wise choices have been considered: consensus vs. majoritarian democracy; consociational vs. other forms of consensus democracy; direct vs. indirect democracy; liberal vs. republican approaches and so on. A second literature has investigated how far democratic processes have already developed in the European arena and how agents have responded to them. It includes studies of European elections, the powers of the European parliament (EP) and the scrutiny roles of national parliaments. A third literature has probed how far preconditions for democratic politics exist (or are ever likely to exist) at Union level. It has centred on political identity, citizen capabilities in relation to Union institutions, and the possibilities and problems of creating a European public space. Each of these lines of enquiry lays the groundwork for an assessment of democracy in the EU in its different way. The first by clarifying what would count as a democratic EU. The second by developing rigorous tools to describe and explain putative forms of democratic process in the European arena. And the third by analysing just how much democracy is reasonable to expect of the Union under any given set of constraints.

A further motive for wanting to study democracy and the EU relates to the profound choices of institutional design currently faced by the Union and all those who are affected by it as a system of rule. At the Nice European Council of December 2000 the heads of government committed themselves to a debate on the future of Europe leading up to an Intergovernmental Conference (IGC) in 2004 that would agree a new Treaty. At the Laeken European Council a year later, they designated a Convention composed of their own representatives, those of the Commission, and those of the EP and national parliaments, to deliberate in public on what options for the future of Europe should be put to the IGC. *Inter alia* the Convention was asked to consider means of improving the democratic legitimacy and control of the main Union institutions, and of developing a European public area (sic.) (Council of the European Union, 2001b).

A standard interpretation is that democratisation burst suddenly on to the EU's agenda of institutional change when the Maastricht ratification crisis of the early 1990s revealed that the stakeholders in a legitimate Union could no longer assume the 'permissive consensus' of the public. It is by identifying the inadequacies of this as history that we can best understand what contemporary challenges of institutional design now require of any academic method for appraising the democratic performance of the Union. Whatever the combination of a quickening pace and a broken consensus did to raise democratisation up the Union's agenda during the 1990s it can hardly be attributed with putting it there in the first place. Direct elections to the EP were first agreed in 1974 and held in 1979. The powers of the EPs have been steadily strengthening in the direction of bicameralism with the Council since 1987. Serious attempts at national parliamentary scrutiny have existed since the first enlargement in 1973. Elements of 'interest representation' have existed from the beginning.

The result is that the debate on how the EU should be further democratised is far from abstract. It is as if a series of experiments have already been set in motion in a somewhat tentatively assembled laboratory for democracy beyond the state. Different ideas of how to proceed further involve different reactions to feedback and rival claims of what works and what does not. Democracy assessment is, therefore, already at the heart of the debate about how the Union should be developed further. Yet there are at least three reasons to question the adequacy of present methods to the task of policy prescription. The following paragraphs elaborate.

The first difficulty is whether methods for assessing the whole and the parts – the EU's overall political system and its particular institutions and processes – are sufficiently linked. In early debates, it was the EU as a whole that was widely said to be in democratic deficit. Although it is only to be welcomed that academic research has moved on from treating the EU as a single unit of assessment, it leaves unresolved the level of analysis problem at the heart of any attempt to appraise the democratic qualities of the EU. One-by-one appraisal of policy instruments or institutions risks excessive disaggregation by failing to pick up those democratic qualities or problems that arise from interactions between the multiple institutions and practices of the Union. What appears to be deficient or satisfactory in the performance of a particular institution may be the other way round once it is remembered how often outcomes are shaped by interactions between Union institutions as much as by the internal procedures of any one body. Yet, judgements about the EU as a whole run the converse risk of excessive aggregation in so far as they are unable to discriminate where in the Union's institutional order, and in relation to which aspects of democracy, problems are most acute. Any method of assessment thus has to achieve the difficult task of being both discriminating and holistic: of cross-checking appraisals at a level of single institutions with those of the political system as a whole.

A second concern is whether there is sufficient integration between analysis of the democratic deficiencies of the EU on the one hand and investigation of its democratic qualities on the other. If the last paragraph indicated the need for any assessment to take account of the internal complexity of the EU, this implies it will also have to accommodate the internal complexity of democracy itself. Democratic rule often involves trade-offs between values associated with democracy itself, and between democratic and non-democratic values. Those trade-offs may, in turn, be made more acute by technological limits to what is institutionally and socially feasible in any place at any one time. Any method of assessment should ideally be able to distinguish 'pure costs' or 'pure deficits' in democratic standards from those that are 'compensated' to the extent that they are incurred in the course of delivering other qualities of government. This is important where the trade-offs in question have been freely chosen by citizens or are defensible in terms of their known values. It is also especially pertinent to the EU. As will be seen later, there are reasons to believe its democratic deficiencies and qualities are internally related in ways that make it difficult to comprehend the one without the other (Lord, 1998a, p. 1).

A third difficulty is whether the normative and empirical study of democracy and the EU take sufficient account of one another's findings. As Richard Bellamy and Dario Castiglione argue (2000, p. 65), much of the empirical literature just assumes what is by no means self-evident, namely that the EU ought to be democratic. Without adequate justification of why this should be so, it is unclear what purpose is served by empirical enquiries into how democratic the EU is in practice. More, however, than being dependent on normative analysis for its point, empirical study relies on it for its direction. The obvious difficulty here is that what counts as a good measure or test will vary with views of how the EU ought to be democratised, if at all (Katz, 2001).

Many shortcomings in present understanding of democracy and the EU can be attributed to attempts to dispense with normative preliminaries to empirical research. Some accounts use one model of democracy to denounce missing standards that may be in the process of being delivered by some other approach to democratic governance that is, arguably, better suited to the EU. Others fail to distinguish necessary and sufficient conditions for democratic rule. An example is the recent popularity of the notion that the distance between Union policies and 'median' citizen preferences can be taken as a measure of the democratic deficit (Crombez *et al.*, 2000, p. 379n). Since even a technocracy or benign dictatorship could achieve an efficient alignment of policy outcomes with citizens' desires this cannot be a sufficient test of democracy.

Still other pitfalls are associated with attempts to evaluate the EU by analogy with other political systems. The main example is implicit in the classic definition of the democratic deficit as a net loss of democracy that comes from transferring powers from state to Union institutions without also democratising the second to the standards of the first. The neatness of this definition gives it a surface plausibility. Yet, on reflection it is full of difficulties. Use of the state as an implied benchmark for a democratic EU is open to the objection that standards of democratic governance may be justifiably different between state and non-state political systems, national and trans-national ones. It is perfectly coherent to believe that one model of democracy is best for the state and a different one – or none at all – is best for the EU.

Moreover, there is a sense in which the classic definition is an unattainable test. Since its Member States have responded differently to unavoidable trade-offs between standards associated with democratic rule, the EU cannot reproduce all the standards to be found in all its Member States in the one political system. The classic definition, taken literally, would mean that the democratic deficit would always exist for someone. If in this way the classic definition is too demanding, in another it is not demanding enough. It does not allow for the possibility that both national and European political systems might be in democratic deficit at the same time, since it assumes that the EU only needs is to be as democratic as the states from which it derived its powers.

Another approach to appraisal by analogy has been to take democracy as it is practised in federal systems as a benchmark for the EU. Indeed, the term 'democratic deficit' was, as Fritz Scharpf observes (1996), originally coined by advocates of a draft constitution drawn up by the Institutional Affairs Committtee of the EP under the largely federalist inspiration of Altiero Spinelli (Corbett, 1988; Karlsson, 2001, pp. 195–8). This plainly narrows the expectation of what the EU should be expected to achieve to a manageably coherent set of tests. But its difficulty lies precisely in how far the term 'democratic deficit' has been appropriated by almost all who have prescriptions to make for the institutional development of the Union. The result is no one standard, let alone the federal one, can provide the basis for a democracy assessment to the satisfaction of all.

If empirical research into democracy and the EU cannot advance very far without spelling out a normative case for why the EU ought to be democratic and on which model, normative theorising about democracy in the EU may fail on its own terms without empirical analysis of what is feasible. As Albert Weale puts it, any 'non-utopian' normative theory is committed to the position that 'ought implies can':

> if we hold to a principle that a certain set of institutions ought to be maintained or brought into being, then we are committed to saying that such institutions can be feasibly maintained or introduced ... thus we should need to ensure that our principles of democratic theory were consistent with what political science currently thinks to be feasible. (Weale, 1999, pp. 8–9)

In the case of democracy this is especially so. For many democratic theorists the most persuasive justifications for democracy are consequential, rather than intrinsic (Weale, 1999, chap. 3; Bellamy and Castiglione, 2000, p. 72). They concern, in other words, the capacity of democracy to deliver outcomes that go beyond the values contained in its own definition. These might include government more or less free of arbitrary domination, superior rights protections, better economic performance and more pacific forms of international relations.

But, if the expected consequences of democracy are a part of its justification, the task of justifying the application of democracy to any one political system such as the EU cannot be complete without empirical research into whether those consequences are realisable in practice. Associated with this problem is a second. If 'ought' really does imply 'can', the non-utopian normative theorist must always be ready to resort to 'second-best' analysis: to be permanently armed, in other words, with a method for identifying what would be the next best to the normatively ideal under any given set of constraints. A process of shunting to and fro between hard-headed empirical analysis of exactly how intractable are constraints and fresh justification of second- and third-best solutions can be expected to feature prominently in the analysis of a problem such as democracy and the EU.

Evaluation in political science

The previous section argued for four improvements in how we assess democracy in the EU. First, we need a method that simultaneously appraises the Union's individual institutions and its overall institutional order. Second we need to distinguish how the Union performs against different attributes of democratic rule such as accountability, representation, participation and so on. Third we need a means of distinguishing democratic deficits that are at least partially compensated by the delivery of other qualities of good governance or even other attributes of democracy itself from those that are pure loss. Fourth we need to link empirical tests to reasoned views of why the EU ought to be democratic in the first place. Even a more modest list of objectives would, however, face the problem that evaluation is one of the more methodologically underdeveloped areas of political science. It has, as Robert Putnam observes (1993, p. 63), become especially difficult to ask 'how well?' are different peoples governed given the inevitable mixture of data collection, causal analysis and normative judgement needed to answer such a question.

> Rigorous appraisals of institutional performance are rare, even though 'good government' was once at the top of our agenda ... the discipline has too readily relinquished this important patrimony of political science – this 'ancient obligation of our craft' – to political philosophers and publicists. (ibid.)

Evaluation has been avoided for fear, on the one hand, of confusing fact and value and, on the other, of reaching conclusions that are no more than the subjective opinion of the researcher (Shepsle and Bonchek, 1997, p. 9; Peters, 1999, p. 13). The first of these reasons for avoiding evaluation is, however, questionable in its logic and damaging in its consequences. As the relevant entry in the Oxford book of philosophy puts it:

> value free political science is only committed to there being no logical connection between factual claims and evaluations. It can admit of any other sort of contingent connection one can dream up. (Ruben, 1998, pp. 465–7)

The only fallacy, in other words, to be avoided is one of claiming that statements of value follow from those of fact or *vice versa*. There is no bar to appraising the one against the other. This is just as well since continued insistence on a firewall between the two disables the study of politics from considering one of the most important questions of politics, namely how do political systems perform against those values their citizens identify with the legitimate exercise of political power (Ostrom, 1998)?

What of the second charge that appraisal can never be more than the personal opinion of the researcher? This is not the place to consider in full the difficult question of whether evaluation – and not just description and explanation – can count as knowledge. Those philosophers who defend this position do so on the grounds that we plainly can recognise degrees of good or bad assessment: some forms of appraisal are more careful in specifying their criteria, in establishing relationships between tests, in gathering evidence and in telling us how conclusions might be reproduced or shown to be fallible. Thus with reference to the two tests used by epistemologists (Moser *et al.*, 1998), appraisals satisfy the *coherence* test of knowledge where they are based on an internally consistent set of indicators and the *correspondence* test where they are supported by externally verifiable data. The rest of this chapter considers how approaches to democratic assessment might meet these two requirements.

Democratic Auditing explained

An early attempt at defining coherent indicators of democracy is to be found in Robert Dahl (1971) as follows: free and fair elections, universal suffrage, the election of key office holders, popular control of the political agenda, access to alternative sources of information, and the freedoms of association and expression (see also Bollen, 1980; Coppedge and Reinicke, 1990). There then followed a series of authors whose main concern was to develop indicators that consolidated or questioned S.M. Lipset's pioneering work (1959) on the economic and societal preconditions for democracy (Diamond, 1992; Hadenius, 1992; Moore, 1995). During the 1990s, pressure to link various kinds of external relationship (candidate status for EU membership, receipt of development aid and access to credit) to good governance required governments and international agencies to develop their own indicators of democratic governance. The EU has itself been a major contributor to the process (Crawford, 1997; Zanger, 2000). What is, however, reassuring is that in spite of some differences between these approaches the assessments they reach of various political systems usually correlate closely with one another, since as Thomas Zweifel has noted (2002, p. 815), most 'indicators of democracy come from a limited pool of common measures'.

Yet, in spite of Zweifel's suggestion that methods of democracy assessment are close substitutes for one another, this book seeks to defend and apply one particular approach to an appraisal of the EU, namely Democratic Auditing. The reason for this, as I hope to show in the next few pages, is that it matters not just what assessment is reached, but how it is reached. For the moment it is sufficient to note that one appeal of Democratic Auditing lies in the coherence with which it derives its indices of democratic performance through a series of steps. It begins by defending a core definition of democracy, goes on to identify a range of mediating values by which the core definition can be realised, and concludes by specifying social and institutional preconditions for delivering each of those intermediating values.

The core definition of democracy from which the Audit starts is 'public control with political equality' (see also Weale, 1999, p. 14). One way of arriving at these minimum conditions is essentially inductive. As David Beetham puts it, it is the absence of public control with political equality that people have historically complained about where democracy has, in their view, been missing (Beetham, 1994, pp. 27–8). Yet, even if historical experience had been otherwise, a moment's reflection reveals the two conditions to be logically entailed in any notion of rule by the people. Whereas democracy is conceivable where citizens do not rule in person, it is inconceivable where they do not control those who take decisions in their name. If, however, some of the people were to count for more for than others in exercising that public control, the resulting system would involve an element of rule of some of the people by others, rather than a straightforward one of rule by the people.

Beetham's second move in developing Democratic Auditing is to note that although public control with political equality forms the core definition of democracy it is possible to have various value preferences for how those attributes should be delivered. He accordingly identifies authorisation, participation, responsiveness, representation, transparency, accountability and solidarity as democracy's '*mediating values*'. As a final move, the Audit uses the means by which each of the mediating values has been delivered in practice to specify detailed tests of democratic governance. At their most detailed these run to 85 tests set out in the following thematic clusters: nationhood and citizenship, rule of law, civil and political rights, economic and social rights, free and fair elections, democratic role of political parties, government effectiveness and accountability, civilian control of the military and police, minimising corruption, the media in a democratic society, political participation, government responsiveness, decentralisation and international dimensions of democracy. The reader can consult the full list in Beetham *et al.* (2002). A more limited set of tests adjusted to the specific challenge of auditing democracy in the EU is set out in the next chapter.

In sum, then, Democratic Auditing promotes *coherent* appraisal by making criteria of democratic performance explicit and by formulating them into a comprehensive check list that clarifies relationships between tests, the principles of democratic governance that underlie each, and the approaches to institutional realisation into which they cluster. In the course of discussing how Democratic Auditing should be adapted to the EU, the next chapter will argue that another of its attractions lies in its what it takes to be evidence *corresponding* to democratic performance. First, however, we have unfinished business with the claim that it matters how a democracy assessment goes about its task and not just what outcome it reaches. Consider the following questions that have framed previous discussions about how best to evaluate the democratic performance of political systems.

1. What should the relationship be between a survey of democracy and its object of appraisal? This is a classic social science question that has implications for what the goals of a Democratic Audit should be and how it should be done. Some social phenomena consist of relatively invariant law-like relationships. Others are made up of frames of meaning and value commitments that may themselves change through the very act of attempting to understand them (see esp. Giddens, 1984, pp. 327–34). In the latter case, social science does not just describe and explain from an external point of view. It is partially constitutive of the very thing that is being investigated.

There clearly is a sense in which a democracy assessment needs to adopt an external and objective view in which it takes political systems as given at the moment of appraisal and concentrates on collecting the data that best describe delivery of individual democratic standards. It also needs to analyse causal relationships if it is to show which aspects of the political system are responsible for which democratic achievements or failures, or, indeed, if it is to be sure that any delivery of standards is not a random event but something that can be reliably attributed to recurring features of the institutional order. In these respects a democracy assessment shares all the normal concerns of analytical political science for accurate description and powerful tools of explanation.

However a democracy assessment can also be a reflective and a diagnostic tool, a means of explicating meaning and of provoking debate. Here it is important to recall just how far democracy involves continuous choice, as to motives or justifications for wanting it as a system of rule, as to priorities and balances between its mediating values, and as to institutional means of realising it. This, in turn, means appraisal in all its forms – and not just that of academic enquiry – plays a number of roles in democratic politics. At its simplest it is a means of taking stock and improving self-understanding: of clarifying the value commitments and choices of means into which members of a democratic polity may have slipped through the cumulative unintended consequences of institutional accretions and imperfectly co-ordinated actions.

At its most ambitious, appraisal of democratic performance is a part of the process of choice itself. Few would want to put all their money on what might be called a *deductive* approach to democracy design in which first principles are seen to translate unproblematically into ideal institutions. Most would probably also want an *inductive* or experimental element in which the rigorously appraised lessons of previous performance are used to frame and critique options for continuing efforts at democratic construction.

Cutting across these two roles is a third. A method of assessment that brings out implicit value commitments and compels all to say how their empirical claims might be verified can be used to improve inter-paradigmatic deliberation between those who disagree as to what form of democracy they want in the future or even what kind of democracy they believe themselves to have been constructing in the past. It should be noted that the cumulative implication of all three roles is that democracy assessment is most likely to be helpful where democratic politics are both nascent and contested, which, we will argue in the next chapter, are precisely the conditions in which the EU finds itself.

The place of academic assessment within a wider social process in which those who live under democratic rule are continuously concerned to appraise their systems of government creates an obligation on the researcher to present findings in a form that aids prescription, choice and deliberation. The continuous co-evolution of democratic practice and values means that any assessment of democratic performance is provisional: even if the empirical characteristics of the political system do not change the relative priorities citizens put on values may do. Thus ideally a democracy assessment should be conducted in a form that can be easily repeated at regular intervals in order to register change over time.

2. What account should a survey of democracy take of contextual factors? Given our argument that democracy has both a core definition that must be satisfied and several mediating values and institutional means that can be freely chosen (see also Schmitter and Karl's (1992) 'radial' concept of democracy) democracy is not as, is often supposed, an 'essentially contested concept'. Rather it is better understood as a 'boundedly contested' one. In other words, a method of democracy assessment can be based on at least two attributes (public control with political equality) that cannot be contested, that must be taken as having universal validity as necessary components of democratic rule and must be delivered by all systems purporting to be democratic in some form or another. Beyond insisting on those two attributes, however, the tests used in any democracy assessment have to be doubly sensitive to context. First, priorities between democracy's mediating values – authorisation, participation, representation, accountability and so on – should not be those of the assessor but of the people who live within the system of rule. Given, as we have repeatedly seen, that democracy has more than one justification, there is no reason why any two populations should have the same goals or values in mind when they choose to adopt it as a system of rule. Second appraisals must reflect what is feasible in a given time and place for reasons we discussed above (Schmitter and Karl, 1992, p. 8).

3. Should a democratic assessment concentrate on inputs or outputs? One view forcefully expressed to me during the preparation of this book is that any attempt to appraise a political system like the EU by focusing on its inputs or procedures is bound to be indeterminate. The problem my critic had in mind was the famous one of 'cycling' (McKelvey, 1976): where preferences are multidimensional (as they are in the EU) it is, as Kenneth Shepsle and Mark Bonchek argue, 'difficult to justify' any procedure for 'group choice' since there will always be 'an alternative some majority prefers' to the decision actually taken (Shepsle and Bonchek, 1997, p. 102). Implicit in this critique is a utilitarian view that the test of democracy is the efficient aggregation of citizen preferences. Such a view that democracy is 'best justified as a political system for the satisfaction of wants' (Plamenatz, 1973, p. 181) is, however, open to the objection that the same legitimation claim could be made of many other forms of rule – an effective and benign technocracy for example – but only democracy is open to being justified in terms of a particular configuration of 'rights and obligations and of procedures that secure those rights' (ibid.). The input measure of democracy turns out to be of the essence after all. It matters very much that there are procedures that allow citizens to join with others to exercise rights to public control as equals.

4. Should measures of democracy be dichotomous or matters of degree? As Zachary Elkins puts it (2000) binary 'yes/no' measures can be defended on the grounds that 'democracy is a question of kind before it is a question of degree'. Moreover, the critical 'pass–fail' threshold may pose fewer measurement problems than attempts to calibrate degrees of democracy. On the other hand, a suspicion that democracy is always an 'unfinished business' (Arblaster, 1987) and that even its core elements of public control with political equality are usually delivered with huge degrees of imperfection makes it hard for academic enquiry to duck questions of how much has been done and how much further there is to go (where and from what point of view)? Whether these are within our measurement capabilities begs the question of whether measuring is what a democracy assessment should be attempting to do. It is to this point we now turn.

5. *Should a survey of democracy be a judgement or a measurement?* Most standards of democracy are stubbornly qualitative in that they literally concern the *felt* quality of relationships between rulers and ruled: whether *they* feel they have a right to public control which they exercise as equals. Yet, there are many ways in which the 'subjective' feelings of those who live under a system of rule of its democratic qualities can be checked and challenged against 'objective', 'external' and comparative measures (see p. 48). A recent conference on the subject was thus almost certainly right to conclude that any satisfactory democracy assessment will have to include a mixture of 'subjective' and 'objective' sources (Centre for Democratic Governance, 2002, p. 2). This has a major implication: whatever the role of statistical indicators in contributing elements of a democracy assessment, the overall appraisal can only be a judgement and not a measurement. At some stage the ensemble of subjective and objective data needs to be assembled and an overall conclusion reached. This inescapably requires multiple judgements, as to the design of each data source, its significance for each test of democratic performance, and any adjudication that may be needed if sources conflict.

The study that follows will, accordingly, avoid the fashion for attaching numerical scores to institutions as part of a democracy assessment. *A fortiori* it will avoid any attempt to sum those scores into some overall quantitative assessment of the political system. Instead it will make no attempt to take appraisal further than a series of qualitative judgements, albeit ones that are informed by quantitative measures where they are available. It seems to me this is at once the most honest and most valuable course. Scoring only offers a form of bogus quantification in the sense that it obscures how far putting a number on an institutional quality is itself a matter of judgement. The summing of scores only compounds the error, since the relative weight that should be given to each attribute of democratic government is itself a value judgement.

If, then, judging is what a democratic assessment is unavoidably about, it is better that we should follow methods of judging and not pretend that we are doing something else, namely measuring. Even though the notion that judging could follow a method every bit as rigorous as their own might seem peculiar to many political scientists, it is hardly so to academic lawyers or philosophers. Moreover, the safeguard against appraisals amounting to no more than the personal judgement of the researcher is, in the end, no different than with any other political science research: data should be collected in forms that can be inspected by others and any inferences or judgements they are used to make should then be recorded in a manner that allows others to say what they think would be a better conclusion from the same data set. As Karl Popper puts it in a remark that betrays the ultimate failure of positivism to discover a science whose chain of reasoning is made up entirely of empirical observations without judgements, 'the *objectivity* of scientific statements lies in the fact that they can be *inter-subjectively* tested' (1959, p. 44 and fn. 1).

Conclusion

The argument that democracy has triumphed everywhere as a source of legitimate rule needs to be treated with care. It disguises how far other disputes about what is an acceptable form of government have been internalised into arguments about what is a proper form of democracy. Within states, it is not uncommon for those who take contrasting views on institutional questions to accuse each other of being undemocratic. It is, however, a peculiar feature of our times that arguments about democracy no longer just take place within the state. Rather, they have begun to focus on whether democracy should apply to political institutions and processes beyond the state and, if so, how?

If arguments about democracy within and without the state are central to modern politics, we need some rigorous means of evaluating it. In introducing the main principles of Democratic Auditing I have argued that it matters how a democracy assessment proceeds. It needs to be in a form that aids prescription and provokes debate; that takes account of the value preferences of those who live under the system being evaluated as to the form of democracy they find desirable; that makes allowance for what is feasible in context; and respects that as long as we define democracy as a unique combination of rights to public control with political equality it is not enough to test the democratic qualities of a political system by its substantive outputs, as opposed to its procedures. It is also important to avoid spurious attempts at measurement that obscure how much any assessment is a judgement. Yet, judgement is not without epistemic standards and responsibilities. It too needs to be informed by coherent criteria and the best empirical data available. It is to how this might be done in the case of the EU that the next chapter now turns.

2
Auditing Democracy in the European Union

Introduction

This chapter discusses how far Democratic Auditing needs to be re-invented at the same time as it is transposed to the EU. The main issues are what criteria should be used to test the democratic qualities or deficiencies of the EU? What should be covered by any democratic audit of the Union? And what in the EU's case should count as evidence of different levels of democratic performance? It follows from what was said in the last chapter that answers to these questions depend on what reasons are given for believing that the EU ought to be democratic and on the feasibility of achieving that outcome. This chapter will thus begin by reviewing justifications for a democratic EU and possible difficulties of achieving it.

Justifications for a democratic EU

Philippe Schmitter is surely right to ask 'why bother?' (2000) to democratise the Union in full and in a hurry when public demand is less than clear, agreement on what counts as a democratic Union is elusive and an evolutionary pattern of democratisation seems plausible. Others might add a further note of caution: 'citizens spend much of their time in organizations where democracy operates only at the margins' (Bellamy and Castiglione, 2000, p. 80). This need not, the argument might go on, be a concern. First, because democracy is not the only desirable form of rule (ibid.). Second, because non-democratic institutions can be required to operate in a framework of rules laid down by democratic ones.

According to the latter view, the need for the Union itself to be a democracy declines in proportion to it remaining within the ultimate controlling power of the democratic states that comprise it. It may even disappear altogether if it is further assumed that the Union is unlikely to be in a position to satisfy the conditions for democracy, whilst the state, in contrast, has reasonable prospects of sustaining those characteristics that have historically made it the most successful milieu for democratic politics. It should, however, be emphasised that this argument presupposes that the Union should be the object of democratic control, even if it questions how far it should be a democracy itself. Even on its own terms it does not remove the need to explain what it is about the exercise of political power by the EU that makes it desirable that it should be consistent with democratic values.

One possible answer to Schmitter's 'why bother?' question is that democracy remains a latent condition for the legitimation of the Union even in the absence of a manifest public clamour for the Union to proceed faster towards democratisation. According to this argument, only crises or hard choices fully test the claims of a political system against ideas current in society of what is needed for the rightful exercise of political power.

However, the relationship between democracy and legitimacy is by no means straightforward in the case of the EU. An indication that the first may be needed for the second is provided by survey evidence which suggests a popular expectation that the EU should be subject to one key attribute of democratic rule, namely public control. A standard Eurobarometer question asks whether there should be a European Government responsible to a European Parliament (EP). This has been approved by a large majority in each survey in which it has been used, even though it is a fair surmise that many respondents would prefer a European executive that did not amount to a 'Government'. It may also be significant that in the year when the EP demonstrated its ability to exercise the key controlling function of forcing the resignation of the EU's executive, it was the only Union institution to improve its rating (by eight percentage points) (Eurobarometer, no. 51, 1999). On the other hand, it is not hard to imagine forms of democratisation that would provide the Union with less, and not more, legitimacy, the obvious example being a highly majoritarian approach that would allow democratic majorities at Union level to over-ride democratic majorities at national level with ease, frequently or for long periods (Dehousse, 1995).

Another possible answer to the 'why bother?' question is that the Union is required by its own stated objectives to be democratic. The following are well-known examples of how democracy has progressively crept into the EU's 'mission statements' over the last decade. In the preamble to the Treaty on European Union (TEU), Member States confirm 'their attachment to the principles of liberty, democracy, and respect for human rights' (European Commission, 1992). The Commission's Strategic Programme for 2000–5 speaks of 'shared values of ... democracy and human rights' being 'best promoted through shared values and institutions'. It then goes on to claim that 'the EU's model of integration is a quarry from which ideas for global governance can and should be drawn' (European Commission, 2000b). Democracy and human rights have likewise been identified as values for export through the Common Foreign and Security Policy and Development Co-operation (Titles V and VII of TEU). They have additionally been refined as preconditions for membership (Copenhagen criteria, European Council, 1993) to the point at which the Commission reports annually to the Council with detailed appraisals of democratic standards in 13 non-EU countries.

Such statements fit the 'end of history argument' that democracy has become a universal principle of good governance, a benchmark for comparing systems and a test for the admissability of relationships with others (Fukuyama, 1989). Those, however, who use the EU to affirm democratic principles bind themselves into replicating those standards in their own behaviour. The only escape from such a 'categorical imperative' would be by claiming that it is enough for Union institutions to be democratic in their effects without being democratic in their internal characteristics. Far, however, from it being possible to take for granted that the Union is a net benefit to democracy in other arenas, some of its features may only complicate and constrain the practice of democracy in its Member States (Lord and Beetham, 2001). Moreover, to the extent that shared attachment to such civic values as democracy may be the only basis for a European identity that is both analytically plausible and normatively acceptable to many Union citizens (Habermas, 1992; Weiler *et al.*, 1995; Weiler, 1997b), it is less than clear that the Union can manage without it in its own institutions.

We can, however, go further than to say that the EU needs to be democratic according to its own standards. It has characteristics that require it to be democratic according to fundamental justifications for democracy itself. Arguments for democracy are of two kinds. *Intrinsic* justifications hold that democracy 'has moral authority' (Ryan, 1998, p. 392) in and of itself, and regardless of its consequences. One such argument runs as follows. It is right that people should make decisions about their own lives. Although there are those who question the ease with which the autonomy of individuals can ever be reconciled with collective decision-making processes to the point at which they can count themselves authors of their own laws (Weale, 1999, pp. 64–8), a counter-argument is that, in a social condition, any meaningful concept of 'person autonomy' *requires* an autonomous public sphere governed by democratic principles: 'the individual liberties of the subjects of private law and the public autonomy of enfranchised citizens make each other possible' (Habermas, 1996, p. 457).

In contrast, the *consequential* argument is that democracy is likely to produce desirable effects beyond those contained in its own definition as public control with political equality. It is often claimed, for example, that democratic systems are better than others at protecting individual rights and avoiding arbitrary domination (Pettit, 1997). Indeed the consequential and intrinsic arguments overlap, since a likely consequence of democratic decision rules is a body of decisions that approximate the autonomous preferences of the ruled in important ways. Public control at least discourages those who hold office from acting only on their personal preferences without any attempt to anticipate the needs and values of citizens. Political equality at least means that each person's preference has the same weight in the whole. The decision-rule 'one person, one vote' re-weights public decisions away from private distributions of power and resources. Deliberative standards fairly applied allow all points of view an opportunity to be argued towards a winning position, regardless of the initial number of their proponents. In addition, a system of government that encourages most decisions to be taken somewhere close to the median preferences of citizens on most issues has the advantage of being the least average difference from what each individual would probably have done if deciding for herself (Powell, 2000).

Thus an *intrinsic* argument for a democratic EU might be that those subject to the Union as a form of rule have become dependent on institutions at a European level for autonomous shaping of their own rights and life chances. A *consequential* argument for a democratic EU might be that it has passed some threshold in the accumulation of power over ordinary lives at which democracy is a useful additional safeguard against the abuse of that power. A good many of its functions redistribute values, resources, entitlements and identities between states, regions, generations, the sexes and social groups. Many of these reallocations may be indivisible or hard to reverse in so far as they lock those affected into remorseless forms of path dependency (Pierson, 2000), though that does not mean that deciding not to decide will not also have the same effects on individuals. Even non-decisions are anything but neutral in their implications (Lukes, 1974). Whilst, however much political systems are inescapably forced to choose between values, democracy can at least be used to control those who make such choices, so they are not merely arbitrary (Pettit, 1997).

Difficulties in making the EU democratic

As seen, any selection of tests for auditing democracy in the EU needs to reflect what is difficult, and not just what is desirable, in applying it as a system of rule to the EU. This follows from our earlier argument (p. 7) that any non-utopian standard of evaluation has to take account of what is feasible. A core difficulty in applying democracy to EU is that it is a non-state political system. This matters since studies of democracy have shown that it was the hierarchical nature of the state that allowed democracy to undergo its 'transformation' from a decision rule occasionally employed by small communities to a form of government widely used in mass modern societies (Dahl, 1989). Whilst, however, the EU is a still more massive political system than the state it is not a hierarchy based on a monopoly of violence and a central locus of decision-making with a sovereign right to regulate all other relationships in society. Although its law takes priority over national law, there is no power of the Union that cannot itself be withdrawn by the agreement of Member States to change the Treaties. Furthermore, that power is dispersed and reliant on the enforcement structures of others, primarily the administrations of the Member States. As Joe Weiler puts it (2002, p. 568) the EU has a 'top-to-bottom hierarchy of norms' but a 'bottom-to-top hierarchy of authority and real power'.

All of this creates a dilemma. A pattern in which mechanisms of public control are dispersed horizontally across particular institutions of the Union and vertically across levels of Union governance will make it hard to apply democracy to the EU through one straightforward process of competition for political power. This has a number of consequences. First the EU is never likely to be a system in which the public has a single clear opportunity to enforce responsibility by, for example, removing a 'government' (Weiler, 1997b, p. 225). Second, there may be too little at stake in any one election or procedure to mobilise high and sustained levels of public participation or even attention to Union matters. Third, it may be difficult to institutionalise political equality as long as the rights of ordinary citizens and their representatives to exercise public control of Union processes are significantly affected by variations in the sub-arenas that give them access to the Union, both variation in the bargaining power of each Member State in Union decision-making and in the internal representative politics of each Member State (see Chapter 7). Fourth deliberation may be too fragmented to be aggregated into a single public space at Union level. We will return to each of these points in the chapters that follow.

The EU, however, is not only a non-state polity. It is also a multi-state, multi-national, non-state polity that operates from beyond the nation-state. This means that in its case democratisation and identity-formation stand in an unusually problematic relationship. Although there are suggestions for how the two might develop in tandem, tensions between them are never far from opposed views of what is needed to legitimate the EU. If the contestedeness of the EU polity includes the very question of whether it should be democratic and how, it is not often on account of disagreement about the value of democracy, but of how a democratic EU should interface with various identities. Claims about identity – actual or aspirational – are often used to argue that national democratic institutions should prevail over European ones or *vice versa*; and in between such 'one size fits all' solutions there is always the possibility that feelings of multi-level identity might be best satisfied by national forms of democratic control for some issues, European-level solutions ones for others.

The complexity of the Union polity is a further reason to expect its democratization to be difficult. Although a political system can be discerned at the core of the first pillar (Quermonne, 1994; Hix, 1999), the Union as a whole is better described as a 'plurality of polities at different levels of aggregation' (Schmitter, 2000). These mix international, supranational and even infranational features (Weiler, 1997b, pp. 276–7). They range, in other words, from practices that resemble classical forms of co-operation between states (international); to those which draw on the supremacy of Union law and process outcomes through a standard set of institutions more or less structured into demarcated functions of government (supranational); to those which organise knowledge and attention around professional and sectoral networks rather than national–European or even public–private distinctions (infranational).

A further source of complexity is that the final impacts of Union policy have to be filtered through domestic political systems. Indeed, most Union policies are not based on an exclusive competence at all, but mingle with national attempts to manage the same problem or issue. We will see how national parliaments, domestic electoral and party systems, and varying patterns of decentralisation within Member

States all mean that the Union is experienced differently depending where an individual is located within its territory. If to implement is to govern, national variations in the character of executive power and public administration will also mean that both the supply and demand for democratic solutions of representation, responsiveness and accountability will vary with who is the local implementing authority for particular Union policies.

Above all, complexity raises a problem of congruity. It is difficult to conceive of structures at Union level that can be guaranteed to match representatives and represented without any risk of some representatives participating in decisions that do not affect their constituents or, conversely, some individuals being exposed to decisions from which their representatives are excluded. Not only is there substantial internal variation in how EU policies are experienced by citizens of the Union itself. There are also significant examples where Union policy is applied extra-territorially to those who have few if any formal rights of representation in its institutions (Kux and Sverdrup, 2000). For example, Schengen agreements on the management of frontiers apply to two non-Member States (Norway and Iceland), but not to the UK or Ireland.

A final difficulty is the relative youth of the EU's polity. Here we need to be aware of theories that emphasise democratisation as an evolution, rather than a design. As James March and Johan Olsen argue (1995), many of the capabilities – rights, trust, identities and knowledge – needed to operate a democracy grow with use (pp. 96–8). More normative issues of who representatives should be and what they should do can only be settled deliberatively and constructively within a given context by those who are subject to the system of rule. It follows that nascent political systems – of which the EU is arguably one – are likely to go through a period of standard setting in which principles of representation are still being defined, contested and negotiated. On the one hand, this makes life more difficult for any survey that travels in the hope that standards by which to judge the democratic performance of the EU have already been unambiguously defined by those subject to it as a system of rule. On the other hand, it means that an assessment of democracy in the EU may itself be in a position to contribute to standard setting. As long as there is sufficient information to make assumptions about the *pro tempore* expectations the public or its representatives have of the democratic performance of the EU, there is much to be said for the argument that it is precisely in the formative stages of democratisation that evaluation is most useful. Since that is the stage when there is most likely to be a number of competing or imperfectly formed claims, and since it is of the nature of democratic prescriptions that they mix empirical claims with those of principle and value, the defining of standards is not prior to the process of assessment. Rather the two need to evolve interactively.

Tests of a democratic EU

So far we have argued justifications for a democratic EU and the difficulties of achieving that outcome need to be reflected in our choice of tests of a democratic Union. However, any claims about the value of democracy, on the one hand, and what is institutionally or socially possible, on the other, need to be coherently related. Discussions about democracy, accordingly, tend to be conducted as debates between competing models. Consideration of which models of democracy should be applied to the EU has centred on the following pair-wise distinctions.

Direct/indirect democracy. Perhaps the most familiar of all distinctions used in the classification of forms of democracy, direct democracy is where the people themselves take major decisions of government. The alternative is that the people exercise control indirectly through elected representatives. Indirect or representative democracies may be further sub-divided into presidential and parliamentary forms. Under presidential systems, a chief executive and a legislature are elected separately. Under parliamentary systems the two are effectively elected together, since a majority of the legislature can make or break governments.

Both presidential and parliamentary forms of indirect democracy have been proposed as solutions for the EU (Bogdanor, 1986). The Laeken declaration asked the Convention on the Future of Europe to consider whether the President of the Commission should be appointed by the European Council or elected either by the EP or by citizens (Council of the European Union, 2001b). Amongst proposals for more direct forms of democracy are Heidrun Abromeit's (1998) suggestion that groups of citizens should be able to petition for referendums to contest EU decisions, and that of Weiler (1997a) and others for a 'legislative ballot' that would allow a certain number of questions (to be decided, once again, by the petitioning of citizens) to be put to pan-EU referendum at the same time as elections to the EP.

Consensus/majoritarian democracy. Majoritarian democracy is where decisions can be taken by a bare majority of the people or their representatives. Its proponents argue that any alternative would amount to a system of minority rule. Consensus democracy is where the aim is to align policies with the greatest number of citizens or their representatives, rather than with the preferences of a simple majority (Lijphart, 1984). Its defenders argue that any alternative allows minorities to be excluded and is not really rule by the people as a whole. Moreover, there, is, in their view, no defensible reason why a bare majority should act as a kind of 'cut-off' point for collective decision if compromises can be made to accommodate a bigger majority without significantly deviating from the preferences of the bare majority. Examples of consensus democracy include super-majoritarian decision-rules (where decisions need the approval of more than 50 per cent), systems of divided government that require concurrent consent across branches and levels of government, consociational systems that guarantee the participation of many cultural segments in public decisions (Lijphart, 1979) and arrangements for the inclusion of opposition parties in some of the tasks of government (Powell, 1989). In a moment, we will give extended attention to proposals for the application of consensus democracy to the EU.

Bargaining/deliberative dimensions of democracy. More abstract than the previous two distinctions, Strategic models of democracy assume that citizens have clear and fixed views of their interests. The main goal of democratic institutions is then to find the most efficient means of aggregating individuals' preferences into collective actions. In contrast, deliberative notions hold that aggregation is only one aspect of a democratic process. If political equality is to mean anything at all, members of a democracy must be able to deliberate what they propose to do in common in a way that abstracts from power relationships between themselves (Habermas, 1996). Moreover, the act of voting – with its hugely coercive implications – is most likely to be acceptable to losers where it is 'never merely voting' unaccompanied by prior 'discussion, consultation and persuasion' (Dewey, 1927, p. 207; Miller, 1993). Although this emphasis on deliberation is often treated as a preoccupation of contemporary political thought, it is in fact of ancient lineage. Thus J.S. Mill argued representative bodies should provide a 'Congress of Opinions' where 'all points of view could present themselves to challenge discussion by adverse controversy'. Those who are overruled should 'feel satisfied that [their opinion has been] heard, and set aside not by a mere act of will, but for what are thought to be superior reasons' (Mill, 1972 [1861], pp. 239–40).

Thus, the common argument of those who urge the application of deliberative to the EU is that representative institutions, participation and even identity formation will be insufficient for a democratic EU if they are used to aggregate preferences alone. Democracy also requires an agreed process for reflecting on preferences before they are transformed into collective action (Eriksen and Fossum, 2000).

The foregoing would seem to suggest there is no manageably simple range of views of how the EU ought to be made democratic against which we can appraise how democratic it is in practice. Yet, on reflection, there is considerable scope to simplify the range of disagreement. First, the strategic/communicative distinction does not so much connote a cleavage line on how the EU ought to be made democratic as two different logics that need to be built into any system of democratic politics (Habermas, 1996). Second, the direct–indirect distinction turns out be relatively weak in accounting for differences in how the EU should be democratised. For example, both the proposals for referendums mentioned earlier *presuppose* a representative process that would be complemented in the one case (by an additional opportunity for agenda-setting that does not depend on representatives) and counterbalanced in the other (by an opportunity to contest the decisions of representatives).

In contrast, the majoritarian/consensus distinction might seem to be the key fault line in the debate on how the EU ought to be made democratic (Katz, 2001). Yet, even that is probably a misunderstanding. Proposals for an elected Commission President or for a strengthened EP would certainly give a greater role to electoral or parliamentary majorities at key moments in the operation of the EU's political system. But those proposals almost invariably assume that a more democratic Commission or a strengthened Parliament would have to operate within a continued separation of powers and achieve the concurrent consent of other actors (such as national governments in the Council of Ministers) with claims of their own to be representative.

In what follows, then, it is assumed that the dominant cleavage on what would count as democratic EU is not between proposals for majority and consensus democracy, but between two versions of the latter. On the one hand, a consociational approach assumes that a democratic Union would be one in which EU institutions can be controlled by representatives of the national democracies of the Union often operating with formally equal decision and veto rights. On the other hand, implicit in another approach to consensus democracy that I term 'concurrent consent' is the additional requirement that representatives of national democracies should not only reach a high level of consensus between themselves but also with those elected for the express purpose of representing the public in Union institutions. Its goal, in other words, is consensus within a divided system of government. Although this would (by definition) require consensus between two representative bodies, there would be nothing to stop those bodies operating internal decision rules that range from simple majoritarianism to unanimity. Supermajorities with varying thresholds (from 50 to 100 per cent) could be used in one of the representative bodies or both, for some issues but not for others and so on. The rules for achieving some kind of co-decision between the two bodies could likewise vary, maybe in a way that is linked to the size and nature of the internal consensus that has to be obtained in each.

Many contributors to the literature have seen consociational democracy as suited to the EU (Chryssochoou, 1994; Lijphart, 1997). In other words, the Union would be democratic in so far as its institutions meet the following tests:

(1) Provide inclusive and proportional representation of office-holders designated by national democracies;
(2) Respect the autonomy of national democratic practices;
(3) Allow representatives of national democracies to retain veto rights in matters they consider of vital importance (Lijphart, 1979, 1997).

A difficulty, though, is that in its original version consociationalism assumes that it is better to avoid communication between publics belonging to different segments of the political system and that elites should, accordingly, be given wide discretion at the level of shared institutions. However, the EU consists of more or less demarcated national-territorial segments whose populations merely feel themselves to be different rather than intermingling cultural communities whose members feel themselves to be antipathetic (Bogaards and Crepaz, 2002). It is thus by no means clear why, in the case of the EU, it should be difficult to make national elites accountable to 'their' publics without igniting the very tensions that the shared political system is supposed to remove. Indeed, a Union managed by national governments without the active scrutiny of national electorates and parliaments would, in the eyes of many, be a cartel of elites, rather than a model of democracy. It could even encourage the opposite result to that intended by *de*-democratisating the state through its participation in the EU, rather than democratising the Union through its control by national democracies (see esp. Lord and Beetham, 2001, pp. 448–9). To avoid these difficulties, this study will assume that the effective control of the Union by national democracies would be best achieved through a 'modified' consociationalism in which the following requirement is added to the three listed in the previous paragraph:

(4) Representatives of national democracies are themselves open to control by their publics or national parliaments in how they exercise the powers and rights of each national democracy within the EU's institutional order.

If modified consociationalism would vest ultimate control of Union institutions in national democracies what arguments might be made for their joint or concurrent control by representatives elected at the Union level as well as the domestic? One concern we will explore in Chapter 7 is that however active and empowered national parliaments are on Union issues, there may be structural constraints on how far the contributions of individual national democratic institutions can add up to an adequate system of public control at Union level. The 'consequential argument' for a democratic EU as a means of avoiding arbitrary domination may thus require a form of 'divided government' in which the controlling powers of national representatives are complemented by those of a representative institution directly elected at Union level. A division of powers between the two kinds of representative would be an insurance against the behaviour of national governments in EU institutions becoming more a part of what needs to be controlled than a means of delivering control on behalf of their electorates and parliaments.

In any case, even if all governments were perfect representatives of their national democracies on Union issues, it is not entirely clear why that should entitle each to unconditional powers in EU institutions. The idea that national democracies voluntarily accept some restrictions on their own operation so that the common institutions can acquire certain normative and performative properties of their own may not be to everyone's liking, but it is hardly incoherent. Such constraints might plausibly include the following. First, the 'constitutional features' of EU law, its supremacy and direct application. Second, use of majority voting to prevent gridlock or situations where a minority can block change to an existing policy that the rest find dysfunctional or unjust. Third, use of the European arena as a guarantee of citizen rights, and as a point of judicial appeal against national authorities. Fourth, commitments to observe boundary relationships between 'soft' and 'hard' forms of nationalism, both within states and between them (Weiler, 1997b). Fifth, certain rules of good-neighbourliness and mutual respect such as deliberation in 'good faith' of policies with cross-border effects (Joerges and Neyer, 1997; Shaw, 1999).

Indeed, for all who agree with Jean-Marc Ferry 2000, p. 10) that European integration has to have a 'double normative reference point' – the rights of national democracies and of individual citizens – the 'intrinsic argument' for a democratic EU reinforces the case for a division in powers of public control between representatives elected at national and European levels. Such an arrangement would allow individuals, who do not agree with the positions supported by their own governments in EU institutions, access to additional representative structures where they can aggregate and deliberate their preferences with the like-minded on a basis that cross-cuts national divisions (Bellamy and Castiglione, 2002, p. 19). The need for such opportunities might be justified by a view of democracy as a decision-rule where no voting mechanism can be used authoritatively until all have had an opportunity to persuade all. It may also be desirable if preferences are, indeed, likely to correlate poorly with national divisions. A paradoxical effect of the subsidiary principle – that the Union should limit itself to those policies that 'cannot be achieved at national level for reasons of their *cross-border* effects' – is that it propels the Union towards a policy agenda that calls the adequacy of national channels of representation into question. 'Cross-border problems' of their nature divide actors not just by nationality but by attitude to such questions as market regulation, management of migration flows, or control of pollution.

Table 2.1 operationalises modified consociationalism and concurrent consent respectively as Democratic Audit tests corresponding to different democratic values. At this stage, the tests are deliberately set at

Table 2.1 European Union Democratic Audit (EUDA) tests

Democratic values	*Modified consociationalism*	*Concurrent consent*
Citizenship	1. How far does the EU respect the autonomy of national practices of democratic citizenship?	7. How far is there an agreed democratic citizenship at EU level and how able are individuals to use it in practice?
Authorisation	2. How far are national democracies able to shape and control the institutional design of the EU by means of their own choosing?	8. How far can individuals and groups influence questions of institutional design at Union level, according to deliberative processes that bring them into direct communication with one another, regardless of boundaries between national democracies?
Representation	3. How far does the distribution of executive	9. How far is the designation of executive and legislative

Table 2.1 Continued

Democratic values	*Modified consociationalism*	*Concurrent consent*
	and legislative office in the EU ensure the inclusive and proportional representation of national democracies?	positions by Member States matched by opportunities for citizens directly to elect representatives of their own at Union level?
	4. How far do representatives of national democracies shape and control Union decisions they consider of vital importance?	10. How far do individuals and groups have means of aggregating and deliberating preferences at EU level (if need be, independently of their national governments)?
Accountability	5. How far are those who hold office or make decisions in Union institutions accountable to representatives of national democracies who are, in turn, responsible to their national publics and parliaments?	11. How far are those who hold office or make decisions in EU institutions accountable to elected representatives of citizens at Union level?
Constitutionalism	6. How far does the EU constitutionalise modified consociationalism or use its methods to constitutionalise other values?	12. How far does the EU constitutionalise concurrent consent or use its methods to constitutionalise other values?

a high level of generality in order to maintain a clear overview of the main contours of the analysis that will follow in the rest of the book. Individual chapters will flesh the twelve tests out and provide further justification for them.

Units of assessment

The previous section proposed that a democratic audit should appraise the EU using indices derived from two distinct standards of consensus democracy: a modified form of consociationalism and a form of divided government based on the concurrent consent of different kinds of majority. But what exactly should be assessed? The ideal would be to define units of assessment that pick up the most likely sources of variation in the Union's performance against the criteria for the European Democratic Audit set out in Table 2.1. That would mean including the pillars, institutions and principal policy instruments of the Union, as well as arrangements for Treaty formation, and a miscellany of more unusual processes. The following paragraphs explain:

Pillars. Since the entry into force of the TEU in 1993 the EU has been divided into three pillars. As shown in Table 2.2, the old European Community (EC) Treaties were incorporated as the first pillar of the new Union. Following the Treaty revision conference at Amsterdam (1997) its policies are now set out in 20 'titles'. Two further pillars – the Common Foreign and Security Policy (CFSP) and Co-operation in Justice and Home Affairs (JHA) – were established within the TEU without being included in the EC Treaties. The pillars can be expected to be a significant source of variation in democratic performance, since, as will be seen, they differ in the powers and roles they confer on each Union institution and in the way in which they combine those bodies into patterns of inter-institutional interaction.

Institutions. The TEU confers the status of Union institution on five bodies: the European Commission, the Council of Ministers, the EP, the European Court of Justice (ECJ) and the European Court of Auditors. It further provides that a sixth body, the European Council, shall 'define

Table 2.2 The three pillars of the EU and their policy content

Pillar 1		*Pillar 2 (CFSP)*	*Pillar 3 (JHA)*
The EC Treaty consisting of the following titles: I Free Movement of Goods II Agriculture III Free Movement of Persons, Services and Capital IV Visas, Asylum, Immigration V Transport VI Competition and Taxation VII Economic and Monetary Union VIII Employment IX Common Commercial Policy	X Customs Co-operation XI Social Policy, Education, Vocational Training, Youth XII Culture XIII Public Health XIV Consumer Protection XV Trans-European Networks XVI Industry XVII Economic and Social Cohesion XVIII Research and Technological Development XIX Environment XX Development Co-operation	Title V of the Treaty on European Union	Title VI of the Treaty on European Union

the general policy guidelines' of the Union. Two other bodies – the Economic and Social Committee and the Committee of the Regions – have various rights to be consulted on Union legislation; and, of course, the European Central Bank (ECB) has now been established with responsibility for monetary policy. The composition and roles of these bodies are set out in Table 2.3. It should also be noted that several other institutions have been established through acts of delegation. Under the first pillar these include a number of specialist agencies such as the European Patents Office, an Office for the Evaluation of Medicinal Products. Under the third pillar, they include Europol (for the co-ordination of national police forces) and Eurojust (for the co-ordination of prosecuting authorities in Member States).

As hinted, the pillars combine the main institutions in different ways. The first pillar is often said to operate the 'Community method', which in its contemporary form might be summarised as follows: the Commission has a monopoly of initiative, the Council decides most matters by Qualified Majority Voting (QMV) of Member States, the EP co-decides a significant proportion of legislation with the Council, and the ECJ has the power to review the conformity of all actions of the other institutions with the Treaties. On CFSP and JHA matters, on the other hand, the Commission only has a shared right of initiative (with Member States), the Council takes most decisions by unanimous agreement of its Members and the EP is only consulted. The ECJ, for its part, has no role in CFSP and it only has jurisdiction over JHA matters where the Council so provides on a case-by-case basis.

Policy instruments. Decisions may be made by the foregoing institutions, but they are experienced by the citizen through the Union's policy instruments, as set out in Table 2.4. Since arrangements for consultation, representation, responsiveness, transparency and accountability differ markedly across the various instruments, the Audit needs to include them as possible sources of variation in the democratic performance of the EU.

Treaty formation. The pillars, institutions and policy instruments may at any one time be the most plausible sources of variation in the democratic qualities of Union rule, but any can be changed by decisions on the overall institutional design of the Union. We will see, moreover, how questions of institutional design raise distinctive issues of democratic choice and control. Treaty formation thus also needs to be included in the Audit. In recent years, Treaty change has been repeated at a frequency approaching permanent revolution: the Single Act (1987), the TEU (1992), Amsterdam (1997), Nice (2000) and the

Table 2.3 The institutions of the EU

Institutions	*Leadership and administration*	*Functions*
Commission	*President* chosen by consensus of the European Council *College of 20* *Commissioners*. The 5 largest Member States appoint 2 each, and the rest 1 each. *Permanent officials* organised into Directorates General (DGs)	*Legislation*. Most pillar 1 legislation can only be initiated by a Commission text. Under pillars 2 and 3 the Commission shares its right of initiative with Member States; *Executive*. The Commission oversees implementation of pillar 1 measures. *Finance*. The Commission presents a draft of the annual budget for approval by the Council and EP. *Representation*. The Commission represents the EU in external negotiations often in conjunction with the Council.
Council of Ministers	'One representative of each Member State at ministerial level authorised to commit the government of that Member State' (Article, 203) Meetings prepared by Presidency National Permanent Representatives and Working groups of national officials	*Legislation*. Decides legislation, subject, where relevant, to the powers of the EP; *Finance*. Sets out five-yearly framework agreements for the financing of the EU, co-decides the annual budget with the EP and has the final say on compulsory expenditures; *Co-ordination*. Co-ordinates CFSP and JHA and takes decisions under a number of economic co-ordination mechanisms associated with EMU; *Representation*. Represents the EU in external negotiations often in conjunction with the Commission.
European Council	The Head of Government of each Member State	Agrees the primary acts of the Union: Treaties, five-yearly budgets and so on. Provides political leadership to the other institutions.

EP	626 directly elected members elected in national constituencies. Organised into: • multinational party groups, • national party delegations • committees	*Legislation*. Can amend or reject much pillar 1 legislation *Financial*. Determines annual budget jointly with Council, with final say on non-compulsory expenditures; *Executive supervision* • Confirms appointment of Commission • Censure of Commission • Investigation (parliamentary questions, special committees of enquiry etc.) • Approval needed for discharge of Commission's accounts.
ECJ	15 judges appointed for renewable 6-year terms by common accord of Member States.	Application and interpretation of Union law
ECB	General Council of 18 Central Bankers. 6 Executive designated by the European Council + 12 national central bankers	• Sets interest rates and other monetary policy for the euro-zone as a whole • Exercises (prudential) supervision of the euro-zone banking system in collaboration with national central banks • Participates in discussions on co-ordination of national economic policies.

Table 2.4 Policy instruments of the EU

	Primary acts (*The Treaties*)
Secondary Acts	*Regulations.* Measures binding in their entirety throughout the Union; *Directives.* Results that national authorities must achieve in a 'form and method' of their own choosing; *Decisions.* Measures that only bind the specific actors to whom they are addressed; *Recommendations* and *Opinions* without binding force
First pillar legislative procedures	Most first pillar legislation can only be initiated by the Commission and be decided with the agreement of the Council. It may however be made by procedures that give varying powers to the EP as follows: *Consultation.* The EP must be consulted but the Council is not obliged to take account of its opinion. (Titles II, IV, IX, XVI, part of VI, VIII, XI, XVII, XVIII & XIX.) *Co-operation.* The EP can reject the legislation provided the Council is not, in turn unanimous in overturning the Parliament's position. The EP can amend the legislation. If the Commission accepts EP amendments, the law passes if the Council either accepts the amended draft by QMV or decides by unanimity to strike out any EP amendments (Title VII). *Co-decision.* The EP enjoys the same rights of amendment as above, but its powers of rejection are stronger. It can reject by an absolute majority of its membership at first reading or a simple majority of its membership at third reading. The Council cannot over-turn that rejection. (Titles III, V, X, XII, XIII, XIV, XV & XX, and part of VI, VIII, XI, XVII, XVIII & XIX.) *Assent.* The EP is able to reject but not amend. This applies, for example, to international Treaties signed by the EU.
Second pillar procedures	*Common strategies* are agreed by heads of government in the European Council on proposals framed by their foreign ministers. Those strategies can then be carried out by the following: *Joint actions.* Particular foreign policy tasks, usually with closely specified objectives, and limited means. *Common positions*, commit Member States to following a Union line in other international bodies and processes.

Table 2.4 Continued

	Primary acts *(The Treaties)*
	The Commission can make proposals for Joint Actions or Common Positions, but it crucially has no monopoly of initiative. Member States can and do make proposals of their own. The EP only has powers to be consulted. The ECJ has no jurisdiction.
Third pillar procedures	*Common positions* and *joint actions* are also used in JHA. In addition, the Council can draw up *Conventions*. These are recommended to Member States, which can decide whether to adopt them according to the rules of their own political systems. The powers of the Commission and EP are much as for pillar two. The ECJ may have jurisdiction where the Council provides on a case-by-case basis.

intergovernmental conference (IGC) scheduled for 2004. Treaty changes ultimately require the unanimous consent of representatives of member governments meeting in an IGC, though they may be prepared by various means, including a deliberative Convention.

Delegation, flexibility and extra-territoriality. Even the foregoing does not capture all that needs to be included in a Democratic Audit of the EU. Recent years have seen a growth in various forms of flexible integration in which some institutions and policies only apply to particular Member States. The most obvious example is Monetary Union. But others are the Schengen Accord, provision for Constructive Abstention in CFSP (Member States that abstain from a policy do not have to participate in it) and a general flexibility clause in the Treaty. A Democratic Audit thus needs to be alive to the possibility that citizens may have different rights of representation and variable access to democratic accountability because they come from countries that participate differentially in European policy regimes. Since, its institutions, conversely, provide governance beyond the EU (as not just beyond the state), the question also arises as to how far they allow voice to those who come under a variety of pressures to adopt Union policies without having the formal rights of representation that come with Membership.

In keeping, then, with the need to address the 'level of analysis' problem set out in the previous chapter, the Audit will cover a number of units of appraisal. Working as it were from the bottom upwards, it will aim to appraise the democratic standards of (a) specific procedures or policy instruments, (b) each institution of the Union, (c) the three pillars (d) the Union as a whole and (e) processes of institutional design. It will also include a number of observations on flexible integration within and beyond the Union, though space will not permit these to be quite as systematically worked out as the main assessments of (a)–(e).

Having settled on the units of assessment, a final question is over what time period they should be Audited. This is less straightforward in the EU than in other political systems, since the institutions are governed by Treaties which, as seen, have changed at frequent intervals in recent years. To allow for consistent and comparable appraisals, this Audit has defined an assessment period from the entry into force of the Amsterdam Treaty in June 1998 to its replacement by the Nice Treaty. Some allusions will be made to earlier institutional mechanisms and, indeed, to future ones envisaged by Nice or contributions to the present Convention on the Future of Europe. But, for the most part, the book seeks to appraise the European Union *à l'Amsterdam*, in the expectation that further Audits may well be needed as the institutions change further, methods of assessment become more sophisticated, and new information becomes available.

Sources of evidence

Having set out tests and considered how the Union should be broken down into units of assessment, we need to ask what should count as good evidence of democratic performance in the case of the EU? Although the only satisfactory judge of the democratic qualities of any political system is the public itself, it is less than clear where to look for evidence of that judgement. Opinion polls are one possible source. For example, one Eurobarometer question measures public satisfaction with Democracy in the EU. This indicates an even split of the public into the satisfied and dissatisfied (Table 2.5). However, a weakness with this question is that it is unclear whether it is a general enquiry about all forms of rule in the EU (national systems included) or a specific one about Union institutions. Another question set out in the bottom half of Table 2.5 probes how often citizens feel they have a say in the decisions of the Union. This paints a bleaker picture.

The rest of the book will make extensive use of opinion polls and other survey evidence. Indeed, it will hopefully, demonstrate how they can be

Table 2.5 Satisfaction with democracy in the EU

Satisfaction with democracy in the EU									
Eurobarometer number	39	40	41	42	43	48	51	54	56
Very/fairly satisfied	44	44	42	37	39	37	42	40	44
Not/not at all satisfied	41	38	42	39	42	44	39	43	38

In your assessment, do European citizens always, never or rarely have a say in the decisions of the EU? (Eurobarometer, 1995, p. 48)

	EU15	*Aus*	*Bel*	*Den*	*Fin*	*Fr*	*Ger*	*Gr*	*Ire*	*It*	*Neths*	*P*	*Sp*	*Swe*	*UK*
1. Always/often	29	25	27	26	23	29	28	34	28	31	24	37	33	14	24
2. Rarely/never	66	63	65	67	70	67	63	51	59	58	70	49	51	78	68
Difference 2−1	−37	−38	−38	−41	−47	−38	−35	−17	−31	−27	−46	−12	−18	−64	−44

mined more deeply for clues than hitherto. But standard opinion surveys are only reliable sources at high levels of aggregation. As soon as they attempt to probe the fine-grained differences between institutions and procedures which we have argued are indispensable to any assessment of democratic standards in the EU, they run into the methodological difficulty that many of their respondents appear only to judge the Union as a unitary actor, and to be somewhat confused by distinctions between its institutions (see Chapter 3). Moreover the evaluative and complex nature of the question 'how well do Union institutions satisfy various standards of democratic government?' means it is just the kind of problem that raises the following objection to 'static' forms of opinion polling: experiments with 'deliberative opinion polling' in which participants respond to a questionnaire, then debate the issue between themselves and call expert witnesses before replying to the same questionnaire for a second time, indicate there can be huge differences between initial and deliberated judgments of the same issue (Fishkin *et al.*, 2000).

The testimony of 'representatives' with the most direct experience of the frustrations and opportunities for mediating citizen demands through the EU's political system would be one way of addressing detailed and disaggregated questions left over by more 'gross' assessments of the Union by public opinion. The Audit thus uses a mixture of documentary sources and interviews to analyse how elite actors appraise democratic standards in the EU. The documents were compiled from those associated with the preparation of the Nice IGC, the Commission's White Paper on European Governance (1999–2001), and the debate on the Future of Europe initiated by Joshka Fischer's (2000) speech to the Humboldt University in May 2000 and then pursued at the European Convention itself (2002–3). They were selected from documents that were either the official position of a body with some kind of representative status (national parliaments, national governments and the EP) or those which summarised or focused the deliberations of one of those groups. Follow-up interviews were then requested with elite actors from the EP, national parliaments, the Commission, Council of Ministers, and the ECB.

An obvious difficulty is that the assessments of 'representatives' can no more be taken at face value than they can be disregarded. On the one hand, such views are important, since bounded rationality means that everywhere citizens acquire much of their understanding of political systems from those who 'represent' them. On the other hand, 'representatives' are themselves interested parties in the outcome of any assessment. Indeed, there is a danger of assuming the very thing that needs to be tested, namely the representative status of those who hold office in the political system that is being audited. Many of the assessments that the elite actors made of their own institutions in the documents and interviews used for this research were predictably self-serving. Others, however, were sharply self-critical, even agonising, reflecting, perhaps, that the capacity of institutions for self-delusion is limited by a long-run interest in aligning themselves with ideas they cannot fully control of what is needed for the rightful exercise of political power in society. One safeguard against more flawed forms of elite assessment is, of course, to give special credibility to these more self-critical contributions. Another is offered by the analytical framework of the Audit itself. In the chapters that follow, use of the European Democratic Audit criteria to interrogate the documentary and interview evidence helps highlight hidden assumptions, internal inconsistencies and evasions. A third safeguard is offered by the shape of the EU's political system. Its dispersion of power between heterogeneous and mutually watchful actors, allows each piece of documentary and interview evidence to be classified either as a 'self-assessment' of standards in an actor's own institution or as a 'peer review' of standards in an interlocutor body. In other words, as we will see repeatedly in the chapters that follow, elite judgements on the democratic performance of the EU can be expected to check and balance one another.

A further safeguard which applies to all kinds of 'subjective' appraisals – whether public opinion surveys or elite judgments – is that at least two forms of 'objective' evidence offer varying degrees of corroboration at little additional effort. One consists of a number of *existing* statistical series on matters as diverse as voting in European and national elections, voting in the EP and (more tentatively) the Council of Ministers, comitology controls on the Commission, questions to the Council and Commission and complaints to the Ombudsman. On the basis of some of these data sets, this book will discuss indicators of:

- Democratic identity (pp. 45–6)
- Trust (p. 48)
- Rights (p. 51)
- Citizens' knowledge and understanding of the EU (pp. 55–6)
- Voter participation (p. 65)
- Proportionality of national representation (p. 100)
- Representatives' role conceptions (p. 127).

A second reality check is provided by case studies of particular Union procedures. In many areas (such as Co-decision or Comitology) the existing literature provides an abundance of case studies. This research however develops some original case study material in relation to procedures that are recent or comparatively less well researched, including the Nice IGC (2000), the Conventions on the EU Charter of Fundamental Rights (1999–2000) and on the Future of Europe (2001–), the Investitures of the Santer (1994–5) and Prodi Commissions (1999) and, indeed, the resignation of the former (1999). Amongst more routine procedures it contains new case study material from recent experiences with the budget and budgetary discharge procedures, Second and Third pillar 'instruments' and the 'monetary dialogue' between the EP and the ECB.

Conclusion

At the beginning of the book we discussed various weaknesses in existing approaches to the assessment of democracy in the EU. This chapter has shown how Democratic Auditing can address those deficiencies. It has specified tests that are clearly derived from contending views of how the EU ought to be made democratic. It has shown how the Union might be assessed at levels of analysis that vary from the aggregate of its institutions to particular policy instruments. And it has demonstrated how different kinds of evidence of democratic performance can be pieced together in a manner that acknowledges the strengths and weaknesses of each. Now that we have set out what a strategy for a Democratic Audit of the EU, we can apply it, to see just how far it can improve our understanding of the problem of democracy and the EU.

3
Citizenship

Introduction

Two of the EU Democratic Audit (EUDA) tests listed on pages 28–9 concern citizenship. That derived from 'modified consociationalism' requires the EU to respect the autonomy of democratic citizenship as defined in each Member State (*EUDA Test 1*). That associated with 'concurrent consent' requires the Union to develop its own form of democratic citizenship (*EUDA Test 7*). The significance of the latter test is that if two sets of representative – one elected at national and the other at European level – really are to influence and control Union decisions, the EU will have to develop its own sense of democratic citizenship sufficient to support the following: a willingness to participate in European elections, a modicum of knowledge of the EU's political system, and a widespread willingness to accept the decisions of representatives elected at Union level as authoritative, even where they check and balance representatives of national democracies.

There can, perhaps, be no better confirmation that 'modified consociationalism' and 'concurrent consent' really are amongst key normative differences on how the EU ought to be constituted that the Treaty on European Union (TEU) obfuscates the positions on citizenship associated with them by announcing the creation of Union citizenship and then going on to stipulate that it will be additional to and not competitive with national citizenship (Article 17)! For our purposes the Treaty provision on citizenship is, however, both too much and too little. It is too little to the extent that much of what might pass for Union citizenship is to be found outside the Treaty. It is too much to the extent that a Democratic Audit need not assess how much substance there is to Union citizenship in general. It need only ask whether the Union has developed those selective aspects of citizenship needed to satisfy its own tests of democratic performance. What follows in this chapter is thus definitively not a discussion of the general problem of EU citizenship but only of those selective parts of the problem that allow us to evaluate whether our Democratic Audit tests are satisfied by the Union as it is presently constituted.

Dealing briefly with the first of our tests – since it seems to be the less demanding of the two – a number of factors suggest the Union does, indeed, respect the autonomy of national citizenship (*EUDA Test 1*). It is for each Member State to decide how to ratify Treaty change, how domestic representative institutions (national and regional parliaments) are to participate in Union decisions, and, to a degree, how national Members of European Parliament (MEPs) are to be elected. In addition, legal definitions of who is a citizen, and of who can vote or stand for public office are matters of national competence, with the exception that the TEU allows EU citizens to stand or vote in the European and local elections of whichever Member State they are resident (A. 18). For the most part, questions of education and culture-including curriculum content with all its consequences for identity formation and the nature of citizenship itself – are likewise national competences.

Yet, the relationship between Union Membership and national democratic citizenship is far from unproblematic. One difficulty is that however respectful the Union may be of national citizenship in practice, the supremacy of Union law means that an over-ride of national citizenship arrangements is always possible. Not only is it difficult to imagine how the Union could do without the principle of supremacy for functional reasons, the European Court of Justice (ECJ) rulings imply, as Pavlos Eleftheriadis puts it (1998, p. 258) 'all national law must give way to Community law, even if the national *constitution* has to be set aside' (see esp. Case 6/64 *Costa* v. *ENEL* (1964) ECR 585, Case 11/70 (1970) *Internationale Handelsgesellschaft* ECR 1125, Case 92/78 (1978) *Simmenthal II*). An implication, as Alex Stone Sweet argues, is that 'supremacy could work to insulate EC law from national rights protection' (2000, p. 171). European Institutions – which are not themselves subject to a legally binding Bill of Rights – could be a source of laws that lack the rights protections that, for example, help define what it is to be a German citizen yet still take priority to the rights enumerated in German Basic Law.

A second difficulty is that membership of the EU may upset some of the institutional balances on which notions of democratic citizenship are predicated in particular Member States. This problem can arise in relation to 'horizontal' separations of powers between the executive and legislative branches of government in Member States, and to vertical divisions of power between their centrally and regionally elected authorities, with European integration, in both cases, strengthening the first element at the expense of the second. Linking this difficulty to that in the previous paragraph, it should be noted that most of the Union laws which take priority over domestic ones are themselves substantially authored by actors drawn from national executives. There may thus be a 'double whammy' in which the executive branches of Member States governments are first of all strengthened at the expense of both legislative and judicial guarantors of aspects of national citizenship (Weiler, 1997b, p. 274). This may, in turn, tempt national executives to move decisions to the European arena, not because they are more likely to achieve the public welfare functions of government there, but for no better reason than that they are more likely to get their way with greater freedom from domestic constraints. Much of this can, of course, be countered by the development of legislative and judicial checks and balances at Union level. But apart from these presupposing a concurrent consent model rather than a consociational one, it begs the question from which we started out, namely of how far legislative and judicial constraints at Union level can be both uniform in their application and cognisant that autonomy in national citizenship practices may require forms of diversity that are challenged by the exposure of the domestic polity to the European.

Indeed, the more the Union becomes a system in which all contribute to decisions binding on all, the harder it may be to maintain the mantra that it is for each Member State to decide its own internal democratic institutions and practices. Since they are in so many ways sub-systems of the EU's own political system – in recruiting to Union office, in determining who participates in the making of Union decisions and in setting patterns of implementation on the ground – it is not always easy to argue that national arrangements are not also of common concern. It was precisely this problem that in 2000 led other Member States to downgrade their bilateral relations with Austria in protest at the inclusion of Jörg Haider's Freedom Party in government and thus indirectly in the Union's own collective decision-making. The Nice Treaty now even allows a four-fifths vote of the Council (with the Assent of the EP) to decide that a Member State is in 'serious and persistent' breach of the principles of the Union and to suspend certain of its membership rights. The votes of the State concerned do not count in the calculation of the majority (new A. 7).

Still, the development of a democratic citizenship at the European level can be expected to present a qualitatively different set of challenges to the mere avoidance of tensions with nationally constituted forms of citizenship. The remainder of this chapter, accordingly, assesses how far the Union has developed forms of identity, trust, rights, knowledge and participation entailed by an 'agreed democratic citizenship of the Union that individuals can use in practice' (*EUDA Test 7*).

Identity

It is often remarked that no 'democracy' can be legitimate unless its 'demos' is agreed to the mutual satisfaction of its participants. Where the right of the unit to make binding decisions is in dispute, no amount of agreement on what would be a democratically impeccable procedure for it to employ can make it legitimate. This is, moreover, the one question that cannot be determined by democratic process itself, since the latter presupposes prior settlement of the very point at issue: namely, who is to be included and who excluded from voting and deliberation (Dahl, 1989).

It might seem that there is little to add to this debate in general or to its application to the EU in particular (Chryssochou, 1994). Whilst, however, the literature on EU demos formation has acknowledged that the substance of identity can be varied and flexible, and a sense of identity can develop from within a political system, it has not fully considered the key point that what is needed by way of a shared identity varies with the type of democracy practised. Thus tests of whether citizens identify sufficiently with the EU to support institutions of concurrent consent at Union level might be twofold: first do they accept that outcomes should be co-determined by representatives of national and European level majorities, rather than the former alone? Second, are they willing to participate meaningfully in whatever elections to executive or legislative offices that are needed to form Union level majorities in the first place?

It is no easy task to discover whether citizens identify sufficiently with the EU to accept decisions made by what might pass for representative structures in the Union arena. Eurobarometer asks respondents to what degree they feel European. It also probes the acceptability of the EU as a framework for collective action without any reference to procedures by which decisions might be made. Answers to the first question are used in the Section A of Table 3.1 to develop an index of identification with the EU. Answers to the second question are then summarised in the Section B of the table which shows that across the Union as a whole a majority of respondents prefer at least some joint decision-making at both levels to action by Member States alone in most policy areas (19 out of 27).

Yet, answers are geographically varied. For example, the number of issue areas where a majority would accept at least some EU involvement rises to 27 in the case of Spain but falls to only 9 in that of Sweden. It seems plausible to imagine different sections of the population moving in opposite directions at the same time, with some embracing a euro cosmopolitanism, while others deepen their commitment to localised forms of communitarianism, defined precisely by hostility to Europeanisation. Although the EU would not be the first territorial unit to find that contending constructions of its own identity are amongst the main cleavages that have to be managed by its shared institutions, the *distribution* of feelings of identification with the political system may be as much a constraint on options for its democratic development as their *level*, particularly when, as will be discussed in the next chapter, geography is the basis for who has vetoes on questions of institutional design.

Of more direct relevance are the questions set out in Section C of Table 3.1, since all probe the willingness of respondents to accept that Union level majorities should determine political outcomes. At first sight the results seem at odds with one another. Questions 4 and 5 (asked as a pair) indicate limits to the acceptability of majority decisions in the form of reluctance to see Member States lose their veto rights in matters they consider to be of vital national interest. Yet Questions 6–8 (also asked as a block) show some willingness to embrace majoritarianism in the form of a preference for a Commission Presidency chosen by a parliamentary or electoral majority of the Union as a whole over one appointed by Heads of Government. Question 9 then confirms an overwhelming public view. that the Commission should have to retain the confidence of the European Parliament (EP). It may just be that respondents were not fully aware of the implication of their answers to these questions. However, an alternative possibility is that elements of majoritarianism at selected points in the EU's political system – such as appointment of a Commission President – would be acceptable precisely if accompanied by safeguards for representatives of Member States at others.

Indeed, it is highly questionable that the Union lacks sufficient identity to support public acceptance of its decisions. There are few

Table 3.1 Public identification with the EU

	EU15	*Aus*	*Bel*	*Den*	*Fin*	*Fr*	*Ger*	*Gr*	*Ire*	*It*	*Lux*	*Neth*	*P*	*Sp*	*Swe*	*UK*
A. Feelings of identity																
1. Index of Feeling of Europeanness (0–1)[1]	0.25	0.23	0.29	0.24	0.17	0.27	0.28	0.20	0.21	0.32	0.35	0.23	0.21	0.28	0.17	0.16
2. Percentage who feel exclusively national	38	45	34	38	55	33	39	48	47	20	26	41	43	28	54	62
B. Acceptance of joint decision-making																
3. Number of issue areas (max 27) where majority accept joint decision-making	19	13	19	12	10	17	20	16	14	23	20	17	21	27	9	10
C. Acceptance of majority decisions																
4. Member States should retain vetoes to preserve essential national interests	50	67	45	71	62	51	51	69	57	51	68	50	44	38	60	47
5. States should drop vetoes to make EU more efficient	25	16	33	18	27	28	30	12	15	25	17	32	15	23	26	19
6. The President of the Commission should be selected by Heads of Govt	14	16	11	22	22	16	13	14	23	15	18	14	21	13	18	10
7. EP should elect President of the Commission	32	31	35	40	35	26	38	35	21	37	30	39	18	25	39	24

Table 3.1 Continued

	EU15	*Aus*	*Bel*	*Den*	*Fin*	*Fr*	*Ger*	*Gr*	*Ire*	*It*	*Lux*	*Neth*	*P*	*Sp*	*Swe*	*UK*
8. Citizens should elect President of the Commission	34	32	36	25	29	41	33	31	28	32	42	31	26	34	29	36
9. Commission should resign if loses confidence of EP (balance of those agreeing over disagreeing)	+55	+61	+53	+70	+75	+55	+63	+54	+50	+64	+70	+50	+42	+58	+66	+31
D. EU citizenship education																
10. The EU should be taught at school (balance of those agreeing over disagreeing)	+71	+77	+79	+82	+82	+73	+72	+70	+79	+81	+87	+83	+79	+70	+87	+50

[1] The index of feelings of Europeanness is calculated from the answers in Eurobarometer 57 (2002) to the standard question in which respondents are asked whether they feel (a) European only (b) in the first place European and in the second place citizens of their own country (c) citizens of their own country in the first place and European in the second place (d) national only. Responses (d) to (a) are scored from 0 to 3 respectively and then expressed as a decimal of the maximum possible score taking into account 'don't knows' for each country.

historical examples of widespread non-compliance of citizens with Union decisions. Since this extends even to cases where an unpopular measure is widely understood to have originated from Union institutions it cannot be attributed to a tendency to experience Union rules as national ones on account of their implementation by domestic agencies. It may just be that the EU does after all have a political system that is broadly compatible with low and uneven levels of identification. Its consensus procedures lighten the need to identify in order to accept.

Trust

As Andreas Føllesdal (2001) has put it, 'trust in the future behaviour of others is the necessary backdrop to both veto and majoritarian arrangements' for democratic institution building at Union level. Participants in any democratic decision-making at Union level have to be able to trust that provisions for majority-voting will not be used to extract rents from minorities, and, conversely, that provisions for the protection of minorities will not be used to lock in policies that later turn out to be dysfunctional, oppressive or unjust to all but the minority that refuses to lift its veto on their reform. In addition, the argument that deliberative standards can soften the trade-offs in democratic institution building and the often coercive implications of using any kind of voting as a decision rule (see p. 24) depends on trust that all other actors will observe those standards in practice. This may be a tall order since deliberative standards are often defined in a way that presupposes a 'high level of virtue': a willingness to reflect on the preferences of others, to reason publicly and to consider the force of the better argument regardless of considerations of power or interest (Rawls, 1993; Habermas, 1996; Elster, 1998).

Clauss Offe (1999) distinguishes various dimensions of trust including the 'vertical trust' of citizens in the institutions and elites of a political system and their 'horizontal trust' in one another. What is, of course, distinctive about the EU is that the 'others' who need to be trusted because they participate in decisions affecting the lives of all include the governments and citizens of other states. Responses to the first four questions in Table 3.2 suggest that at first blush 'vertical trust' in the institutions of the EU is higher than that of most citizens in their own national governments and parliaments. However, at least one source of mistrust is revealed by answers to question 8. Large states are widely

Table 3.2 Trust in Union institutions and in other EU nationals

	EU15	*Aus*	*Bel*	*Den*	*Fin*	*Fr*	*Ger*	*Gr*	*Ire*	*It*	*Lux*	*Neth*	*Por*	*Sp*	*Swe*	*UK*
Trust in EU																
1. Balance of those trusting over those not trusting EU.	+9	−6	+14	+5	−10	−4	+4	+24	+28	+42	+35	+14	+47	+26	−29	−22
2. Balance of those trusting EP over those not trusting it.	+30	+14	+31	+28	+24	+28	+31	+38	+52	+59	+50	+37	+46	+36	+11	−3
Trust in national institutions																
3. Balance of those trusting over those not trusting their national government.	−12	+5	−3	+19	+16	−33	−14	−16	−4	−20	+48	+30	+1	+3	+14	−23
4. Balance of those trusting over those not trusting their national parliament.	+5	+14	−3	+34	+13	−26	−3	+6	+2	−10	+39	+26	+11	+4	+25	−13
Trust in other EU nationals																
5. Percentage of those who fear living in another EU country because of being treated as a foreigner (Eurobarometer, 1995, p. 47).	56	48	48	51	40	50	53	60	41	59	40	47	48	73	52	62
6. Percentage of those who fear living in another EU country because of being disadvantaged (ibid.).	49	37	39	47	38	41	37	47	40	55	36	35	45	75	49	62
Fears																
7. EU will mean loss identity/culture. (Balance of those agreeing over disagreeing.)	−12	−23	−32	−10	−15	+3	−25	+19	+1	−39	−13	−12	+8	−25	+3	+28
8. Big states impose decisions on small. (Balance of those agreeing over disagreeing.)	+14	+12	+17	+36	+49	+19	−12	+37	+27	+11	+26	+41	+32	+9	+51	+28

suspected of using Union institutions to 'impose decisions' on smaller ones. Only in Germany does a majority of respondents fail to see this as a difficulty. In Denmark, Finland, Greece, Netherlands and Sweden particularly large numbers of respondents agree that it is a reason for fearing integration.

On the question of 'horizontal trust' Eurobarometer has not directly asked how far Union citizens 'trust people' from other Member States since 1990 (Niedermayer, 1995). Indirect evidence is, however, available from a 1995 survey that asked respondents about fears that would inhibit them taking up their rights to reside in another Member State. This probed how far different EU nationalities trusted others to treat them impartially and not as 'foreigners'. Around half of the overall Union population (Table 3.2, lines 5 and 6) lack that feeling of trust, rising to 73 per cent amongst Spanish respondents.

If, as argued above, members of a shared democratic process need to be able to trust one another to observe deliberative standards, it is worrying that a further survey (Eurobarometer, no. 55, 2001, pp. 76–8) shows that only 26 per cent of respondents have any interest in 'taking part in discussions about Europe' while 62 per cent are 'not interested'. Moreover, even amongst the former group 'exchanging my views with other people living in our country' or 'with national politicians' are more popular motives for dialogue than 'exchanging views with people living in other countries' or with 'politicians from other countries' or even with 'EU politicians such as Commissioners and MEPs'. If such findings are to be taken at face value, they indicate that any delivery of deliberative standards in the European arena may for the foreseeable future have to rely on the elite level unsupported by the popular. Indeed, they support the view that it is precisely reciprocal recognition between individuals from different Member States which is the weakest part of the notion of EU citizenship as it has so far developed (Hitzel-Cassagnes, 2000, p. 20; Shaw, 1997).

Other possible measures of the two dimensions of trust are more behavioural. Drawing on the observation that trust is equivalent to 'low investment in information, monitoring and sanctioning' (quoted in Offe, 1999, p. 46) we might take as a possible sign of horizontal trust the significant discretion that Member States of the EU seem to allow each other to implement their contributions to commonly agreed decisions. On the other hand, the profusion of comitology controls around the Commission might indicate a low level of vertical trust in the Union's supranational executive. Telling evidence of this difference in trust is provided by Fabio Franchino who has constructed a 'discretion index' and applied it to a sample of EU legislation. He finds that the discretion index is just 4.4 per cent when the Council of Ministers delegates executive powers to the Commission, compared with 16.2 per cent when delegation is to Member States acting individually (Franchino, 2001, p. 25).

Rights

Since it presupposes elements of election, referendum or deliberation at Union level, a concurrent consent standard of European democracy requires the classic freedoms of expression and association, as well as rights to the impartial and effective administration of elections. Enjoyment of these rights in relation to the Union arena is largely derivative of national arrangements. A good starting point is, therefore, with independent surveys of how the foregoing rights are delivered within Member States. On the whole, these surveys indicate that EU Member States score well by international comparison. Under Freedom House scores for overall political rights and civil liberties, all EU Member States score between 1.1 and 1.3 on a scale of 1.0 to 7.0 (Freedom House, Annual Freedom in the World Country Scores 1972–3 to 2001–2).

However, it is instructive to analyse outstanding concerns. One Freedom House survey appraises media freedom under the following heads:

- legal restrictions (mainly defamation laws);
- political pressures, controls and violence;
- economic pressures on content (mainly concentration of media ownership in the hands of a few).

Table 3.3 shows that in several EU countries economic pressures are the only significant blemishes on media freedom. Part of the problem is that several Member States are relatively small markets in which it is difficult for a wide range of media companies to compete against one another with economies of scale. However, the election in Italy of the Berlusconi Government demonstrates a further difficulty: some Member States have insufficient safeguards against the possibility that control of sections of the private and public media may be merged as an outcome of the democratic process itself. Freedom House notes that in addition to Berlusconi's private holdings, the state-owned TV network and three radio channels fall within the responsibilities of his government (ibid., p. 33). An example of how this source of media unfreedom may impact directly on citizens' access to information on the EU is that

Table 3.3 Measures of media freedom in EU Member States (Freedom House, 2002)

	Aus	*Bel*	*Den*	*Fin*	*Fr*	*Ger*	*Gr*	*Ire*	*It*	*Lux*	*Neth*	*Por*	*Sp*	*Swe*	*UK*
Restrictiveness of laws 0 (free)–30 (un-free)	10	2	1	1	2	2	16	5	2	3	5	3	1	1	4
Political pressures on media freedom, 0 (free)–40 (un-free)	6	2	1	3	5	8	6	4	11	4	4	5	9	2	7
Economic pressures on media freedom, 0 (free)–30 (un-free)	8	5	7	6	10	5	8	7	14	7	6	7	7	5	7
Overall score on scale of 0 (free)–100 un-free	24	9	9	10	17	15	30	16	27	14	15	15	17	8	18

Radiotelevisione Italia (RAI) – the most watched of the Italian TV chains – was one of the few in the Union not to transmit the precise words that Berlusconi used to insult a German MEP in a speech to the Parliament in his role as President of the Council in July 2003.

The remaining two sources of an 'un-free' media – legal restrictions and political pressures – are low on average across the Union. But they can reach significant levels in particular Member States. Some problems may be idiosyncratic or the fault of actors other than the state. An example of the first is that the French Government, requires journalists to register and runs a scheme for their financial support. By all accounts this is innocuous in practice but the potential for abuse is clear. An example of the second is the targeting of Spanish journalists by ETA terrorists (ibid., p. 46). Other country case studies are, however, more worrying. Freedom House observed in the case of Greece:

> Although the Constitution guarantees freedom of expression, the government often ignores that right. In March the government closed 66 radio stations in Athens, claiming they interfered with frequencies used by the new airport…This set off clamorous bids for licences and permitted the authorities to select which news channels should be licensed and which not.

Such interferences may, moreover, have a direct bearing on how citizens and Union institutions are linked to one another in public debate. The Freedom House report goes on to cite an example of how the Greek government brought – but repeatedly delayed – a prosecution against an individual for circulating a report of an EU institution on ethnic questions in Greece (Freedom House, 2002, pp. 20 and 30).

It may not, however, always be enough to rely on rights established within national arenas. Some original rights may need to be defined at EU level if there is to be equal and effective participation of individuals in a Union-based democratic process. This raises the question of whether the Union has a means of defining such rights that is itself democratically defensible. As will be discussed at greater length in Chapter 8 the ECJ is a major originator of rights in the European arena. It has attempted to infer rights from the Treaties, from the common traditions of the Member States and from what the latter have agreed in subscribing to the European Convention on Human Rights (ECHR). This however raises two difficulties. One is whether the ECJ's is more focused on using rights to build a polity and an identity than for the specific purpose of protecting individuals against the abuse of political power.

A second is that the ECJ is, of course, an unelected body. Although it is not unusual for unelected judges to develop a substantial rights jurisprudence in democratic political systems, this is usually conditional on an elected legislature always being able to exercise an over-ride for which it is itself electorally accountable. A problem, therefore, for the EU is that the judicial role in the origination of rights may be far more developed than the legislative. The EP cannot overturn ECJ decisions at all, and the European Council can only do so if it is unanimous, with the result that the ECJ is hardly in the analogous position of national courts of having to anticipate some median representative or voter in its rights jurisprudence.

We will see at greater length in the next chapter how the Cologne European Council (1999) agreed to deal with these difficulties by appointing a Convention to draw up a Charter of Rights specific to the Union. The Convention drew its representation from national governments, national parliaments and the EP. By all accounts it achieved some success in applying deliberative standards (relatively free from considerations of power and interest) to the framing of rights. It was also able to decide a text by consensus (see esp. Schönlau, 2001). However, it is open to the criticism that it remained, none the less, an elite exercise that attracted little public attention beyond already organised groups of civil society. In addition the Charter remains to be authoritatively adopted and incorporated into the Treaty. At the time of writing, it has no effect unless the ECJ chooses of its own accord to take into account in developing its own rights jurisprudence. This, as Joe Weiler points out (2002, p. 575) creates a contradictory result from the point of view of democracy assessment: either the Charter is ignored or it is taken into account in spite of the fact that it is not constitutionally authorised.

Knowledge and understanding

Democratic citizenship plainly requires knowledge of the political system. Choices between candidates and parties in European elections, and associational activity in relation to Union institutions, imply an instrumental understanding of how the EU's political system can be used to promote particular needs and values. Individuals should at least have sufficient grasp of means–ends relationships in the European arena to put all choices available to them in an ordinal ranking, even if the precise consequences of each option are unknowable. Deliberative ideals – such as an ability to reflect on the arguments of others – are even more demanding of citizens' understanding. Some of the limited evidence of whether individuals do indeed have sufficient knowledge and understanding to exercise those citizenship roles and capabilities presupposed by the EU's political system are set out in Table 3.4. Section A of the table simply reproduces a subjective measure of how much respondents think they know about the Union, and uses it to compute a 'balance' and an 'index' of how self-confident they feel in their knowledge. Across the Union as a whole those who do not feel self-confident in their knowledge of the Union outnumber those who do by 43 per cent. In no Member State is the balance positive, yet it varies hugely from −5 per cent in Austria to −65 per cent in the UK. The index of self-confidence likewise averages 0.36 across the Union, with variation from 0.27 (UK) to 0.46 (Austria).

Citizens do not just lack confidence in their own knowledge about the EU. Objective tests show they really are poorly informed. Richard Sinnott has analysed replies to 30 Eurobarometer questions that test citizens' knowledge of the EU. He found two-thirds of respondents had 'no', 'little' or not very much knowledge. In contrast, knowledge of national political systems was 'high to very high' (see discussion in Blondel *et al.*, 1998, pp. 92–9). Sinnott's approach demonstrates the value of not merely aggregating citizens' knowledge of the EU into a single score, but of distinguishing different kinds of understanding of the Union's political system – of its institutions, of its policies and of its *dramatis personae* – and then drawing inferences from patterns of weakness or strength. Since public understanding of these dimensions has recently also been tested by a series of 86 focus groups from right across the 15 Member States of the Union and 9 candidate countries – the Commission's Optem survey (European Commission, 2001b) – it is possible to complement Eurobarometer statistics with more qualitative and spontaneous evidence of where gaps in citizens' understanding of the EU are most glaring.

Knowledge of EU institutions

Section B of Table 3.4 shows many citizens claim to have 'heard something' about what are probably the five Union institutions most likely to influence their lives. However, the distribution of Citizen awareness across Member States and particular institutions is significant. The average level of awareness of the five institutions varies from 90.6 per cent in Luxembourg to just 61.4 per cent in the UK.

It is also questionable how far the EU's political system is understood in the same way across national arenas. Although it is a structure in

Table 3.4 Public knowledge of the EU

	EU15	*Aus*	*Bel*	*Den*	*Fin*	*Fr*	*Ger*	*Gr*	*Ire*	*It*	*Lux*	*Neths*	*Por*	*Sp*	*Swe*	*UK*
A. Self-perceived knowledge																
Percentage of those rating their own knowledge of the EU as:																
(a) Almost nothing	21	10	21	10	18	20	14	17	28	17	17	22	32	22	13	37
(b) A bit	50	41	45	54	51	54	48	50	47	48	55	46	50	57	60	45
(c) Quite a lot	26	41	32	33	29	24	31	30	21	31	22	31	16	18	26	16
(d) A great deal	2	5	1	3	2	1	4	2	3	2	6	0	2	2	1	1
Balance (c + d) – (a + b) (Eurobarometer 57)	**−43**	**−5**	**−33**	**−28**	**−38**	**−49**	**−27**	**−35**	**−51**	**−32**	**−44**	**−37**	**−64**	**−59**	**−46**	**−65**
Index of respondents self-confidence in their knowledge of EU.[1]	0.36	0.46	0.37	0.43	0.38	0.35	0.41	0.39	0.33	0.39	0.39	0.36	0.29	0.33	0.38	0.27
B. Awareness of institutions																
Percentage of those who have recently heard of:																
Commission	78	87	85	92	95	82	84	81	86	80	94	84	81	80	85	73
Council of Ministers	63	76	72	77	76	54	54	68	67	73	83	66	76	78	90	36
ECJ	73	84	77	95	79	67	77	67	67	57	90	78	70	62	71	56
ECB	67	84	71	82	91	67	81	56	84	76	89	83	76	75	80	56
EP	89	90	92	98	97	92	84	81	95	93	97	96	87	90	96	86
Ave of above	**74**	**84.2**	**79.4**	**88.8**	**87.6**	**72.4**	**76**	**70.6**	**79.8**	**75.8**	**90.6**	**81.4**	**78**	**77**	**84.4**	**61.4**
Committee Regions	27	47	31	33	40	27	27	29	31	26	39	13	49	42	24	12
Convention (Eurobarometer 57)	28	41	35	39	34	32	21	29	32	26	48	28	47	42	28	14
Index of specificity of citizens' assessments of the EP	0.26	0.26	0.16	0.33	0.28	0.21	0.33	0.22	0.26	0.24	0.31	0.30	0.16	0.18	0.30	0.26

Table 3.4 Continued

	EU15	Aus	Bel	Den	Fin	Fr	Ger	Gr	Ire	It	Lux	Neths	Por	Sp	Swe	UK
C. Awareness of policies																
Agriculture/Fisheries (Optem, Focus Groups)	13	X	X	X	X	X	X		X	X		X	X	X	X	X
Education/Culture	4		X								X		X	X		
Energy	4	X	X			X				X						
Employment	3							X		X	X					
Environment	7	X		X				X	X		X	X			X	
External Security	4	X			X									X	X	
Health/Consumers	6	X				X	X		X			X	X			
Human Rights	2							X	X							
Internal Security	7	X				X		X		X	X	X		X		
Monetary (euro)	13	X	X	X	X	X		X	X	X	X	X	X	X	X	
Single Market/Trade	7		X	X	X	X						X	X		X	
Social	7	X	X					X					X	X	X	X
Structural/Regional	6				X		X		X					X	X	X
Transport/Infrastructure	3	X	X									X				
Total number of Union policies recognised		9	7	4	5	6	3	6	6	5	5	7	6	6	7	3
D. Country rankings																
Self-perceived knowledge		1	9	2	8	11	3	5	13	5	8	10	14	13	4	15
Awareness of 5 main EU institutions		5	8	2	3	13	11	14	7	12	1	6	9	10	4	15
Attention		4	11	3	6	9	12	1	14	2	6	15	10	9	7	14
Awareness of own country's Presidency of the Council		6	7	5	2	14	13	5	9	12	11	5	9	10	1	15

[1] Index of Self-confidence is computed by scoring responses from 0 (know almost nothing) to 3 (know a great deal) and then expressing the result as a decimal of the maximum possible score.

which outcomes are shaped by interactions between institutions as much as by decisions within any one body, Member States vary in how far their citizens have a comprehensive, rather than a selective, ability to recognise the main Union institutions. In some (Austria and Luxembourg), public recognition is relatively even across all five main institutions of the EU. In others (France and the UK), there is a wide difference in levels of recognition of individual Union institutions. The example of the ECB illustrates that knowledge of Union institutions may not even correlate with membership of them. Respondents in Denmark, Sweden and the UK are equally above or below the EU average in their recognition of the ECB (of which their country is not a member) as they are in their recognition of the other four institutions in which their countries participate fully.

The fact that the Council of Ministers has the lowest public recognition amongst the main institutions arguably means that citizens' understanding of the EU's political system is in inverse proportion to the actual distribution of power (Blondel *et al.*, 1998, p. 93). Indeed those claiming to 'have heard something' about the Council of Ministers fall to particularly low levels in at least three out of four of those large Member States – France, Germany and the UK – that are best placed to exercise its powers as measured by voting weights. This has serious implications. First, citizens are likely to exaggerate the powers of the Commission and EP and underestimate those of the Council in a manner that leads to misattribution of responsibility for outcomes. Indeed, the Optem survey found that UK focus groups tended even to 'confuse' the Commission 'with the Union as a whole' (p. 71). Second, claims that the Council can function as a 'representative body' are not yet underpinned by public consciousness of it. Again, the Optem focus group findings drive the point home:

> Only the Commission and Parliament are recognised as institutions, even though the public barely know what they do. Sometimes the Court of Justice is also recognised, though it is commonly confused with other international or European Courts. The Council of Ministers is not generally known, the European Council even less so.

As suggested by this quotation, the standard Eurobarometer which asks respondents whether they have recently heard anything about the EU institutions is too superficial to test understanding of them. A more occasional Eurobarometer question asks respondents whether they have particular likes and dislikes about the European Parliament. This is used in the last line of Section B of Table 3.4 to construct an index that shows that public assessments of the Parliament are lacking in specificity (only 0.26 on average across the Union as a whole), even though the EP is also the Union institution of which Eurobarometer respondents claim to be most aware.

Only the Optem survey (rather than the aggregate Eurobarometer results) comes close to testing public comprehension of the composition, powers and roles of the Union institutions, as well as demarcations between them. Understanding seems least deficient on questions of institutional composition. Focus groups in several Member States identified Commissioners as nationally appointed and the EP as comprising directly elected MEPs. Many were also aware that national leaders and other ministers meet to discuss Union questions but few named those gatherings as the European Council and Council of Ministers respectively or understood them as structured parts of the Union decision-making process. Many of the focus groups seemed to assume that Member States watch the EU from the sidelines, rather than participate as decision-makers. Indeed, understanding of roles was reported as patchy, and that of 'interactions' between institutions as almost non-existent.

Knowledge of actors

If citizens have poor understanding of the EU institutions and the distribution of power between them, they also have difficulty putting a 'face on the Union'. As Blondel *et al.* (1998, p. 96) point out even Jacques Delors enjoyed lower public recognition than national ministers of finance and foreign affairs – let alone Prime Ministers – at the end of his ten-year tenure of the Presidency of the Commission. Documents produced by the Commission agree that the seeming facelessness of the institutional process is a source of alienation from it:

> People do not know the difference between the institutions. They do not understand who takes the decisions that affect them. They expect Union institutions to be as visible as national governments ... People are dissatisfied because they fail to understand the Union's objectives and are often unable to put names and faces to tasks. (European Commission, 2000d, pp. 4–5)

Of course, another dimension to understanding the *dramatic personae* of Union politics is to have knowledge of which other countries are

Member States. Given that democracy is rule by others, it would be a concern if citizens had difficulties naming the other Member States whose representatives participate in decisions binding on all. One of the few pieces of evidence on this score is the survey for Blondel *et al.* (1998, p. 96) which indicates that respondents commonly identify around a half of EU Member States and that some – France and Germany – are almost recognised as being fellow Members. Beyond that, however, confusion lies.

Nor, indeed, would citizens even seem to have much understanding of their own somewhat limited role in the EU. Eurobarometer 47 tested public awareness of eleven EU 'citizenship rights'. Average awareness was just 34 per cent. The least known of the rights (recognised by 23–25 per cent of respondents) was, in fact, the one which relates most directly to the democratic process, namely that of any EU national to stand and vote in the local or European elections of another Member State if resident there. A further survey (Blondel *et al.*, 1998, p. 93) indicates that answers to the question 'who elects the EP?' are only slightly better than random although many respondents presumably have themselves taken part in European elections.

Knowledge of policies

If individuals seem to lack understanding of the input side of Union politics – of the institutional opportunity structure to channel, aggregate, consult or deliberate individual preferences – do they at least have some knowledge of its outputs: of what 'public goods' it provides or of what allocations of value its institutions make? At first sight, citizens would seem to have better understanding of at least some of the policies and outputs of the Union than the processes by which they are produced. Some of the Union's outputs – the CAP, the Euro and the Single Market Programme – seem to be fairly widely known. Otherwise, understanding of what the Union does is patchy, once again across national arenas, but also between policies themselves (Table 3.3, line 5).

Even if citizens had more understanding of the output than the input side of the EU's political system, it is unclear how reassuring that finding would be. It could even be read as confirming that citizens have a fatalistic conception of themselves as objects rather than actors in the Union polity, and that, they, accordingly, regard it as a technocracy, rather than a democracy. To the extent that such a supposition discourages participation in debate or investment of effort in the acquisition of knowledge of how the Union works (European Commission, 2001b) it is in danger of being self-fulfilling. It is to the question of the 'developmental dimension' of democracy that we now turn.

Developmental democracy?

All the foregoing is based on snapshots from various surveys. If, however, we are to judge whether the cognitive shortcomings of democratic citizenship are likely to be permanent or temporary, we also need insights into how knowledge of the EU changes over time. One possibility is that the knowledge required for equal and effective democratic citizenship is a capacity that grows with use (March and Olsen, 1995, pp. 96–8). As David Held puts it (1996, p. 313), 'we learn to participate by participating': each act of participation improves the continuing ability of citizens to use the political system to aggregate and deliberate their preferences. Even a more passive growth of public knowledge of the EU with time seems plausible. First, the proportion of those who have been affected by EU institutions and policies for a significant part of their adult lives rises the longer a country has been a Member of the Union. Second, most complex systems eventually lend themselves to a language of simplification. Third, average levels of educational attainment are still rising across European societies. Bernard Wessels claims to have found some evidence for a 'diffusion model' in which understanding of the EU is becoming less uneven between social groups: 'the impact of stratifying characteristics – education and occupation in the social realm, degree of political involvement in the political realm – on attitudes towards the EC has declined. The Community has become more familiar to all groups in society…' (Wessels, 1995, p. 135).

Yet, even if sections of society are becoming less unequal in their understanding of the Union, it is less clear how far overall levels of public awareness of the EU are on a rising trajectory. One cause for pessimism is that survey respondents do not seem to have become any more self-confident over time in the assessments they make of their own knowledge of the Union. It may, of course, just be their feelings of what they ought to know keeps expanding in a knowledge-based society. Another indicator, however, suggests their environment is becoming less 'information rich' on EU questions, maybe not because there is objectively less information available on the Union, but, as much as anything else, on account of the huge competition any topic has in struggling for attention in a media culture that it at once fragmented and saturated. One indicator which is useful because it is based on a question regularly asked by Eurobarometer since 1977 is the percentage of those claiming recently to have heard something about the EP. Figure 3.1 shows how positive answers have followed a consistent pattern. They regularly fall to a trough 12–18 months before European elections and then increase significantly at the time of the poll. On the one hand, this would seem to confirm European elections do promote political socialisation. On the other hand, that effect would not seem to be lasting. Each spike in awareness of the EP has failed to produce any long-term uptrend. As Blondel *et al.* put it (1998, pp. 86–7):

> it is surprising there is little or no evidence of a cumulative increase in the awareness of media coverage of the European Parliament over the last two decades: in 1994 awareness of the European Parliament was only marginally ahead of what it had been in 1977, two years before the first direct elections.

Indeed, peaks in 'awareness of the EP through the media' were lower during the European elections of the 1990s than in those of the 1980s, suggesting either declining media coverage or diminishing citizen interest (Eurobarometer, no. 52, 2000, p. 79). In fact, it is by no means far-fetched to expect understanding of the Union to fade with time. One of the main educational experiences available to Member societies is accession itself which, in many cases, involves negotiation of several Union policies and then a referendum.

Another way of appraising the likely stubbornness of low public understanding of the EU is to probe possible causes of the problem. Here it is worth considering four (partially overlapping) possibilities: poor understanding is sustained by institutional features of the EU itself, by variations in the willingness of national government to inform their

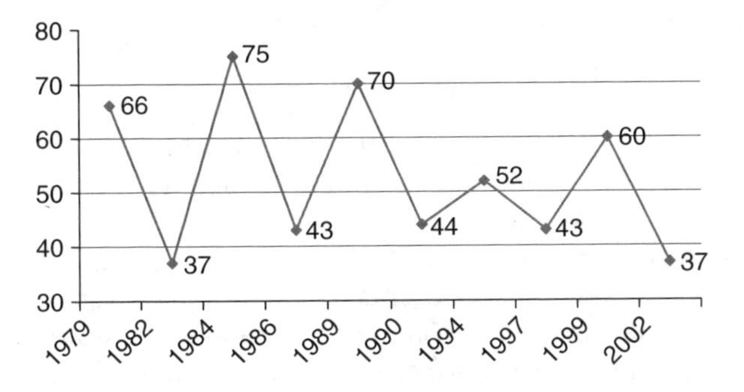

Figure 3.1 Percentage of those who have recently heard about the EP through the media (various Eurobarometers)

own citizens on Union questions, by variations in the motivation of individual citizens or by the media. The first and fourth of these possibilities are analysed later in this chapter. The second – and to a lesser extent the third – can be approached by ranking countries (see Table 3.4, Section D) by how their citizens score according to the following:

- General self-perceived knowledge of the EU.
- Average awareness of individual Union institutions.
- Assessments of their own attentiveness to EU questions.
- Awareness of their own country's Presidency of the Council. This last can be taken as a proxy for how willing Member States are to publicise their own participation in the EU.

Spearman rank coefficients calculated from Section D of Table 3.4. indicate that variations in self-perceived knowledge of the Union are modestly correlated to variations in the willingness of governments to publicise national participation in the EU (as indicated by public awareness of Council Presidencies) and strongly related to individual 'attentiveness' or cognitive mobilisation. Awareness of Council Presidencies may incidentally suggest that the quality of national political systems as arenas for political socialisation into the Union may have something to do with the size of Member States. The publics that are least aware of their own country's Presidency of the Council are all those of the larger Member States: UK (15th), France (14th), Germany (13th) and Italy (12th).

It is, of course, the media as much as political elites that shapes opportunities for the development of a European democratic citizenship through learning about the EU. Media representations of the EU have recently been the subject of rigorous forms of content analysis (de Vreese, 2001; Garcia and Le Torrec, 2003). Amongst the main findings of these studies are the following:

(1) Citizens claim to gain more of their information about the EU from audio–visual than print media, and to put significantly more trust in its reliability (various Eurobarometers).
(2) Regardless of source, media coverage of the EU tends to be sporadic and 'events based'. Those events divide into major launches of new policies (the Euro or enlargement), the more theatrical moments in the political cycle (European Councils and to a lesser extent European elections) and crises (BSE). Coverage is not only light and intermittent, it is also variable in quantity across Member States.

Fascinating data compiled for five Member States by Guillaume Garcia and Virginie le Torrec (2003, p. 119) put the average coverage of the EU by hour of televised news at 7.5 per cent with the following distribution between countries: Germany (10.6 per cent), France (10.1), UK (7.4), Italy (6.9) and the Netherlands (2.4).

(3) The probability of an EU matter receiving media coverage rises if it involves conflict, personalities, finance or 'real life situations'. Thus, clashes between heads of government in European Councils and the adoption of the euro in particular businesses or communities were amongst the most widely covered EU stories during 1999–2002.

(4) It is rare for news coverage of the EU to be 'purely' European or national in character. Rather, it follows two kinds of framing: a form of 'internalisation' in which a Union policy is illustrated through its application to a 'real-life situation' within the Member State; and a form of 'externalisation' in which the handling of domestic issues is put in a European context, usually through country-to-country comparisons with our 'European partners' designed to bring out qualities or deficiencies in national policy delivery. None of this framing is innocent. Given the predominantly national character of the European media, it contributes, to there being as many European public opinions as there are Member States. Le Torrec and Garcia describe this 'as a logic of national appropriation of European affairs' (2003, p. 121). They find crucially that the EU tends to be presented as an object of national policy rather than a shared political system (p. 125) and that common problems are differently defined. Thus, BSE was a public health problem for the French media, and one of rural employment for the British. Moreover citizens watching different national media are likely to develop different institutional understandings of the EU. The number of EU-related news items that make no mention of institutions is only 13 per cent in Germany, but it rises to a massive 56 per cent in the UK. Moreover, supranational institutions are more than four times as likely to be mentioned than intergovernmental ones in the UK. In Germany the ratio is closer to 2 : 1 (p. 127). As argued earlier, this matters if the EU is to be understood as an inter-institutional political system, whose decisions are not those of 'another', but, in part, of national governments themselves, to whom citizens can look to provide representation on the one hand and take responsibility on the other.

(5) Although European elections are the one opportunity for mass democratic participation in the Union, they cannot be assured of significant coverage in all Members States. In a comparative content

analysis of the British, Danish and Dutch media, Claes De Vreese found that the key Dutch TV networks 'mentioned the [1999] elections only once, on the evening prior to Election Day'.

An interesting footnote to our discussion of the development of civic capabilities in relationship to the Union arena is, however, provided by returning to Table 3.1. on page 46. Answers to question 10 suggest there is little principled opposition to a European democratic citizenship. To the contrary, there are high and uniform levels of support for the inclusion of information about the EU in school curricula.

Participation

The main opportunity for citizens to participate in the EU arena is through five-yearly elections of representatives to the EP. Turn-out is significantly lower than for national general elections. This section analyses electoral abstention and participation, and appraises whether low turn-out is either a defect in its own right or an indicator of the underdevelopment of other aspects of democratic citizenship at Union level (Table 3.5).

Table 3.5 Turn-out to European elections

	1999 Elections for European Parliament (1)	*Turn-out to immediately prior national general election (2)*	*Difference 1 & 2 (3)*	*Participation of non-nationals in elections 1994 (4)*
Austria	49.4	86.0	−36.6	7.9 (1996)
Belgium	90.9	90.5	+0.4	5.1
Denmark	50.5	86.0	−35.5	24.8
Finland	30.0	65.3	−35.3	22.0
France	46.7	67.8	−21.2	3.4
Germany	45.19	82.2	−37.01	6.6
Greece	70.3	64.2	+6.1	1.5
Ireland	50.7	68.5	−17.7	44.1
Italy	69.8	82.8	−13.0	1.8
Luxembourg	86.6	86.7	−0.1	6.5
The Netherlands	30.0	73.4	−43.4	Unknown
Portugal	40.0	66.3	−26.3	2.3
Spain	64.3	77.3	−13.0	12.6
Sweden	38.8	81.4	−42.6	24.0 (1996)
UK	24.0	71.5	−47.5	1.9
EU Mean	49.6	76.1	−27.5	

According to a slightly different measure to that used in Table 3.5, average participation in the 1999 European elections was 52.8 per cent. This was 24.3 per cent less than average of participation in the most recent general elections in Member States. If however we exclude cases where voting is compulsory (Belgium, Greece and Luxembourg) the average turn-out figure falls to 51.2 per cent and the shortfall from participation in national general elections rises to 25.9 per cent. If we also exclude Italy on the grounds that voting was compulsory there until 1993 and habits die hard, the averages are 47.6 and 29.5 per cent respectively. Indeed, there are only three Member States where more than half of the population registered to vote in European elections actually did so in 1999 (Denmark (50.4 per cent), Ireland (50.7) and Spain (64.6)), once all cases where present and previous compulsory voting may have affected participation are ignored.

As this suggests, there are also significant variations across Member States. In Spain the shortfall from participation in the most recent general election was a comparatively modest 13.0 per cent. Yet in Germany, Sweden, the Netherlands and the UK, participation in the 1999 European elections was respectively 37.01, 42.6, 43.4 and 47.5 per cent lower than for the preceding general election. Intriguingly there are also differences within states in turn-out for European elections. The most extensive study of the problem (Blondel *et al.*, 1998) points out that even within the Eastern part of Germany, turn-out for the 1994 election exceeded 70 per cent in two Länder. Yet, it fell below 50 per cent in a third. There were likewise variations of up to 30 per cent between regions of Spain (pp. 32–3).

A further concern is that turn-out to European elections is not only relatively low. It is also apparently declining. Over the last 20 years it has been 65.8 (1979), 63.7 (1984), 63.6 (1989), 58.4 (1994) and 52.8 (1999). At first sight, this seems to show that as the EP has become more powerful, voters have participated less! It also appears to be an accelerating down-trend. Indeed, the two themes came together in June 1999: the most precipitous decline to date in participation in European elections occurred just three months after the Parliament demonstrated its capacity for the first time to force the resignation of the Commission.

Yet, the evidence for declining turn-out is not straightforward. Mark Franklin (2001) points out that it is not only the powers of the EP that have changed since 1979, but those who elect it. The five most recent additions to EU membership have diluted the number of countries affected by compulsory voting. Nor is this the only factor that distorts the figures. A second is that participation in any one European election is affected by the average proximity of Member States to the last possible date for the next general election. A third is that first-time voting in European elections is associated with a once-off novelty value that temporarily boosts turn out. Once these factors are taken into account, Franklin computes 'corrected figures' for turn-out in European elections as follows: 53.9 (1979), 61.0 (1984), 59.8 (1989), 53.9 (1994) and 54.8 (1999) (ibid., p. 301). In short, the downtrend disappears. Then, of course, we need to ask whether trends in turn-out to European elections are any different from changing patterns of participation in elections in general. The 'headline figures' for participation in European elections have fallen more steeply than turn-out to national elections since the late 1970s, but Franklin's 'corrected' figures outperform national benchmarks.

Accepting that the level of turn-out to European elections is low even if the direction of change is unclear, what does this mean for our democratic assessment of the EU? Amongst reasons for equating low turn-out with poor democratic performance are, first, that it is one of the most distinctive qualities of democratic systems that they use elections to choose office holders and confer consent in the same act. Not only, then, does the EU score rather poorly in the proportion of key office holders who are specifically elected to exercise political power through its institutions. But the somewhat narrow front over which popular election operates at the level of the EU's political system itself – a mere section of the legislature and no part of the executive – seemingly struggles to register the active consent of more than half of those registered to vote. Second, low participation may impoverish elections as sources of information about the needs and values of citizens. Third, it may increase randomness of outcomes. Fourth, it may blunt incentives for those seeking re-election to anticipate the preferences of a wide cross-section of voters. Fifth, and related to the last, it may be associated with biases and political inequality in the representative process, for example where some social groups are more likely to be amongst the abstainers than others.

On the other hand, low participation may even be associated with the healthy functioning of a political system. Although much bemoaned, convergence by representatives on positions favoured by the median voter is a sign of efficient political competition, even though it may also depress voter participation. A further consideration we will examine in a moment is that low turn-out may be associated with pluralist systems of divided government. Yet, such systems may be the best means of achieving public control and equality of representation in certain kinds of society.

How do EP elections fit into this debate? We will later show European elections, are indeed, poor sources of information and incentives.

However, this has more to do with 'second-order' characteristics of European elections that may not be as closely connected as was once believed to poor participation (see esp. Blondel *et al.*, 1998). It would likewise be hard to argue that the EP has been weakened in its self-confidence or its inter-institutional relationships by a perception that it lacks public consent. Its often impressive capacity to press legislative amendments on the Commission and Council probably has more to do with the procedural design of decision rules and the coherence of its party and committee systems than the EP's claims (or lack of them) to electoral authority. Poor electoral participation could, of course, be taken as weakening consent for the Union as a whole, rather than for the role of the EP in particular. Yet the empirical grounds for such a claim are shaky (see p. 68) and, in any case, the Union is insulated from such an effect precisely by the understanding that consent for its overall institutional order derives not from periodic elections but from Treaties controlled by Member States.

Indeed, lower participation in European than Member State elections is, in a sense, only to be expected, given the different shapes of their political systems. The practice of using national general elections as a benchmark to appraise turn-out to European elections is only reasonable to the extent that the electorates are almost identical and considerations such as the sense of sociological obligation to vote are, therefore, the same. It is unreasonable to the degree that political systems at the two levels are so fundamentally different as to ensure wide differences in what is 'at stake' in the two sets of elections: Member States elections allow voters to choose the executive and the legislature at the same time. European elections, on the other hand, only allow voters to choose one part of the legislative power. Incentives to participate are systematically stronger in the first case than the second. If European elections are compared with others on a basis of most like political system – rather than most like electorate – it is by no means clear that participation is wanting. Turn-out to US Congressional elections is, for example, the same or lower than for EP elections.

But even accepting that modest participation levels are a consequence of a system of divided government that may have been chosen for the EU for good reasons, are some groups more likely to respond to the reduced incentives to turn-out than others in a manner that distorts representation? The allocation of a set number of seats to Member States means that one measure of relative representation in the EP – that of nationalities – cannot be affected by the large cross-country variations in who takes part in European elections. Another form of relative representation – that of social and economic groups – is, however, exposed to differential patterns of voter turn-out. Table 3.6 takes four sociological categories from Eurobarometer data and calculates the difference between those who participate most and least in European elections. It shows that men are marginally more likely to participate than women (+3 per cent), the well educated are moderately more likely to participate than the less educated (+8 per cent) and that high-paid professionals and middle-aged persons are substantially more likely to participate than the economically disadvantaged and the young (+17 per cent in both cases). The last suggests that in keeping with general trends any rise in abstention from European elections has been concentrated on younger age cohorts. Older voters have continued to participate as before (Bréchon, 1999, pp. 5–6).

Even if it is debatable how far modest participation in European elections should in itself be taken as a defect in democratic performance, does it provide further clues about the under development in the European arena of the various components of democratic citizenship considered earlier in the chapter? Here there would seem to be at least three possibilities, namely that participation is linked to low identification with the European arena, to poor knowledge of how it works, and to institutional defects that would make any sense of European citizenship difficult to exercise even if it existed.

The empirical evidence does not seem to support the view that EP elections are a kind of running plebiscite on European integration and

Table 3.6 Differential participation in 1999 European elections according to sociological characteristics. Eurobarometer, no. 52, p. 85

	% claim to have participated in 1999 elections	*Difference*
Education		
Educated beyond age of 20	66	8
Educated to age of 15	58	
Occupational status		
Manager	64	
Unemployed	46	18
Age		
Over 55	62	
18–24	45	17
Gender		
Men	58	3
Women	55	

that modest participation can be taken as a sign of dissatisfaction, low identification or even hostility to the very idea of applying democratic politics to the EU by means of a directly elected Parliament (Niedermayer, 1990). A Eurobarometer survey shows that only 11 per cent of those who do participate in European elections give demonstration of support for integration as a reason for voting, and only 8 per cent mention support for a stronger EP as a factor. Conversely only 6 per cent of abstainers give hostility to integration as a reason for not turning out, while only 4 per cent claim to be dissatisfied with the EP (Eurobarometer, no. 52, 2000, pp. 86–8).

There would, on the other hand, seem to be a strong relationship between how knowledgeable of the EU individuals perceive themselves to be and the likelihood they will vote in European elections. On average those with 'low' self perceived knowledge of the EU rank the probability of their participating at just 5.81 on a scale of 1 to 10, whilst those in the 'high' category rank the probability of their voting at 8.45 (Eurobarometer, no. 57, 2002, p. 98).

The third possibility we need to consider is that modest turn-out to European elections is caused by institutional factors. These might be characteristics of the Union itself – about which more in a moment – or of Member States on which European elections depend for at least three forms of 'intermediation' (Franklin, 1996). National electoral systems are used to administer the poll, to aggregate the votes and allocate seats. National political parties structure voter choice. And national media provide most of the information during the campaign.

National parties have been criticised for 'making a parsimonious effort' to the point at which one can ask whether there 'has really been an election at all' (Delwit, 2000, p. 310). The difficulty with low profile campaigns is that it may be necessary to pass a certain 'threshold of visibility' in order to achieve 'cognitive mobilisation' (Gerstlé *et al.*, 2000). Indeed, the same criticism might be made of national media, on the grounds that coverage fails to provide a steady debate or build up to the poll.

There are also reservations about dependence on national electoral systems. If we are to believe the 40 per cent or so of abstainers surveyed by Blondel *et al.* (1998, p. 53) who claim that circumstances, and not unwillingness, are the main obstacles to their participation, we also need to question whether national authorities who administer European elections do everything possible to facilitate turn-out and to adapt it to the exigencies of modern life. European elections are held in June when many voters are already on holiday, and Member States that do not have a tradition of polling on a Sunday have a lower turn-out than those which do (Blondel *et al.*, 1998). Mikko Mattila estimates that just 'holding elections during weekends and having multiple constituencies in all countries could increase the turnout by approximately ten percentage points' (2003, p. 449). As this suggests, specific difficulties that are minor across the Union as a whole, are significant in particular Member States. Registration difficulties are more serious in Britain, France and Spain than elsewhere. Discontent with the electoral process is mentioned by 26 per cent of voluntary abstainers in France, in contrast to only 8 per cent across the Union as a whole.

In addition to these apparently trivial but cumulatively significant causes of low turn-out, it is often argued that it is a structural problem that European elections are organised into national constituencies, even though they are choices about an EU institution. Since they are contested by domestic political parties, the counting of votes by Member State (or in a form that makes it easy to work out what the total is for each national party across the country as a whole) means that European elections are an unusual form of national general election: everyone votes at the same time for more or less the same menu of parties that dominate national politics, but without any risk that legislative or executive power will actually change hands.

We will debate the implications of this at some length in Chapter 4. For the moment it is sufficient to note the claim that it depresses participation in European elections by confusing the whole nature of the exercise: an election that is about representation in the European arena is forced back into a straightjacket of domestic political competition. Whilst, however, this may affect the quality of electoral participation (assuming we are prepared to make the value judgement that individual *ought* to vote on European issues) it is less than clear that it affects its level.

In particular it is questionable that the most plausible alternative – the allocation of seats at Union level – would produce a higher level of participation. By allocating seats by Member State and thus encouraging national parties to operate as mobilisers for European elections, present arrangements at least go with the grain of established patterns of 'brand recognition'. A key point here is that theories of 'partisan dealignment' only posit a decline in the proportion of voters who identify with a political party or vote for it out of habit. They imply neither the complete disappearance of such voters nor the unimportance of brand recognition amongst those who pick and choose in different ways at different elections.

If it is unclear that similar familiarity with voters would be enjoyed by the pan-European party federations (which would presumably be used to contest seats allocated in proportion to total votes cast right across the Union). It is also unclear that a contest whose outcome is decided at EU level would benefit from feelings of civic obligation to vote that have developed through political socialisation into the national arena. An important point here is that there is a key difference between reasons why people do not vote in European elections and reasons why they actually do so: whereas abstention is conditioned by a bewildering array of factors, participation is primarily motivated by just one: a feeling that voting is an obligation (Eurobarometer, 2000, no. 52, pp. 86–9).

Concluding briefly with features of the EU's political system that may discourage electoral participation we have already reviewed the impact of its divided system of government. In Chapter 5 we will also ask whether the preference of the EP for consensus over competition is also a cause of poor electoral linkage. A third argument is that participation is discouraged by a chain of representation that is so long that the EP appears 'remote' and 'abstract in its representation of the people' with the result that it fails to catch their attention or play a 'public forum function' (Weiler, 1997b, p. 274). Indeed, the ratio between population and representatives averages 600 000. On the other hand, MEPs who participated in this survey differed in their own assessment of whether this really is a problem. One MEP put the contrary view as follows:

> It is a big mistake to believe the closer the level of government is to the people the greater is the capacity of the representative. Problems that affect people have a variety of dimensions of which the localised is just one. MEPs have a unique capacity to represent people in the management of problems of transnational scope that touch ordinary lives.[1]

Amongst examples of a transnational 'case-load' cited by this respondent and other MEPs were interventions on behalf of citizens concerned about the cross-national recognition of qualifications, the entitlement of one partner to pension rights acquired by the other in another Member State, and, of course, access to justice in other Union countries.[2]

Conclusion: the 'no demos' thesis revisited

It is one thing to observe that the EU makes decisions that profoundly affects the lives and values of individuals. It is another to show that it engages with them as citizens. This chapter has appraised the Union against two tests of democratic citizenship. Using a test derived from 'modified consociationalism' *(EUDA Test 1)* the chapter confirms the sensitivity with which national definitions of democratic citizenship are for the most part treated by Union institutions. Yet there are two difficulties:

- The claim of the Union to have a law that takes priority over national law extends to constitutional provisions including, for example, Bills of Rights constitutive of national citizenship.
- However much care they take to avoid intentional encroachments on national arrangements for democratic citizenship, Union institutions may have unintended consequences for them. By altering balances in domestic arenas between executives and legislatures, and the centre and the regions, they change how the individual is governed within Member States.

Much of this chapter has, however, been concerned with a second test, namely whether the EU has developed an agreed form of democratic citizenship of its own that individuals can use in practice (*EUDA Test 7*). Its conclusion is that democratic citizenship at Union level remains problematic in relation to the following measures:

- Identification with the EU remains weak and uneven.
- Existing evidence only allows us to make tentative judgements whether there is adequate trust in institutions or between co-participants for effective democracy at Union level.
- Rights needed for the exercise of democratic citizenship at Union level are still open to some degree of arbitrary interference at national level, though this is rare in practice. Progress towards the agreement of a Bill of Rights at Union level has been mixed. At the time of writing the Charter remains in legal limbo, available for use by the ECJ, but not formally incorporated into the Treaties.
- Low public knowledge of the EU's political system is a particular concern given that citizens are called upon to elect the EP every five years. Of course the cognitive capabilities presupposed by many models of democracy (both aggregative and deliberative) would in their pure form be immensely burdensome of any citizenry. They are, therefore, normally met through mechanisms of simplification and intermediation. But that only raises the questions how far have such mechanisms developed in the European arena? We will examine this in Chapter 5.

- Low voter turn-out to European elections may not be as troubling as it often appears to be, but what is clear is that the progressive empowerment of the European election since 1979 has hardly inspired an increase in participation.

The first component (low identity) is often taken to mean that the EU has no 'demos'. The 'no demos' argument might, in turn, suggest our Democratic Audit need proceed no further. Whatever subsequent chapters may do to show that Union institutions satisfy certain procedural condition of democracy, this chapter has seemingly demonstrated that it fails the membership conditions: it does not rule over a group of individuals that consider themselves to be a 'people'. However, the problem is at once more and less serious than this suggests. It is more serious to the extent this chapter has discovered a second reason to doubt that the EU has a 'people', namely a citizenry that lacks the civic capabilities presupposed by its putatively representative or participatory institutions. Indeed, it has been argued that it is here (rather than in any insufficiency of identity) that the 'no demos' problem really lies. On the other hand, the seriousness of low identification with the EU is reduced by the absence of any evidence that it translates into widespread refusal to accept its decisions as collectively binding (see p. 57). Not the least reason why that aspect of the Union's under-developed demos has limited practical implications is that the Union uses consensus procedures that reduce the need to identify in order to accept. It follows that weak identification with the EU's political system makes it more and not less important for any Democratic Audit to focus on Union institutions and their procedures. It is to this task the remainder of the book now turns.

4
Consent

Introduction

Most accounts of democracy in the European Union (EU) jump straight into an appraisal of standards under a given set of Union institutions. This omits the prior and arguably more important question of whether the processes by which Union institutions are formed are themselves democratic. Of course, not all matters of institutional design are determined by 'decisions' as opposed to adaptation, *bricolage*, or cumulative unintended consequences. As with many other political orders, academics debate whether 'evolution' or 'moments' have been the more important (Ackerman, 1998) in shaping the EU's institutional development (Christiansen *et al.*, 2001; Moravcsik, 1998).

Amongst mechanisms by which the Union makes choices about institutions are Treaty formation, the interpretation of Treaty texts by the European Court of Justice (ECJ), inter-institutional agreements between the Commission, Council and Parliament and definitions by each of those bodies of their own rules of procedure. This chapter will concentrate on Treaty formation. Chapter 8 will consider the role of the ECJ. Chapters 6 and 7 will have much to say about inter-institutional practices. This chapter opens with a discussion of what democratic standards should be expected of procedures for choosing EU institutions. It then goes on to review the main stages in Treaty formation, namely Intergovernmental Conferences (IGCs), ratifications by referendums and national parliaments, and recent experiments in the use of Conventions to deliberate options for Treaty change.

The EU, democracy beyond the state and the problem of institutional choice

Any political system needs a means of deciding what Rawls calls the 'circumstances' or basic conditions of politics (Weale, 1999, p. 8), including rights, duties, rules of the game and distributions of authorised power. It follows that there are two forms of consent giving in any democratic system: first, consent to an institutional design; and, second, consent to particular political leaderships that assume powers allocated under that institutional design.

The two kinds of consent raise distinct issues for democratic politics. One reason for this concerns the non-neutrality of institutions. Once chosen, institutions mobilise biases that are hard to reverse. They lock actors into forms of path dependence by encouraging citizens and society to sink investments in particular capabilities or patterns of organisation, further development of which offers increasing returns, deviation from which incurs exit costs (Pierson, 2000). Another striking aspect of the non-neutrality of institutions is that wherever politics are multidimensional (there is more than one scale of values that actors care about) the key determinant of outcomes is not the preferences of actors but the rules by which those preferences are aggregated (McKelvey, 1976). Indeed, institutions often have circular, self-perpetuating characteristics. They shape identities by which they and their policy addressees bond together as a group; norms by which behaviour and performance, including their own, are judged (March and Olsen, 1995); causal beliefs about economy and society that guide demands for collective action (Kahnemann *et al.*, 1982); and feedback loops by which citizens can respond to past experiences with a political system by feeding new inputs into it (Easton, 1957).

A key difference between the EU and its Member States is that the latter focus the politics of consent on periodic opportunities for voters to choose political leaderships. The former focuses them on questions of institutional design. Whereas national politics are dominated by the choice of governments within more or less agreed political systems, the EU does not have a political leadership that is popularly authorised as a whole or specifically for the purposes of exercising power in its institutions. Yet, it often calls upon the public or its representatives to authorise redesigns of its institutions, which have been frequent in the last twenty years with the Single Act (1986), the Treaty on European Union (1992), the Amsterdam Treaty (1997) and the Nice Treaty (2000), and a fifth Treaty change in preparation at the time of writing. Not only is the EU probably a more self-consciously designed political system than many of its Member States, there is also something to be said for prioritising forms of consent-giving differently at the two levels. As long as there are good reasons for the EU to operate a form of consensus democracy, there will be limits to how far its political leadership can be chosen and changed as a collective. On the other hand, a focus on giving consent to choices of institutional design is understandable in so far as the institutions of European integration are more contested than those of its Member States. That is to say they are less likely to be seen as 'natural' and 'given', and more likely to be regarded as intentional acts of contemporaneous will formation.

How should a Democratic Audit go about appraising mechanisms for choosing EU institutions? One test is that institutions should be selected by a means that allows the people to see themselves as authors of those institutions (Habermas, 1997). There are also good reasons for believing that ideal conditions for authorising political systems should be power blind and to some degree interest blind. All prospective members of a political system should be equals at the point of consent-giving. Not only is political equality a part of the core definition of democracy (see p. 10), but any process of authorisation, if it is to be acknowledged as just, needs to avoid the circularity of assuming the very power distributions that are to be authorised. Since, moreover, institutions are intrinsically non-neutral and difficult to reverse, it becomes all the more important that there should be equality of voice and choice at the moment they are established. Given that institutions are supposed to be useful it may be a bit much to expect those forming them to operate from behind a 'veil of ignorance' (Rawls, 1993) as to their likely distribution of benefits. But even the most hard-bitten utilitarian would be pushed to deny that any process of choosing institutions should enable those expecting to live under them to answer two questions and not just the one that is associated with a calculus of interests: the question 'how will *I* benefit?' will always need to be accompanied by the question 'how can *we* agree [on] ways of regulating our lives in common that we all acknowledge as legitimate?' (Habermas, 1996). What is distinctive about the latter question is that it cannot be answered by the exercise of power or by reference to personal benefits but only by deliberation of shared values.

Such ideal conditions of institutional choice are everywhere difficult to deliver. Political systems are ships that need to be built at sea. The double move of aggregating interests in different institutional solutions and deliberating shared criteria for acknowledging them as just is hard to execute. Indeed, many systems face the problem of how to deal with contradictory but equally reasonable views of what is needed to make them legitimate (Rawls, 1993). Not only does the EU clearly fall into that category (Lord and Magnette, 2004), but commentators continue to dispute whether choices about EU institutions acts of delegation or of constitutionalisation (Moravcsik, 1998; Pollack, 1997a; Weiler, 1999, 2002)? Whereas constitutionalisation connotes a decision to establish an institutional order that has some autonomy of its parts and a legitimacy of its own in its origination and enforcement of norms, delegation connotes a decision to lend powers and legitimacy to another body only so long as it performs a specific mandate that is not of its own choosing. Whereas constitutionalisation entails a decision to combine with others in a polity that will play some part in defining the rights, values and identities of all, delegation implies no more than a contract to create a shared institution to solve a handful of collective action problems of a practical nature.

Widespread use of the term 'Constitutional Treaty' indicates a studied ambiguity on the issues raised by the last paragraph, a huge agreement to disagree, only made possible, as Joe Weiler has so cogently argued (2002), by a 'constitutional tolerance' between those who could, if they really wanted, explore the explosive consequences of contradictions between understandings of the EU as delegated and constituted authority. We will return to this problem in the conclusion. For the moment it is sufficient to note that it renders forlorn any expectation of identifying just one set of standards by which to assess the democratic qualities of procedures by which Union institutions are chosen. If the choice of EU institutions is an act of delegation it would be sufficient to appraise procedures used by the following Democratic Audit test set out on p. 28 *How far are national democracies able to shape and control the institutional design of the European Union by means of their own choosing (EUDA Test 2)?* If, however, the design of EU institutions amounts to constitutionalisation, it will also be necessary to show that individuals can engage directly at Union level to shape and control the rights, values and identities (Wiener and Della Salla, 1997) by which they are constituted into a new polity; and that they can do that deliberatively as equals. This implies a very different test, namely: *How far can individuals and groups influence questions of institutional design at Union level, according to deliberative processes that bring them into direct communication with one another, regardless of boundaries between national democracies (EUDA Test 8)?*

Intergovernmental conferences

If democracy at Union level is to follow the national experience in being fashioned out of pre-democratic political forms (Manin, 1997) the latter, in its case, will surely be international conferences traditionally used by states to negotiate Treaties. The procedure for using Treaty changes to make decisions about EU institutions is as follows: changes to EU Treaties have to be unanimously agreed by a 'conference of the representatives of the governments of the Member States' commonly known as Intergovernmental Conferences (IGCs). They then have to be 'ratified by all Member States in accordance with their constitutional requirements' (Article 48). Any one Member State or even the Commission may submit proposals for the amendment of the Treaty, and a simple majority of Member States is sufficient to convene an IGC. Some of the most trenchant critiques of democratic deficits in European integration have been directed at IGCs as means of making institutional choices. The following are examples:

1. Decisions about EU institutions are made over the heads of the people who have few opportunities to shape the agenda of institutional choice or participate in any deliberation of options. Citizens do not appear to have much say in how they are constituted into a European political system (Wiener and Della Salla, 1997). Those who see EU Treaties as having constitutional features find, it disturbing that they should be produced by the secretive proceedings of an international conference (Curtin, 1993, p. 66). The opacity of the Treaty formation process deprives the Union of many of the benefits of public authorisation such as a clear understanding of what an institution is for, of how to judge its performance and of whom to hold responsible for what. Thus the seeds of many of the democratic deficiencies most commonly alleged against EU institutions may be found in impoverished opportunities for public participation and debate in the processes by which they are designed in the first place. A stronger version of this criticism is that publics have not just been left out, they have been deceived on questions of EU institutional design. Elites have preceded by stealth without fully informing their publics, all in the expectation that the lock-in effects of institutions would make them hard to change once citizens woke up to the European political system that had been constructed behind their backs.

2. IGCs fall foul of the argument that those who are likely to hold power in institutions should not have the decisive say on questions of institutional design (Elster, 1998, p. 117). In assigning powers to Union institutions, IGCs do not just assign them to the supranational Commission, European Parliament (EP) and ECJ, but, crucially, to the collective of governments in the Council and European Council, much the same actors, in other words, as those who negotiate Treaty change. Whether Treaty ratification by national parliaments or referendum is an adequate check on this is a matter we will examine later on.

3. IGCs have no moments of power or interest blindness. The Liberal Intergovernmentalist account of Treaty formation (Moravcsik, 1998) argues that outcomes of IGCs follow the power and preferences of the largest three Member States at most, sometimes just the largest two. Since these are best placed to manage on their own or bilaterally, smaller Member States have little alternative to accepting that if European integration is to be used to solve collective action problems, it will have to be on the terms of the larger. This should be a caution to those who confuse Liberal Intergovernmentalism as an explanation of European Integration with Consociationalism as a normative standard for democratic rule by the Union. Far from the one delivering the other, the two could not be further apart. The latter if it is to be a democratic standard is committed to political equality between its units of value, which, in the case of the EU, would be the Member State democracies of the Union.

4. IGCs are governed by decision-rules that make no distinction between first-time agreement and subsequent amendment of the Treaties. In both cases, unanimous consent of Member States is needed. This allows a few who benefit from an established policy to veto its alteration even where it has become oppressive to others. Fritz Scharpf describes the problem thus

> In an ideal-type majoritarian democracy, decision-rules do not discriminate between actors seeking to change an existing policy and others defending its maintenance. However as constitutional checks and balances and the number of veto players increase, symmetry is lost to the advantage of the defenders of *status quo* policies. In the European Union this asymmetry is in fact more extreme than in any national constitutional democracy ... As a consequence policies will be maintained and need to be enforced even though there would be no chance of having them adopted now under the original decision rules, or even by a plurality vote. (Scharpf, 2003)

It might be objected to this that the EU should not follow majoritarian but consensus standards. But therein lies the rub: if it is accepted that the EU ought to be run as a consensus democracy, it is hard to justify decision-rules that in observing the formalities of unanimity in fact sustain outcomes that are not even favoured by a bare majority, let alone a supermajority. Although minority protections are a part of consensus democracy it is important that they should not be confused with minority 'rule': it is by no means clear that rights or entitlements will be at stake in all attempts to block Treaty change and, even where they are, the frustrated majority may feel at least as strongly that its rights are being disregarded by the *status quo* as the protected minority feels it has an entitlement to defend. The EU may well have to address the symmetry of rights between those 'seeking Treaty change' and those seeking 'Treaty maintenance' in the future as the number of veto players grows with enlargement and the weight of the *status quo* increases with the *acquis* of previous Treaty formation. The decision rule for constitutional change in many Federal systems is a simple majority of the whole and an oversized majority (maybe 80 per cent) of the component states. If that is too overtly Federal for the Union it could consider some combination of the following: sunset clauses on existing Treaty provisions, so that it is renewal of the *status quo*, rather than its amendment, that requires unanimous consent; greater use of flexible integration, enabling particular groupings of states to contract into agreements that can subsequently be changed by less than unanimous agreement (Scharpf, 2003); and 'lighter Treaties' that seek to specify less policy detail in a format that can only be changed by subsequent Treaty amendment.

Some of the foregoing difficulties were brought out by the one IGC within the period covered by this Democratic Audit (1998–2003), that concluded by the Nice European Council (December 2000). The main outcomes of the IGC were as follows.

- The number of Commissioners was equalised at one per Member State. Council votes and EP seats were allocated as set out in Table 5.1. Overall, this was a re-weighting of the Commission in favour of smaller states, and of the Council and EP in favour of larger ones.
- Majority voting and Co-decision were extended but only modestly. One observer summarises the outcome thus: 'Nice was able to remove from unanimity to Qualified Majority Voting (QMV) only 27 (and not the most important) of the 75 remaining items. The Co-decision procedure became applicable for only seven provisions that changed over from unanimity to QMV. The IGC was unable to extend the Co-decision procedure to legislative matters which already come under the Qualified Majority rule, like agriculture and trade policies' (Yataganas, 2001).
- The Council would henceforth need a double – and possibly even a treble – majority for QMV decisions. The majority would have to include between 71.31 and 73.91 of the bloc votes allocated to Member States (depending on which of the anticipated accession

countries joined) and a majority of Member States. Any Council Member would, in addition, be entitled to request 'verification' that it represented at least 62 per cent of the population of the Union.
- The European Union Charter of Fundamental Rights was not incorporated into the Treaty.

These outcomes provoked much soul-searching about the process of Treaty formation by IGC. Far from meeting deliberative ideals, it would be hard to present Nice as a principled reshaping of Union institutions in accordance with explicit criteria that were either publicly defended or consistently applied. As a Member of the Swedish negotiating team has put it: 'there were no objective criteria for the changes. The degressivity [of the voting weights in the Council and EP] is not consistent. The proportion between an increase in the population ... and the increase in weights is erratic' (Moberg, 2002, p. 275). Moreover there were anomalies in the treatment of the accession states. Romania was given fewer votes in the Council, and the Czech Republic and Hungary fewer seats in the Parliament, than their population benchmarks amongst existing Members States (Gray and Stubb, 2001). Nice thus failed to represent those who were not 'at the table', those who were likely to be affected by its decisions without having formal rights of representation there. One explanation is that 'conflict avoidance' substituted for deliberation of institutional principles. Thus Moberg continues

> All parties were aware that the issue of voting weights was the most sensitive of the conference ... [but] there was very little common analysis.... Delegations were not always fully aware of the effects of various proposals. The French Presidency did not present any concrete proposals until the final meeting at Nice. The package was wrapped up after other issues had been thrown in. (Moberg, 2000, pp. 265–6)

Another explanation is that there was a logic to what was decided at Nice, but it was presentational rather than principled. Thus George Tsebelis and Xenophon Yataganas argue that the decision to adopt a triple majority rule for voting in the Council could only have been optimal from a point of view of allowing each government an element of 'cover' in presenting the deal domestically (Tsebelis and Yataganas, 2002, p. 293). The majority of Member States criterion allowed small state governments to fend off criticism for agreeing to a re-weighting of Council votes in favour of the large. And the 62 per cent of population criterion helped the German government avoid criticism of a re-weighting that did not address the under-representation of a reunified Germany.

To reach a definitive assessment we need, however, to be clear that IGCs neither stand alone in the process of Treaty formation nor have they remained fixed over time in relation to the procedures that precede and follow them. For example, the Amsterdam IGC was prepared by a 'reflection group' consisting of two representatives of each head of government, a representative of the Commission, and two observers of the EP. As we will see, this arrangement has now been replaced by an experiment with a Convention that is public and more diverse in its composition. A second source of variation is that whilst it seems now to be the norm to use referendums to ratify accession to the EU (nine out of ten countries due to accede in 2004 scheduled referendums), countries vary in whether they use referendum or parliamentary vote to ratify subsequent Treaty changes. It is to Treaty ratification that we now turn.

Treaty ratification

One advantage of using referendums to ratify Treaty change is that they provide a direct and compelling form of consent to decisions on European integration: the question is taken on its own and referred directly to the public. Yet the empirical evidence suggests that such opportunities for deciding a particular question of European Integration on its own merits do not translate unproblematically into patterns of voting uncontaminated by domestic considerations. Franklin *et al.* (1994, p. 487) found that in all countries which put the Treaty on European Union (TEU) to referendum, 'yes' and 'no' votes were significantly correlated with the popularity of the domestic governments of the day and with patterns of partisan support within national politics: 'yes' voters were four times more likely than 'no' voters to be supporters of parties of government. It is not only elections to the EP – but referendums on issues of European integration – that would seem to have the second-order characteristic of being dominated by some other political game.

Another advantage of using referendums is that EU Treaties do not simply transfer powers between the national and European levels of government. As seen, national governments are amongst the principal beneficiaries of the act of delegation, since they participate so intimately in the exercise of many of the powers transferred to the Union. The result is that EU Treaty changes can also redistribute powers within Member

States, from legislature to executive and from regions to the centre. To the extent that national parliaments are 'executive dominated', parliamentary ratifications of EU Treaty changes effectively allow governments to approve extensions to their own powers, albeit at a risk of electoral cost.

Referendums at least do something to take the decision out of the hands of governments, though how much depends on the discretion left to governments to determine timing, the nature of the question and even whether an issue of European integration is to be put to referendum at all. Needless to say this varies markedly across Member States. Only in Ireland is there a constitutional requirement to decide all EU Treaty changes by referendum. Other Member States, notably Germany, have taken a principled position against the use of referendums. In between are many Member States where the use of referendum requires a judgement of whether the Treaty change is sufficiently contentious. Denmark in 1987 raised the further possibility of a referendum being used to appeal to the people to reverse a parliamentary vote against ratification. In still other cases, the conditions that determine the calling of referendums are unclear and suspicion remains that they are used more opportunistically than in search of authentic public authorisation.

Opponents of integration frequently complain of referendums being used to put the same question back to the electorate until it gets the desired result. From another point of view, however, sufficient adjustment to proposed Treaty changes (as effectively happened when the Edinburgh European Council had to find a means of dealing with the rejection of the TEU by Denmark in June 1992) to convert sufficient 'no' voters into 'yes' voters to obtain ratification is a defensible exercise in democratic responsiveness.

An argument often made for ratification by national parliaments is that Treaty changes are complex deals spanning many policies and institutions. They are not, in other words, easily reduced to a simple 'yes'/'no' choice of a referendum question. Of course, the force of this argument is reduced to the extent national parliaments are themselves only given a take it or leave it choice over Treaty texts negotiated by the European Council. Yet, it does not disappear altogether. National parliaments are able to amend national enabling legislation if not the Treaty itself, and many have used ratification to demand an amelioration in their own powers of decision and participation on EU matters. Moreover, a law of anticipated reactions may operate in which the negotiations themselves are used to align draft Treaties to the risks of domestic rejection. In this respect, ratification by national parliaments and by referendum offer contrasting strengths and weaknesses.

National parliamentary ratification offers the possibility of continuous and structured dialogue between the ratifier and negotiator throughout the process of Treaty formation. Up to the time of the TEU there was much unevenness both within and across Member States in the participation of national parliaments in the negotiation of Treaty changes. Thus the British Government's boast that the House of Commons debated the negotiation of that Treaty for 204 hours over 23 days (House of Commons Debates, 20 May 1993, col. 381) has to be qualified by its refusal to make available to parliament what was perhaps the most important document to the Political Union negotiations, the draft Treaty produced by Luxembourg Presidency in June 1991 (quoted Sverdrup, 2002, p. 128). By the time of Nice, however, it was common for most national parliaments to receive reports, question ministers and debate options for institutional change throughout the negotiation of Treaty change. A questionnaire conducted by the Swedish Presidency of Conference of the Parliaments of the EU (COSAC) found that several (Austria, Belgium, Italy, Germany, Luxembourg, Portugal and Sweden) passed plenary resolutions or adopted committee reports (as many as 20 in Finland's case) on issues such as the incorporation of the Charter into the Treaties, the scrutiny role of national parliaments themselves, and delineations of competence in EU decision-making. Indeed, it is possible for a national parliament to sustain influence right up to the 'endgame' of IGC negotiations. The European Affairs Committee of the Swedish Parliament held 'telephone conferences with the Swedish negotiators' in the final stages of the Nice negotiations (Sveriges Riksdag, 2001).

During the preparations for the Nice IGC several national parliaments also included some element of 'public hearing' in their deliberation, though, it has to be said, with varying degrees of originality and openness to spontaneous influence from those outside organised channels of civil society. Amongst the most adventurous were the Scandinavian national parliaments all of which 'took public hearings to the people' by organising them in a number of provincial centres. For its part the Irish Parliament 'placed an advertisement in national newspapers inviting written submissions by members of the public who might wish to convey their views on the matter'. In so doing it thought it was responding to a complaint that in considering the Amsterdam Treaty it had only 'invited presentations from organisations it knew would be interested' and not from the 'public in general' (ibid).

How national parliaments participate in the formulation of negotiating positions for IGCs depends, however, on the nature of executive–legislature relations in Member States. Some national parliaments make representations that reflect high levels of control over their own business and the inclusion of parties of opposition in opportunities for policy shaping. Thus during the Nice IGC the European Affairs Committees (EAC) of the German Bundestag was sufficiently emboldened by an inter-party consensus to put the incorporation of the European Union Charter on Fundamental Rights on to the agenda for plenary debates no fewer than four times. In more majoritarian systems any national parliamentary influence is likely to be confined to the governing majority and is unlikely to be deliberated or even transparent to the wider representative body. Thus the outcome of the Maastricht European Council was hostage until the last moment to a parallel negotiation between the British Prime Minister and a Cabinet Minister (Michael Howard) who would probably have resigned with significant support from the wider parliamentary party had the UK not secured an opt-out from the social chapter of the TEU (Forster, 1999, p. 92).

In contrast to the continuous but calculable pressure on governments to align IGC outcomes to national parliamentarians responsible for ratification, the appeal of referendums lies precisely in greater uncertainty: with less control or information about the views and behaviour of the ratifier or even of who exactly the latter will be once the vagaries of voter participation and abstention are taken into account, governments may have to anticipate a wider range of possible objections while negotiating Treaty changes. Before concluding that the strength of each mode of ratification is the other's weakness, we need, however, to note that they are not altogether mutually exclusive. Not only are many referendums on EU Treaty change only advisory, national parliaments may have an impact on the negotiating dynamics of IGCs, even where it is acknowledged that a referendum will be decisive in providing authorisation. This follows from the finding above that significant numbers of voters will follow the position in a referendum of the parliamentary parties they support.

Overarching problems specific to using referendums and national parliaments to authorise Treaty changes are difficulties common to both. As seen earlier, both methods of ratification limit the role of the public or its representatives to a 'take it or leave it choice' structured by others. In other words they confer veto powers but only limited and indirect agenda-setting powers: the power to say 'no' is more evident than the power to shape the choice itself. Indeed, as also seen, the formal position is that national parliaments and electorates can only accept or reject, and not amend, what has been negotiated by the European Council. This is a constrained choice indeed where Treaties are complex package deals in relation to whose individual elements national parliaments and publics might in an ideal world want to choose differently; and, particularly for small Member States, where the *fait accompli* of a package defended by a united front of governments weighs heavily against the uncertainties of provoking a crisis in the integration process, or even of raising questions about the continued membership of countries unable to ratify. Both methods of ratification also fragment debates on institutional questions on national lines rather than bring them together into a European public space. Habermas has thus argued 'a real advance would be for national media to cover the substance of relevant controversies in other countries, so that all national public opinions converge on the same range of contributions to the same range of issues' (Habermas, 2001). It is, however, worth noting that the first problem has been softened somewhat since Treaty ratifications have ceased to be single shot games (Sverdrup, 2002). This allows some scope for rumblings of discontent from previous ratifications to feed into agenda-setting subsequent Treaty change.

Towards the convention method

The foregoing criticisms of Treaty formation imply a need for greater participation of the public or its representatives at an earlier stage than ratification. Footprints of autonomous organisations of civil society are to be found in the TEU (Mazey and Richardson, 1996, p. 126). Yet, the Reflection Group phase of the Amsterdam IGC (1995–6) probably provides better evidence that EU Treaty formation is now a target for lobbies and advocacy coalitions. In their study of the phenomenon, Sonia Mazey and Jeremy Richardson found contributions addressed the shape of integration including deepening, enlargement, variable geometry and subsidiarity (ibid., p. 130). They did not, in other words, merely enumerate narrowly defined wish-lists. Moreover, many were 'bargainable and tradable', open-minded and focused on influencing the 'framing' of problems at an early stage of discussions about Treaty change.

Lobbies and advocacy coalitions can, however, only bring greater pluralism to the framing of options for institution design. They cannot in themselves provide the structured representation and deliberation needed to make the process of agenda-setting more democratic. It was in part to meet this difficulty that the EU has recently experimented with Conventions. The Cologne European Council (European Council, 1999a) appointed a convention to draft an EU Charter of Fundamental Rights. The Laeken European Council (European Council, 2001) appointed one to consider options for the institutional development of the Union after 2004. The latter produced a draft constitution that inter alia seeks to

- redefine the values and objectives of the Union;
- incorporate the Charter of Fundamental Rights;
- classify competences as those exclusive to the Union, those shared between the Member States and the Union, and those where the Union is merely an arena for the co-ordination of national powers;
- change procedures for designating the political leadership of the Union by creating a more fixed Presidency of the European Council, creating the post of European Foreign Minister, strengthening the powers of the Presidency of the Commisison, and clarifying the linkage between the choice of Commission President and the outcome of European elections;
- change decision-rules through further extensions of majority voting and Co-decision, and, crucially, through a simplification of QMV thresholds to a majority of Member States representing at least 60 per cent of the Union population;
- alter how Member States are represented in Union institutions by removing the right of each state to a voting member of the College of Commissioners and by asserting that representation in both Council and EP should be based on the principle of digressive proportionality (European Convention, 2003c).

Table 4.1 shows how the composition of the two conventions was similar in all but two important respects. On the one hand, the Charter Convention had more choice over its own leadership. The Cologne mandate left it to choose its own Chair and envisaged a Praesidium consisting of the Chair and four others elected from each of the 'delegations': national parliaments, representatives of heads of Government, the EP and the Commission. In contrast, the leadership of the Constitution Convention was largely shaped by the decision of the Heads of Government to designate a President and two Vice Presidents who would then be joined by nine others in a Praesidium. Since it was stipulated that the nine had to include the representatives of the Heads of the three Governments due to hold the Council Presidency during the lifetime of the Convention, the latter was only able to choose six out of 12 Members of its own Praesidium. On the other hand, the Laeken declaration did at least allow 13 candidate countries' representation in the Constitutional Convention on the same numerical basis as existing

Table 4.1 Composition of the Conventions

	Charter Convention	*Convention on the future of Europe*
Designated leadership	—	President (V. Giscard D'Estaing) and 2 Vice Presidents (G. Amato and J.-L. Dehaene) appointed by European Council
National Parliaments	30 (2 representatives of each national parliament)	30 (2 representatives of each national parliament)
Representatives of the Heads of Government	15 (1 per Member State)	15 (1 per Member State)
European Parliament	16	16
European Commission	1	2
Candidate countries	Not full Members	39 (2 representatives of each national parliament and one of each head of government)
TOTAL of ordinary members	62	105
Praesidium		
	The Chair of the Convention + The elected chairs of the four 'delegations': National Parliaments National Governments European Parliament European Commission	The President and two Vice Presidents + Representatives of the heads of the three Governments due to hold the Council Presidency + 6 chosen by the Convention

Members, even though it also established they could not prevent existing Members reaching agreement. In contrast, the mandate from the Cologne European Council establishing the Charter Convention only allowed for an exchange of views with candidate countries.

A number of claims have been made for how the 'Convention method' can improve democratic standards at the agenda-setting stage of IGCs. One is that Conventions are more diverse in their composition than IGCs and thus widen access to the agenda of institutional change. Representatives elected by the public to national parliaments are for the first time directly included in face-to-face discussions in a setting that involves others from right across the unit of shared rule. Since each national parliament is allocated two representatives who in turn have two alternates, parties of opposition are also included in a deliberation on EU Treaty reform previously monopolised by national parties of government with access to the Council of Ministers and European Council. Indeed, in the case of many national parliaments, the two Convention Members (or four including alternates) have attempted to speak to positions developed by their EACs on which all parties are represented.

Although the Convention method is some way from achieving a veil of ignorance or from excluding those who will exercise power in Union institutions from their design, the inclusion of national parliamentarians at least puts some pressure on 'insiders' to justify what they want from institutional design to representatives elected at another level of government whose powers are more likely to be circumscribed than expanded by Treaty change. Moreover, the closer the European Council keeps to the Convention text, the more national parliaments will find that the text they are called upon to ratify resembles that to which they had input at the agenda-setting stage. Andreas Maurer has used data from written contributions and amendments to analyse how active were different categories of representative in the two Conventions. Amendments to the Charter Convention indicate parity of activity between national governments, national parliamentarians and Members of the European Parliament (MEPs). By the time, however, of the Convention on the Future of Europe, written contributions from national parliaments matched those of the EP and national governments put together (Maurer, 2003c). This would suggest, first, growing familiarity and confidence on the part of national parliaments with their inclusion in the Convention method; and, second, that they have, indeed, found it worthwhile proactively to shape options for the design of EU institutions.

In comparison, say, with the reflection group which prepared the Amsterdam Treaty, the Conventions have also given greater weight to MEPs in their role as representatives elected at the level of the Union itself. Above all, they have included them as full members and not just observers. In all, the Conventions have diluted the control of national governments over the agenda of institutional change by shrinking their direct representation to between 15 and 25 per cent of the total, rising at most to 50 per cent if national parliamentarians from government parties are also included, and delegates from candidate countries disregarded.

The decision of both Conventions to proceed by consensus also precludes monopoly control of any one group, such as national governments, on the agenda of institutional change. Although the meaning of consensus was imprecise in both cases, it would have been hard to claim consensus in the face of widespread disagreement from any one of the main constituencies, namely the national parliamentarians, the MEPs or national governments themselves. Yet, from another point of view, the organisation of the Conventions around institutional interests, albeit of public representatives directly or indirectly elected to various levels and branches of government, is a source of criticism. Neither Convention was a cross-section of society, gender-wise, sociologically, professionally, ethnically or generationally. Nor did either have a democratic mandate beyond a task designated by the European Council, and the appointment of individual members by elected parliaments and governments. The whole and the parts both operated at the end of extended lines of delegation from voters. It is by no means clear that if the European public were asked directly to elect a Constituent Assembly it would choose a body whose composition resembles the Convention. Rhetorical conflations of the two terms need to be treated with caution.

Another claim is that Conventions are better settings than IGCs for the application of deliberative standards to EU Treaty change. Both conventions made self-conscious attempts to operationalise deliberative standards. Possible evidence of success is provided by the comparative ease with which the Charter Convention developed a code of EU rights, in contrast with several failed attempts even to put such an initiative on to the agenda of Treaty change when it had been assumed that any negotiation would have to be between representatives of heads of government.[3] This is consistent with the view that bargaining formats will struggle to answer certain questions of institutional design and that the Convention method has allowed the Union to plug the gap.

Yet, neither Convention made a full transition from bargaining to deliberation. As will be discussed more fully in a moment, any notion that deliberation and bargaining could be neatly separated into two distinct phases corresponding to Conventions and IGCs was always likely to prove problematic. In the Constitution Convention, deliberations often showed an awareness of who were likely to be pivotal or strategic actors under the decision-rules of the subsequent Convention–IGC. Paul Magnette takes up the story

> On each and every subject, the British Government drew lines in the sand. It clearly indicated, through its representative in the Convention, the limits it would not surpass. President Giscard implicitly encouraged this attitude by giving Peter Hain a key position

> in the debates so that some observers called him the 'shadow President' of the Convention. The Conventionals were induced to anticipate the IGC and limit their ambition. Deliberation took place under the shadow of the veto. (Magnette, 2003b)

Although there were efficiency gains from limiting discussion to an envelope of negotiable solutions, it is less clear this corresponded to the deliberative ideal of a free-range public space in which all options can be considered and all views and representatives are equal, whether pivotal or not. Indeed, strategic behaviour can be seen in the internal dynamics of the Conventions, even where there was no evident need to anticipate the external bargaining contexts of subsequent IGCs. Justus Schönlau's research of the Charter uncovers an example of a straightforward vote trade in the form of an agreement by the centre right and left of the EP delegation to support the positions of the other on religious rights and the right to strike respectively (2001, p. 139). Yet, discovery of instances of strategic behaviour does not of itself prove absence of deliberative standards. Jon Elster, for example, argues that what matters is what he calls the 'civilising effect of hypocrisy': a deliberative process succeeds not where it removes all self-serving behaviour but where it compels designers of institutions to justify their proposals as if they are capable of benefiting the unit as a whole and not just themselves (1998, p. 104).

A third claim is that the Convention method improves on IGCs in providing publicity in the literal sense of the term. Reflection Groups may well have deliberated extensively but they did so behind close doors. Their members never had to justify their positions in public. On the other hand, there is little evidence that either Convention penetrated deeply into public consciousness. During 2002–3, the Constitution Convention was included in the somewhat 'soft' Eurobarometer question which asks respondents whether they have recently heard anything about various Union institutions. At the time the Convention was being launched to some fanfare, only 28 per cent gave a positive answer against an average of 74 per cent for the main four institutions of the Union (see Table 3.4). This was no higher when the Convention reached the end of its work than at the beginning. As one of its senior members admitted, the Convention failed to reach an audience much beyond those whose attention is already mobilised around Union matters:

> If there has been one disappointment, it has been that such an important and innovative process did not become more widely known. Although the Convention has been easy to follow for those

> with an interest in the Union, polls suggest that many of the people in Europe appear not to have heard about it. (Brian Cowen, Irish Minister for Foreign Affairs, 3 July 2003)

Indeed, there may even have been a tension between hopes of greater publicity and of superior deliberation. Those who achieve deliberative ideals risk becoming somewhat self-referential in their discussions, since a commitment to reflect on one another's preferences may absorb attention to the exclusion of responding to outside audiences; and a commitment to building consensus can be hard to combine with more attention grabbing forms of political competition. Both Conventions employed a variety of devices to avoid becoming cocooned in their own deliberations, as did many of their individual Members. But this only suggested a further tension: 'organised' patterns of engagement with civil society are not always 'spontaneous' and 'authentic'.

Although both Conventions were transparent in their debates and documentation, they were opaque in their decision-rules. In the case of the Charter Convention, the European Council stipulated that 'when the Chairperson, in close concertation with the Vice Chairpersons, deems the text of the draft Charter elaborated by the body can be subscribed to by all the parties, it shall be forwarded to the European Council' (European Council, 1999b). This established two things and left a third unclear: it clarified that the Charter Convention should proceed by consensus and that the Praesidium would be the judge of whether a consensus had been achieved, but, it failed to specify exactly who 'all the parties' were whose agreement would be needed. Schönlau observes what followed

> the Praesidium interpreted the notion of 'consensus' pragmatically by stressing the need to achieve unanimity between the four constituent delegations of the Convention [the European Commission, the European Parliament, national governments and national parliaments] rather than between all sixty-two Convention Members. In fact the final draft of the Charter was approved by acclamation without vote. (Schönlau, 2001, p. 144)

The decision-rules of the Constitution Convention were likewise imprecise. Giscard only provided a negative and not a positive definition of the consensus the Convention would need to reach agreement. In specifying that consensus would not be the same thing as unanimity and that the Convention would not take votes, he implied that consensus would be some kind of a feel for an oversized majority in favour of a particular position, without commenting further on how oversized such a majority might have to be, whether it would have to include various elements of the Convention regardless of its size, and crucially, for a deliberative convention, whether the nature of reasons given for dissent would have any role in judgements of whether consensus had been achieved.

However, a definitive assessment of whether the Conventions have raised democratic standards requires an analysis of where they stand on a continuum between substituting for IGCs as a means of making institutional choices, complementing them in some kind of a balanced relationship, or just providing a public relations exercise behind which old methods of Treaty formation continue unchanged. One view is that Conventions will tend to dominate IGCs, as long as texts agreed by the second are the starting point for the first. A game-theoretic basis for this predicts Convention texts will operate like focal (or 'Schelling') points in a landscape to which players keep returning since they solve co-ordination problems and avoid joint gains being consumed in distributive arguments. A more normative perspective is that members of the European Council seeking to deviate from Convention texts will come under pressure to give public justifications for doing so that command at least as much public credibility as that element of the Convention's deliberations they want to discard.

A contrary view is that the Conventions will either prove inconsequential or to have been mere façades for the continuation of IGC-style bargaining by other means. Everyone knew from the moment the Constitutional Convention was called that it would be followed by an IGC, and that the outcome of the Charter Convention could likewise only be incorporated into the Treaties by an IGC. Both were, in a sense, the first stage in a two-stage game. As with all such games, it would be a struggle to preserve the autonomy of the first stage and prevent it being played to the rules of the second. The Giscard Praesidium, in particular, was often suspected of being more interested in steering outcomes past Member State vetoes than in interpreting a consensus from the deliberations of its own membership. Giscard assumed the same brokerage role as Council Presidencies during IGCs, including a tour of national capitals to clarify boundaries of negotiability. In the meantime he kept discussion of specific institutional proposals to the final three months of the Convention, albeit reassuring the plenary that this was sound deliberative practice (European Convention, 2002a, May Plenary Report, p. 2) and not a cover for carrying on an intergovernmental negotiation behind its back. Yet some Members of the Convention were unconvinced that the final outcome followed a deliberative routine in which the Praesidium listened and then proposed. In a concerted letter of protest to Giscard the Benelux representatives claimed his proposals bore little relation to deliberations within the Convention itself.

It seems to me that both these arguments are in danger of missing the point. What for, a start, seems difficult to dispute is that both Conventions moved beyond the specifications of the European Councils that established them. By asking it to identify and 'make more visible' the overlapping rights that were common to the rights jurisprudence of all Member States the Cologne European Council seemed to imply that the Charter Convention should neither originate rights nor adjudicate between them (European Council, 1999a). Yet it did both (Schönlau, 2001). Likewise the Laeken declaration only asked the Convention on the Future of Europe to consider options for institutional change. By deciding to present those options in the format of a Constitution, the Convention took a step change. Indeed, it can and has been argued that if it had proposed no change to the status quo but concentrated all its efforts on formulating the latter into a Constitution, it would still have taken a step of huge significance. The scope of Conventions to innovate is neither unconditional nor non-existent. Even if it were the case that they have to behave as if they are 'agents' to Member State 'principals', that would still give them scope to calculate where the marginal cost of the latter ignoring their recommendations exceeds the marginal return, bearing in mind that there will be divisions amongst the Member States themselves and that the calculation can be affected by the characteristics of the Conventions themselves, their composition, their public nature, their scope to turn the tables on the European Council by offering that body one of the package deals that it is so accustomed to serving up to others, their deliberative standards and the justifications they offer for their conclusions.

Conclusion

Returning, then, to the Democratic Audit criteria with which we began this chapter:

How far are national democracies able to shape and control the institutional design of the European Union by means of their own choosing (EUDA Test 2)? Each national democracy has a double veto over Treaty formation: any elected national government can veto change, so can the national parliament or public of each Member State, depending on what procedure is used for ratification. There are, however, two difficulties. First, political equality may be formal only: national democracies vary in the bargaining powers they bring to Treaty formation and in the ease with which they can veto in practice. Second, national governments have hitherto had more agenda-setting powers in relation to Treaty formation than either their national parliaments or publics. Recent experiments with Conventions purport to remedy this, though some improvement was already in the offing as a result of the iterative nature of Treaty formation, and, in any case, Conventions are better conceived as deliberative exercises at the level of the shared political system, rather than protective devices for single national democracies.

How far can individuals and groups influence questions of institutional design at Union level, according to deliberative processes that bring them into direct communication with one another, regardless of boundaries between national democracies (EUDA Test 8)? As long as publics and their representatives were only involved at a ratification stage that was itself fragmented by national arena, it was unlikely that Treaty change would be deliberated in a European public space. Recent Conventions have innovated in this regard, but their representativeness is open to question, given that they are unelected and designated at several removes from the electorate. Moreover, their deliberations, though successful in engaging across national boundaries, have been on behalf of the public, rather than with the public, or even with the attention of the public. They have created a 'European space' for consideration of institutional issues, though, not as yet, a 'European public space' for doing so.

5
Representation

Introduction

The spatio–temporal limits of politics thrust representation to the centre of debates about democracy. Most commentators assume that even in smaller and simpler political systems than the EU there is little alternative to conducting democracy through representatives. Ideas for returning significant areas of decision-making to citizens are thus often proposed as supplements or correctives, and not as alternatives, to representation.

Yet, political theorists disagree in well-known ways on who representatives should be and what they should do. Some hold there are particular human needs that can only be understood by representatives who resemble the represented. Others argue that what matters is not resemblance but mechanisms that make it likely that representatives will act on the preferences of the represented. Still others doubt if even that is necessary. Representatives may be expected to use their judgement in ways that may be unpopular with the represented (Burke, 1975 [1774]), provided they comply with the act of trust by which the representative function was conferred and they have periodically to justify their decisions on pain of losing office.

Amongst further questions are how far should representatives take public decisions themselves or merely have some ultimate controlling power over those who do, in fact, govern (Mill, 1972 [1861])? Second, to what degree should representatives compete or co-operate with one another? Should they, in other words, concentrate on bargaining the often divergent preferences of those they represent, or do they also have a role in discovering through their deliberations commonly agreed norms on the basis of which members of a community can agree to regulate aspects of their lives in common (Habermas, 1996)? Third, should there be just one kind of representation in a political system or several? If the latter, what relative weight should be given to the different principles of representation, bearing in mind that there may be limits as to how far different forms of representation can be delivered through any one political system (Schattsneider, 1960).

On top of such familiar problems with the concept of representation is a difficulty associated with its specific application to the EU. There is a sense in which the Union is attempting to develop standards and mechanisms of representation at a moment when representation is itself becoming more difficult. As the chair of the European Parliament's Constitutional Affairs Committee recently put it: 'the institutions of representative democracy are going through a phase of serious difficulty ... for reasons that are linked not only to the peculiarities of European integration ... but also to profound changes in our societies' (European Parliament, 2001f, p. 11).

This chapter and the next will attempt to cut through the foregoing indeterminacies by making two working assumptions. First, that the common feature of all concepts of representation is some notion of 'standing in for others' (Weale, 1999, p. 112). Those who do that in relation to the EU's political system include office holders with formal rights to participate in Union institutions, groups of civil society which organise autonomously to influence the Union, and those who span both categories to the extent that their involvement in Union decisions is deliberately encouraged by EU institutions.

Second, it is assumed that if asked what representatives should do at Union level, most of those who are subject to it as a system of rule would give answers that have something to do with the distinction between consociationalism and concurrent consent used elsewhere in this book. In other words, most expectations of how citizens and societies ought to be represented in EU institutions are likely to presuppose high levels of agreement either between those 'standing-in' for the national cultural segments of the Union or between those capable of articulating Union-level cleavages that cross-cut Member States (such as left–right values) or some mixture of the two. This chapter will, accordingly, ask how far territorial, ideological and sectoral patterns of actor participation in the Union singly and cumulatively satisfy consociational or consensus standards of representation? We will address these questions with the help of the following tests from Chapter 2.

Modified consociationalism tests. How far does the distribution of executive and legislative office in the EU ensure the inclusive and proportional representation of national democracies (*EUDA Test 3*)?

How far do representatives of national democracies shape and control Union decisions they consider of vital importance (*EUDA Test 4*)?

Concurrent consent tests. How far is the designation of executive and legislative positions by Member States matched by opportunities for citizens directly to elect representatives of their own at Union level (*EUDA Test 9*)?

How far do individuals and groups have means of aggregating and deliberating preferences at EU level (if need be, independently of their national governments) (*EUDA Test 10*)?

National territorial representation

In one way or another, the Union provides territorial representation of its Member State democracies across the range of its institutions. One question to ask is how these arrangements satisfy the conditions for what we have termed a modified consociationalism: inclusiveness, proportionality, veto rights and the connection, in turn, of national actors who participate in Union institutions to their own publics and parliaments?

Inclusiveness

On the assumption that it is the dominant branch of modern government, consociationalism anticipates representation through the inclusion of each territorial segment of a political system in its executive. A little noticed aspect of how the EU automatically achieves such power-sharing is that its executive power is structurally divided between the national and European levels (Hix, 1999, p. 21). As will be seen, the Commission's role in framing policy initiatives is significantly guided by advisory committees on which Member States are represented and by the Presidency conclusions of European Councils, where, of course, national Heads of Government decide by consensus. Moreover, Member States enjoy the often significant discretionary choice of means and timing that comes with being the authority that executes policy on the ground. Although they are overseen in this role by the Commission, they themselves participate in shaping any criteria by which their implementation is monitored, once again through committees on which they are all represented (see pp. 137–8).

Not only does the Commission share executive power with the Member States. It is itself constructed on Grand Coalition principles of power sharing between actors recruited from each Member State. Under the pre-Nice arrangements that form the basis for this Audit each Member State designates one or two Commissioners depending on its size.

Since an initiative can only be adopted as a Commission proposal by a majority vote of the College, each nationally designated Commissioner participates across the range of policy and not just in relation to her own portfolio, though even the allocation of jobs is often matched to the policy priorities of particular Member governments. As a matter of convention the Presidency of the Commission rotates between categories of Member State, for example, the small and the large, northern and southern. Since 1994, efforts have also been made to appoint Commission Presidents from former Prime Ministers who, it is argued, have the advantage of understanding the concerns expressed by each national head of Government in previous discussions of the European Council. Even at an administrative level there are national quotas for recruitment of officials.

Attempts to construct the Commission as a 'power-sharing executive' inclusive of actors from all Member States may seem incompatible with its independence. Yet, the latter only requires that the Commission should not take instructions from any source, not that it should be unconnected to those on whose behalf it makes decisions.

Representatives of all Member States are likewise guaranteed a high level of control over the legislative outputs of the Union. The Treaties – made by the unanimous consent of national representatives and ratified by their domestic democratic institutions – constitute the primary legislation of the Union. Procedures – such as majority voting on the Council and Co-decision between the Council and the Parliament – only apply at a level of legislation that is secondary in the sense that it can only be introduced where there is a clear legal base in Treaties to which all national segments have at some stage consented. Moreover, each Member State is guaranteed participation in that secondary legislation. Most specific measures introduced under the Treaties require the approval of the Council of Ministers. Even in cases where governments no longer have an absolute right of veto over secondary legislation, neither rules nor practice favour easy agreement of decisions without a near consensus of governments. In addition, all Member States have equal access to the Presidency of the Council and its agenda-setting powers. The Presidency rotates between them on a six-monthly basis, though it should be noted that the draft Constitution proposes to change this.

National–territorial inputs to the Union's legislative powers are likewise made via the European Parliament. Member States form the constituencies for elections to the European Parliament with each receiving a fixed allocation of seats (Table 5.1). Most MEPs owe their election to parties that are represented in national parliaments. Although they form

Table 5.1 Representation of Member States on the Council and EP, and its proportionality to population size

	The Council								*The European Parliament*					
	A *% Population of EU 15*	B *% Population of EU 27*	C *QM votes pre-Nice*	D *% QM votes pre-Nice*	E *Deviation from proportionality (D−A)*	F *QM votes post-Nice*	G *% QM votes post-Nice based on EU 27*	H *Deviation from proportionality (G−B)*	I *EP seats pre-Nice*	J *% EP seats pre-Nice*	K *Deviation from proportionality (j−A)*	L *EP seats post-Nice*	M *% EP seats post-Nice*	N *Deviation from proportionality (M−B)*
Aus	2.1	1.7	4	4.6	+2.5	10	2.9	+1.2	21	3.4	+1.3	17	2.3	+0.6
Bel	2.7	2.1	5	5.8	+3.1	12	3.5	+1.4	25	4.0	+1.3	22	3.0	+0.9
Den	1.4	1.1	3	3.5	+2.1	7	2.0	+0.9	16	2.6	+1.2	13	1.8	+0.7
Fin	1.4	1.1	3	3.5	+2.1	7	2.0	+0.9	16	2.6	+1.2	13	1.8	+0.7
Fr	15.7	12.2	10	11.5	−4.2	29	8.4	−3.8	87	13.9	−1.8	72	9.8	−2.4
Ger	21.9	17.1	10	11.5	−10.4	29	8.4	−8.7	99	15.8	−6.1	99	13.5	−3.6
Gr	2.8	2.2	5	5.8	+3.0	12	3.5	+1.3	25	4.0	+1.2	22	3.0	+0.8
Ire	1.00	0.8	3	3.5	+2.5	7	2.0	+1.2	15	2.4	+1.4	12	1.6	+0.8
It	15.4	12.0	10	11.5	−3.9	29	8.4	−3.6	87	13.9	−1.5	72	9.8	−2.2
Lux	0.1	0.1	2	2.3	+2.2	4	1.2	+1.1	6	1.0	+0.9	6	0.8	+0.7
Neth	4.2	3.3	5	5.8	+1.6	13	3.8	+0.5	31	5.0	+0.8	25	3.4	+0.1
Por	2.7	2.1	5	5.8	+3.1	12	3.5	+1.4	25	4.0	+1.3	22	3.0	+0.9
Sp	10.5	8.2	8	9.2	−1.3	27	7.8	−0.4	64	10.2	−0.3	50	6.8	−1.4
Swe	2.4	1.9	4	4.6	+2.2	10	2.9	+1.0	22	3.5	+1.1	18	2.5	+0.6
UK	15.8	12.4	10	11.5	−4.3	29	8.4	−4.0	87	13.9	−2.1	72	9.8	−3.4

themselves into transnational party groups in the Parliament itself (Table 5.2) MEPs usually join or leave those groups as national party delegations and not as individuals. The most important of those groups put a high value on including at least one major party from each Member State. That, for example, was a factor in the progressive merger of Christian Democrats and Conservatives during the 1980s and 1990s to form an enlarged European People's Party (Jansen, 1996; Johansson, 1997). Both the EPP and the Party of European Socialists (PES) have covered all Member States in each of the last two Parliaments. The European Liberal and Democratic Reform (ELDR) and Green groups are not far behind, respectively with 10 and 12 national parties amongst their membership in the 1999–2004 Parliament.

Indeed, the groups are structured as conglomerates of national representatives. Decisions on how to vote are taken by the bureaux on which each national party is represented. Most groups attempt to agree by consensus of national party delegations and even those that practice majority voting only do so as a way of resolving deadlocks and with the understanding that whole national party delegations are entitled to dissent from a group whip in a plenary of the Parliament. On one interpretation, the groups exist primarily to reduce the transactions costs that MEPs recruited from national parties face in using the powers of the EP (Hix, 1999, p. 59). Although we will see how national party delegations are, in turn, constrained, it seems clear they form something of a second party system behind the dominant organising framework of the EP, namely the transnational party groups (Lord, 2002). Such a dual structure allows nationality to continue to play a key role in how political opportunities are distributed in the Parliament. In addition to the key determinants of influence – committee positions and rapporteurships – being allocated to transnational groups in proportion to their strengths (Corbett *et al.*, 1995, p. 128), national party delegations expect to be the beneficiaries of a second subdivision within the groups of such agenda-setting opportunities.

Proportionality

A consociational standard not only requires the inclusion of all cultural–territorial units in key institutions and decisions. It also requires their proportional representation. In fact, the Union mixes principles of parity and proportionality in the representation of its Member States. Parity implies Member States should be equally represented regardless of their country size. Examples include Treaty changes, European Council decisions, Common Foreign and Security Policy (CFSP) and Justice and

Home Affairs (JHA) decisions, and access to the rotating Presidency of the Council of Ministers.

Proportionality, on the other hand, implies representation weighted to the population size of Member States. Both the bloc votes used for QMV in the Council of Ministers and the allocation of seats in the EP are based on qualified proportionality. Each Member State receives a minimum of Council votes or EP seats. Thereafter, its representation increases roughly in proportion to its population.

Since this Democratic Audit is of the Union as defined by the Amsterdam, pre-Nice allocations of Council votes and EP seats will be used in the discussion that follows. However, the reader need only refer back to the case study of the Nice negotiations in the previous chapter for evidence of how difficult it has been to escape some of the problems raised here. The implicit rule before Nice for determining EP representation is that each Member State receives six seats and then one more for each:

500 000 of population between 1 and 25 million;
1 million of population between 25 and 60 million;
2 million of population above 60 million.[4]

A like exercise is complicated in the case of the Council, but ignoring for the moment the cases of Germany and the Netherlands, each Member State receives a minimum of two votes and then roughly one more for each:

3 million of population between 3 and 15 million;
8 million of population above 15 million.

Yet, there are important differences between the EP and Council. First, the trade-off between equal representation of states and proportional representation of population is steeper in the case of the EP. The composition of the EP is more proportional to population than is the distribution of QMV votes between members of the Council. This is, of course, consistent with the notion that whatever the need for both institutions to reflect both principles of representation, the priority for the Council is the representation of states, whilst that for the EP is the direct representation of citizens.

Moreover in the instance of the Council a case can be made for giving small states some procedural compensation for the greater probability of large states being pivotal to inter-state bargaining. Power indices provide a striking, if somewhat crude, illustration of the problem. Even with present levels of over-representation of small states, the large are more than three times as likely to be pivotal to winning majorities in the Council than, say, Denmark, Finland and Ireland (Hix, 1999, p. 70). As Axel Moberg (2002, p. 262) points out, 'the under-representation of larger countries is not very great. The over-representation of small countries is much greater. But precisely because they are small, this does not to any degree affect the under-representation of the larger countries.'

Even if we accept it is justified, it is important that any trade-off between the representation of states and populations is consistent. The test of this is that the representation of each Member State should rise in a straight line in proportion to population once it has received a minimum allocation of votes in the Council and seats in the EP. As Figure 5.1 shows, there are significant deviations from such an ideal.

Although Moberg is correct that the large states are not drastically under-represented as a group, Germany in particular plainly is under-represented on the Council. Moreover, the principle of over-representation of small states is compromised by the fact that it is not they but some of

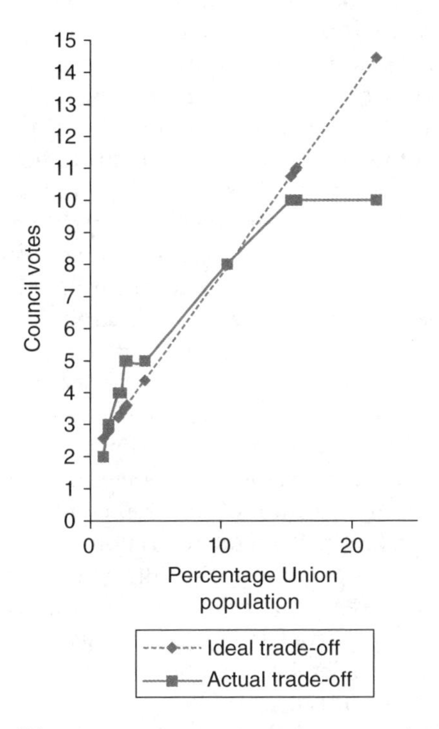

Figure 5.1 Trade-off between representation of states and populations on the Council. How far does the practice deviate from the ideal?

the middle-sized countries such as Belgium, Portugal and Greece that receive some of the most generous allocations of Council votes in relation to population size. The clustering of states into 'status groups' has been one obstacle to a linear relationship between representation and population. It has thus proved difficult to decouple the voting weights of Germany, France, Italy and the UK even though they have ceased to be countries with similar populations since the reunification of Germany. In addition some governments seem to fear that conceding a higher voting weight to a neighbouring country would provoke domestic criticism (Moberg, 2002, p. 270). This may have sustained an anomalous parity in the representation of Belgium and the Netherlands, as much as France and Germany.

However, it is arguable that anomalies in Member State representation in the Council cannot be assessed in isolation from the Union's wider inter-institutional balance. Given that QMV is usually only employed where the EP also has significant legislative powers, a case can be made that the representation of any one Member State in EU decision-making can only be appraised as a joint product of its bloc vote in the Council and its allocation of seats in the EP. Indeed, the notion that EP seats may be considered 'compensation' for under-representation in the Council has been implicit in arrangements for adjusting Union institutions to the reunification of Germany. Whilst Germany's allocation of Council votes has remained pegged to those of France, Italy and the UK, it has twice been allocated extra seats in the EP (Maastricht and Nice).

A counter-argument, is that notions of 'compensation' confuse two things which ought to be kept separate, since the EP is structured for transnational ideological representation, rather than the representation of Member State democracies. A second difficulty is that EP seats can only be used to compensate for the under-representation of a Member State in Council votes where QMV decisions of the Council also require the approval of the Parliament (by Co-decision or Assent). We will see in Chapter 7 that there are still some areas where this is not the case.

Quite apart from any question of how representation in the Council relates to that in the EP, the Parliament has pointed out that the level of disproportionality to population in the allocation of its own seats has not changed much since it was first elected in 1979. What, in its view, is anomalous about this is that it has in the meantime changed from a largely 'consultative assembly' to a body with real legislative powers (European Parliament, 2000a).

Yet, the Parliament is probably close to the limits as to how far its composition can be made proportional to population within a system in which Member States form the constituencies for European elections. A minimum number of MEPs have to be allocated to each Member State if the 'the least populous' is to have a 'minimum representative base' (European Convention, 2002c, p. 8), and a 'meaningul European election'.[5] Otherwise 'political pluralism in the representation of certain smaller Member States' will be 'difficult to maintain' (European Parliament, 2000a). Thus, for example, the proposal to cut the representation of Luxembourg from six to four would raise the threshold any one of its political parties needs to cross to obtain representation in the EP from 16.67 to 25 per cent of the vote.

Veto powers

A third requirement of consociational representation is that cultural–territorial units should preserve veto powers in matters *they* consider of vital interest. In his role as a Swedish official who took part in the Nice negotiations on the allocation of decision rights in the Council (p. 261), Moberg argues that Member States care more about levels of protection that flow from arrangements for forming blocking minorities than about the 'positive' power to shape outcomes by combining into winning majorities.

As seen, instances in which representatives of each national democracy retain a veto include Treaty changes and CFSP and JHA decisions. In cases where QMV applies (mainly pillar one) they have varying opportunities depending on their size to participate in a bloc veto. Under present rules 71 per cent of bloc votes (62/87) are needed for a measure to be carried, and 29 per cent (26/87) are needed for it to be blocked. Germany, France, Italy and the UK all have 10 votes; Spain has 8 votes; Belgium, Greece, the Netherlands and Portugal all have 5 votes; Austria and Sweden 4 votes; Denmark, Finland and Ireland 3 votes; and Luxembourg 2 votes. It follows that.

A. the three largest countries cannot block a decision on their own;
B. the five largest countries cannot make a decision on their own without the support of at least five others;
C. the five smallest countries cannot block a decision on their own (Schmitter and Torreblanco, 2001);
D. the smallest group of member states needed to carry a measure represents 58 per cent of total Union population;
E. the smallest group needed to block a measure represents 12 per cent of total Union population (European Commission, 1999b).

On the other hand, it is misleading to focus only on the smallest possible coalitions in terms of population. If all combinations of member governments that can pass a measure under QMV (using Amsterdam voting weights) are analysed by population, only 5 per cent represent less than 70 per cent of Union population. Conversely, 178 represent more than 80 per cent of Union population, and the median winning coalition represents 78.5 per cent, or significantly more than the 71 per cent of the bloc vote itself. In the handful of cases where a measure can be passed by less than 70 per cent of Union population, 16 out of 22 require almost all small and middling states to vote in favour of a measure that was opposed by at least two out of four of the large members. The only occasion on which such a coalition is at all likely is when size is itself a motive for voting one way or another, which it hardly ever is on normal, as opposed to constitutional, questions.

Although, of course, only the formal rules define the veto *rights*, the risk of Member States having to accept a law against their wishes is lower than implied by the rules. A key data set has been compiled by Mikko Mattila and Jan-Erik Lane (2001) from a total of 1381 legislative acts adopted by the Council during the period 1994–8. This evidence reveals voting is unanimous in between 75 and 85 per cent of cases per year, even where QMV is available. Moreover, in around 60 per cent of the 15–25 per cent of cases where the Council fails to achieve unanimity, there is only one dissenting member, and in around 80–90 per cent there are only two. Around 75 per cent of votes in the Council are unanimous, 90 per cent involve agreement between at least 14 member states, and 95 per cent agreement of at least 13 member states (Mattila and Lane, 2001, pp. 40–3).

In other words, even where QMV is available, Member States prefer to decide by consensus, and to legislate against the wishes of one of their number less frequently than the rules permit. In only around one per cent of cases is the Union's legislation passed by a minimum winning coalition under the rules. This is in stark contrast to models of legislative politics that predict such coalitions will dominate, since actors will seek to maximise pay-offs to themselves by excluding others from joint gains.

It may, of course, be that these figures understate the true level of majoritarianism. On the one hand, consensus may be formed in the 'shadow of majority voting'. Member States rationally anticipate which of their number can form minimum winning coalitions under QMV, extract what concessions they can, and then fall in behind the majority to avoid any domestic political costs of seeming to be on the losing side of a Council vote. A second hypothesis favoured by Mattila and Lane themselves is that elaborate arrangements for preparing Council decisions through working parties and then the Committee of the Permanent Representatives of Member States (COREPER) allow for a high level of vote trading in which apparently high levels of consensus conceal how far Member States accept sub-optimal outcomes in some areas in order to get what they want in others.

However, there are two very different reasons for suspecting that the 'preference for unanimity' in Council voting is sincere and not strategic. On the one hand, case studies (Lewis, 1998) emphasise that the Council has a cognitive, and not just a bargaining, role. Although it deals with many matters where its members have well-defined interests in outcomes, it handles others where objectives or methods are untested, and pay-offs are uncertain or difficult to measure. Governments may, therefore, invest time in comitology committees, Council working parties, COREPER, and the Council itself not to bargain already-formed preferences, but to help one another establish and monitor the consequences of collective actions, without which it is difficult for them to form preferences in the first place. Preferences and assessments that are formed collaboratively are intuitively more likely to conclude with consensus decisions than those which are bargained competitively.

Second, members of the Council may have a normative preference for unanimity (Bostock, 2002, p. 220). Much of this would seem to be delivered in practice through what Jeffrey Lewis (2002, pp. 291–2) describes as COREPER's 'dense normative environment ... of diffuse reciprocity and thick trust ... [leading on to a] consensus reflex'. Such a normative preference for unanimity need be no more real for being conditional. It may, for example, quite coherently require certain reciprocal obligations from dissenting minorities, such as a willingness to justify their opposition and to strive imaginatively for solutions that can accommodate all points of view.

Cognitive and normative explanations of consensual voting in the Council are, moreover, likely to be related. It is where preferences are ill-formed and interests uncertain, that political behaviour is most likely to be shaped by norms (March and Olsen, 1995). A final point is that a certain flexibility in how quickly Member States move from an informal preference for decision by consensus to formal provisions for decision by qualified majority allows some scope for deliberation on a case-by-case basis of which decision-rule is going to be used in practice, taking specific circumstances and actor sensibilities into account (Miller, 1993). It certainly allows a time dimension to be introduced, where unanimity must be attempted authentically before majority voting is recognised as acceptable.

Regional representation

The analysis so far has taken it for granted that the Member State is the only unit that should be entitled to territorial representation. Yet, contributions to recent debates on the future of Europe indicate a number of reasons why regional and other sub-national authorities may want flexible and independent means of influencing Union policy that allow them to differentiate themselves both from their own governments and one another. Indeed a number of distinct clusters of regional interests are already implicit in ways in which sub-national territorial units organise themselves in relation to the EU arena, as follows:

1. The Assembly of European Border Regions (AEMBR) – forms one distinct group. Increasing EU responsibility for the management of external frontiers and prospective enlargement of the Union mean that these regions are drawn together by common concerns.
2. A second group overlapping with the first, but by no mean co-extensive with it, consists of geographically peripheral regions. This group is organised into the Association of the Outermost Regions (ARUP), the Conference of Peripheral Maritime Regions of Europe (CPRM) and the European Association of Elected Representatives from Mountainous Areas (AEM). What makes these regions unusual is the extreme sensitivity of their economic and social conditions to particular Union policies such as the Common Agricultural Policy (CAP), the Fisheries Policy and the Regional Structural Funds. They are the main exceptions to the rule that territorial units only have diffuse interests, while sectors have concentrated interests, in the determination of Union policy.
3. A third group consists of closely interdependent regions from more than one Member State. Some of these have attempted to form themselves with varying degrees of success into Inter-regions (INTEREGs).
4. The development of EUROCITIES reflects a growing perception that cities have distinct interests in European integration centred around environmental issues, urban regeneration and immigration and asylum policies.
5. The final group consists of regions with elected governments of their own. An important subset of these consists of the presently 51 regions of the Union that have legislative powers in their Member States. These are organised into Conference of European Legislative Assemblies (CALRE) and Co-ordination of Regions with Legislative Power (REGLEG). The interest of these regions in being able to represent

> themselves at Union level is constitutional and not just to do with policy. They are concerned to ensure transfers of legislative competence to the EU and do not redistribute law-making powers within the state. Through their involvement in the Council of Ministers, national governments may acquire opportunities to shape legislation which do not belong to them domestically, but to politicians elected at the regional level.

In addition to the demands of particular regions to represent their distinct preferences in relation to Union policy, the Commission has argued that responsiveness in general would be enhanced by a direct interface between Union institutions and those territorial units of governance that are closest to citizens (European Commission, 2001f, p. 6). In addition, trends towards regionalisation and decentralisation mean increasingly that it is often sub-national authorities, and not just Member States, who are the EU's 'partners in implementation'. Their resources are used to deliver Union policies on the ground (Committee of the Regions, 1999). Thus, on principles such as 'no taxation without representation' or 'those who are touched by policy should have some voice in its determination' a case can be made for the structured access of representatives of local and regional communities to EU policy-making.

The Union's attempts to develop a regional tier of representation within its own institutions have however only met with mixed success. The TEU introduced a Committee of the Regions (CoR) that has to be consulted where policies are introduced under various Treaty articles. However, the EP has expressed what is probably a widespread view that 'despite the creation of the CoR regional authorities all too often feel sidelined'. In the EP's view 'tensions' have been 'caused by the Committee's own make-up: 'the Prime Ministers of the largest regional governments sit next to mayors of small towns' (European Parliament, 2002a, pp. 5, 10). As this observation suggests, the diversity in the sub-national composition of Member States makes it hard for the Union to structure regional and local authorities into a single representative institution to the satisfaction of all. A measure of heterogeneity emerges from the CoR's classification of the sub-national structures of Member States into the following four types.

- Federal (Austria, Belgium, Germany)
- Regionalised Unitary (Spain, France, Italy and the UK)
- Decentralised Unitary (Denmark, Finland, the Netherlands and Sweden)

- Centralised Unitary (Greece, Ireland, Luxembourg and Portugal). (Committee of the Regions, 1999)

But even this is a crude simplification. Variations in the powers of regions to make legislation, tax and spend, sign Treaties of their own, and participate in national policy formulation cross-cut the CoR's classifications. Then there are distinctive issues raised by Member States that are asymmetrically decentralised such as the UK, Spain and Finland. To top it all, the regions of Europe vary from those that are little more than administrative creations to those whose sense of identity approaches nationhood. Another key difference is between regions many of whose inhabitants are to varying degrees opposed to the existing structures of their Member States, and those who are not.

This diversity means that whatever structure the EU devises for the representation of regional and local authorities, the latter will vary in how far it is worth their while responding, by mobilising attention and resources. Of course, the Union could incentivise regional participation in its institutions. But this only raises a further problem. Some mechanism to include regions in Co-decision, for example, would multiply veto points and require centralised decisions on which regions should count and for how much in Union decisions. Thus the EP has concluded that it would be hard to progress the involvement of regions beyond consultation. Yet it goes on to argue that even within that constraint much more could be done than at present (European Parliament, 2002a). Representatives of several regions would agree. The following, for example, is the shopping list that the Catalan Parliament presented to a public hearing on the preparation of the Commission's White Paper on Governance.

- The Committee of the regions should be directly elected.
- The Commission and Council should have to give a direct explanation for why they do not follow a recommendation of the Committee of the regions.
- COSAC should be extended to include regional assemblies with legislative powers.
- Regional, and not just national, parliaments should have rights of scrutiny where they, and not Member States, are the implementing authority, or where they would have been the legislating body had their country not joined the EU.[6]

A number of attempts have been made to get round the elusiveness of a 'one size fits all' solution to the problem of how to represent regions at Union level. One has been to adapt Member States' own rights of representation to give regions access to Union institutions. Thus the German Government often includes representatives of the Länder in its Council delegations and the *Grundgesetz* now requires it to negotiate collectively with the Bundesrat or individually with the Länder where the latter have mixed or exclusive competence respectively. Likewise, Spain has established a special 'Sectoral Conference' that its central government is expected to use to negotiate with the seven autonomous regions on EU matters. Belgium, for its part, has taken regional participation to the point at which the regional governments hosted and chaired several Councils during its last Presidency (*La Libre Belgique*, 1 July 2001). Several Member States (Belgium, Germany, Italy, Spain and the UK) also structure the distribution of their EP seats so that some or all of their regions have assured representation there. It should, however, be noted that this is only mathematically possible for those that are either large Member States or have comparatively few regions.

Since engagement with the Union through Member States is not, however, to the liking of all regions, two more 'do it yourself' solutions have emerged. One has been a proliferation of regional representations in Brussels. These allow regions a more 'pick and mix' focus on particular Union policies than would be likely through structured participation in a collective process such as the CoR or through access negotiated with their own governments. A second more tentative solution – much discussed at the time of the Commission's White Paper on Governance – consists of 'partnership contracts' between the Union, and local and regional bodies. These would have the advantage of allowing relationships between the Commission and regional and local authorities to vary somewhat with the sub-national structures of Member States, but with the disadvantage that only Member States can be held legally responsible for implementation.

Interest representation

Regardless of the relative merits of Member States and regions as intermediaries between citizens and Union institutions it is doubtful whether any system of territorial representation could satisfy all the representative needs of citizens in relation to the European arena. As seen, a fundamental difficulty is that the needs and values of citizens on European questions may cross-cut national and territorial divisions. Interest representation would be one means of channelling into the European arena what Philippe Schmitter (1992, p. 400) calls the 'transversal preferences' of 'Euro-proletarians (sic.), Euro-professionals, Euro-consumers, Euro-enviromentalists, Euro-feminists, Euro-regionalists, Euro-youths or just plain Euro-citizens'.

Several studies demonstrate that at least some forms of interest representation are already well developed in relation to the European arena (Greenwood, 1997). Given that the Union tends to make specialised forms of policy for particular sectors, use of organised interests to undertake much of the intermediation between society and EU institutions might be defended on the following grounds. First, that citizens and groups should have influence in proportion to how far they are affected by a policy; second, that a preponderance of regulatory over redistributive policy-making (Majone, 1996), means Union decisions often have concentrated effects for small groups and only weak or diffuse ones for society as a whole. Under such conditions mass representative institutions might even seem singularly unjust, since such institutions count preferences by their number. They do not weigh them by their intensity.

Interest representation can also provide that element of continuous linkage between society and governance needed to compensate for the intermittent nature of electoral choice, or, in the case of the EU, the lack of an electoral connection much concerned with Union issues themselves (see p. 119). An organised civil society may also have a role in developing those capabilities of democratic citizenship needed for mass representative politics that Chapter 3 found to be lacking. Alex Warleigh (2001, p. 621) rightly draws lessons for the EU from an earlier literature that identified experience of a political system, as much as education in its rules and values, as the basis of any political socialisation (Almond and Verba, 1963). Moreover, liberal democracy's peculiar alchemy lies in an organised civil society that can at once engage with a political system while retaining a critical independence of it (Bauman, 1999, pp. 154–5).

The early European Communities attempted to institutionalise interest representation through the Economic and Social Committee (ESC) which the Treaties require to be consulted on a range of legislative measures. However, in spite of attempts to update its role and composition the ESC was constructed on corporatist assumptions that interest representation would be effectively delivered through tripartite discussions between the political authority on the one hand, and the 'peak organisations' of employers and labour unions on the other.

In practice the main axis of interest representation in EU policy-making has gravitated towards a system of network governance. Self-organised networks have developed around specific policies. These consist of actors who are mutually dependent on one another for the delivery of their goals and who cross-cut the branches and levels of Union governance as well as the divide between public and private interests (Peterson, 1995a). Given that functionalities of delivery and patterns of interdependence vary by policy and sector, networks are not only informal they are also heterogeneous in how they configure interest representation.

To their defenders, policy networks may lack qualities associated with structured forms of mass representation through elections, parties and parliaments. But the converse is also true. More hierarchical systems of representation can be deliberatively undemanding. It is sufficient that policies are part of a programme supported by an elected majority regardless of how well individual elements have been scrutinised and justified to others. A controlled majority is often able to shut down discussion on no better basis than because it is the majority. Under well-functioning networks, on the other hand, each policy has to be freshly justified to independent actors whose only basis for agreement is mutual persuasion. Christian Joerges and Jürgen Neyer (1997) provide a bold statement of this point of view:

> core institutional elements of the EU should be read as supranational versions of deliberationist ideals and interpreted with a view to comprehending some shortcomings of the constitutional national state ... the new emphasis is on the development of ... a culture of inter-administrative partnership which relies on persuasion, argument and discursive process ... rather than on command, control and strategic interaction.

Representation through such networks is also likely to be pareto superior to representation through hierarchies. Since *ex hypothesi* all members of networks are necessary for the delivery of the goals of all other members, there is no other basis for collective decision than an outcome that leaves each at least as well off as before. Since all network members are expert in the policy area, the means for speedy identification of positive-sum solutions co-exists with the incentive to search them out. In addition, networks help deliver another quality of the European arena, namely a choice of access points for those seeking representation there.

Yet, for all their ingenuity, there are limits to the democratic representation that can be delivered through networks. Elite accommodation over the heads of the represented is not acceptable merely because networks contain a wide range of actor types or proliferate choice of access points to Union decision-making. One issue is how accountable are network members to those they represent. Empirical evidence suggests that where

NGOs develop at European level they perform in some isolation from the mass membership (Warleigh, 2001). They would not seem as yet to have contributed to political socialisation and demos building. Another danger is that instead of balancing and checking one another, networks or their members may collude to suspend competitiveness between themselves, to reduce prospects of challenge from the constituencies to which they are supposedly accountable and to freeze new entrants out of access to the benefits of engagement with the political system.

Indeed any form of interest representation at Union level raises familiar problems of how to.

- Represent the diffuse public interest (Pollack, 1997b) that is left over after individual lobbies have influenced the political system without regard for the cumulative external effects of their specific actions.
- Allow organised private interests access without capture of what is after all a public process.
- Avoid reproducing the inequalities already to be found in society. The difficulty of how to represent those for whom the marginal cost of self-organisation is greater than the marginal return (Olson, 1965) is especially acute in the case of a political system that is both transnational and large-scale. Indeed it seems likely that for many interests such a cut-off point coincides with the migration of policy from the domestic to the European arena. The degree to which sectoral interests vary in their capacity to organise in the European arena was underscored by the following contribution to this survey:

> There are some sectors where there is almost no established consultation, and some attendant danger of pre-empting what a specific set of stakeholders would find appropriate to their sector were they ever to organise. In other cases, consultees are virtual partners in governance.[7]

Attempts have been made to consider how these difficulties might be circumvented. The argument that properly constituted networks could have normative and representative qualities of their own, even if they are not those of mass democratic structures, has found some support in the Commission. A study co-ordinated by the Forward Studies Unit (FSU) urges a radical rethink of what is needed for 'legitimate rule production'. In place of structures in which elected representatives 'formulate broad policies in legislative chambers, oversee their detailed implementation by bureaucratic departments' and 'impose a particular understanding of the problem and the means to resolve it', the study argues that social actors should negotiate forms of self-regulation between themselves, with Union institutions only intervening to ensure the following conditions of fairness:

- inclusiveness of representatives of all those affected by a rule;
- compensation for inequalities in 'cognitive resources';
- substitution of public reason for purely sectional patterns of preference formation.

Actors, the study urges, should be asked to 'clarify the presuppositions they bring to a particular issue', to reflect on the 'contingency of their models', and to 'demonstrate the coherence of their constructions, not only in terms of their initial positions but in terms of positions of others as they have evolved during a process of collective learning' (European Commission, 1997).

But here is the rub that casts doubt on how far a system of interest representation can ever be satisfactory if attempted as an alternative, rather than a dietary supplement, to more conventional and structured forms of mass representation based around elections and parliaments. The FSU's approach is impregnated with criteria for how the political authority should deal with civil society. Should the Commission set those standards on its own? Or should it be accountable to a representative body in determining them? In the end, interest representation presupposes parliamentary representation, as the Commission was forced repeatedly to emphasise in its defence of its Governance White Paper to the EP.[8] It is to an appraisal of how far the Union has achieved representation through conventional means of parties, elections and parliaments that the analysis now returns.

Ideological representation

The shortcomings of interest representation are normally met in a representative democracy through a system of parties. These compete around broad programmes of government and are awarded with political office in proportion to votes received from politically equal citizens (one person, one vote). Their role in bundling issues into broad programmes deals with the problem just discussed that key choices of value are not just to be found in the management of one policy or sector but in trade-offs between several. Parties can also facilitate responsible government. To the extent they are coherent, a vote for a party programme is a form of *ex ante* public control that requires those who compete for office to set out a stall for public inspection. Scope to hold a party collectively responsible for its record – with reputational costs and benefits sometimes persisting for decades – is, conversely, a powerful instrument of *ex post* accountability (Ranney, 1962).

Moreover parties are radical simplifiers that allow citizens to participate in complex democratic systems with only minimal information. Any two voters from any part of the political system can without ever being aware of one another's existence solve co-ordination problems by aggregating their preferences behind the same party programmes on offer. In addition, parties lighten cognitive demands to the point at which citizens may only need to know what is the ordinal (i.e. relative) position of parties along one or two key dimensions of political choice (such as left–right), or whether a party is in government, and thus responsible for present levels of performance, or in opposition, and thus a plausible vehicle for regime change.

Against this background it is often considered a serious defect in the EU's capacity to deliver representative politics that it does not have political parties of its own. The degree to which the EU is a 'partyless' political system incapable of delivering ideological representation is, however, by no means straightforward. A series of new party political formations has developed whose primary purpose is to exercise influence over the institutions of the European Union. As set out in Table 5.2., these consist at the time of writing of five federations of national parties and seven multinational party groups in the EP some of which correspond to the federations.

Table 5.2 The party politics of the EU

Party federations	*European parliament party groups*
European Peoples Party (EPP) (Christian Democrats & Conservatives)	European People's Party
Party of European Socialists (PES)	Party of European Socialists (PES)
European Liberal and Democratic Reform Party (ELDR)	European Liberal and Democratic Reform Party (ELDR)
European Federation of Green Parties (EFGP)	Greens/European Free Alliance
European Free Alliance (EFA) of Regionalist parties	
—	European United Left (EUL)
—	Union for a Europe of Nations (UEN)
—	Europe of Democracies and Diversities (EDD)

This can be seen as a complete party structure in two senses. First it covers most ideological groupings common to the member societies of the Union: Christian Democrats and Conservatives, Socialists and Social Democrats, Liberals, Greens, the Far Left and Eurosceptics are all to some degree organised at the European level. The only exception is the Far Right that has only occasionally managed even to form a group in the EP, largely because transnational self-organisation is an unlikely activity for often nationalist political parties (Lord, 1998b, p. 130).

Second, the federations and groups feed into several institutions of the Union. They are most obviously organised in the EP. However, the federations also hold summits prior to meetings of the European Council (Hix, 1995). This allows national party leaders who are not represented on that body to discuss the agenda with those who are. Although it is difficult to find firm empirical evidence of the overall frequency with which members of the European Council or Council of Ministers align in a manner that corresponds to the party composition of national governments (even with the publication of voting records of the latter), there are cases where party politics would seem to have been a basis for coalition formation. Thus the EPP 'win' at Maastricht (1991) on the adoption of a model of Monetary Union that emphasised fiscal and monetary rigour is often contrasted with a PES 'win' at Amsterdam (1997) on the adoption of an Employment chapter (Johansson, 1999).

Within the EP in particular there are indications that the EU's party system has stability, cohesion and defined dimensionality. Most national parties are now aligned with their preferred party group. After a period of concentration when national parties migrated from small to large groups and from the peripheries to the centre of the Parliament (Bardi, 1996), changes of affiliation have slowed since the mid-1990s. Indeed, most MEPs now come from national parties whose federations require a commitment that any candidate elected in their name will join a designated parliamentary group. Yet, in spite of absorbing a larger number of national parties to the point at which the larger groups even include more than one party per Member State, the cohesion of the groups – as measured by the frequency with which their members vote with one another – has stabilised around 90 per cent since the early 1990s, a high figure for a Parliament of fluid alignments and without the disciplines that come with the need to sustain a government in office. Voting behaviour reveals two further patterns. First, MEPs from the same transnational party are much more likely to vote with one another than those from the same nationality. Second, MEPs are mainly interested in making left–right choices. No other alignment – not even pro–anti further European integration – comes close to rivalling 'left–right' as the main focus for party political activity at Union level (Hix, 2001).

The development of party actors specific to the EU is firmly underpinned by the powers and decision rules of Union institutions themselves. These encourage party actors to ensure they are at least as well organised as their rivals to influence the policy outputs of Union institutions. On the assumption that party actors are motivated by a mixture of office and policy-seeking goals, even those who care more about national than European politics have to adjust to the shrinking number of *domaines reservées* where policy-making is so concentrated within the domestic arena as to require little attention to the European. With the empowerment of the European Parliament, even those with access to the Council of Ministers – and with a preference for that body as a locus of decision and representation – have to acknowledge legislative outcomes are only partially determined there.

Not only do individual national parties have to adjust to Europe. Few have much margin to function as 'structure-makers', as opposed to 'structure-takers' in relation to pre-existing transnational party formations at Union level. While it is true that the groups in the EP are collectively constrained by their component national parties and have only limited autonomous means of rewarding or sanctioning the loyalty of their members, there has been insufficient attention in the literature to the converse problem of just how far national parties are individually constrained by the transnational party alignments and organisational structures to be found in the European arena.

The probable reason for this neglect is that the systemic constraint of national party delegations by transnational party groups lies not in conventionally understood party disciplines, but in the smallness of those delegations in relation to the Parliament as a whole. The average size of a national party delegation is only five or six Members in a Parliament where absolute majorities are needed to exercise several key powers (i.e. regardless of the turnout, 314 have to vote 'yes'). Moreover, fluid voting alignments mean few national party delegations can expect to be pivotal for long (though there are exceptions, about which more in a moment). In addition, existing formations (the EP groups and federations) represent sunk investments in the development of elaborate co-ordinating mechanisms. These arguably benefit from increasing returns with use (Pierson, 2000) which breakaway groups of national parties seeking to reconfigure the Euro-party system might struggle to replicate from scratch.

Yet, the representative qualities of the EU's party structures as just portrayed are open to question. No citizen has the opportunity to vote directly for the transnational party groups in the EP and the only mass membership parties with roots in civil society are national ones. Instead the EU operates a 'split-level' party system. This centres on a division of labour in which national parties structure voter choice whilst representatives only join transnational party groups once they arrive in the Parliament.

The key question is whether this split-level party system provides an adequate electoral link between the represented and their parliamentary representatives. Scepticism has centred on the second-order character of European elections (Reif and Schmitt, 1980). Although recent research has questioned whether low turnout can be attributed to a perception that the EP is unimportant (Blondel *et al.*, 1998) it leaves intact that part of second-order theory which predicts that the behaviour of both voters and parties is significantly shaped by domestic issues and national patterns of political competition, even though European elections are the only opportunity the voter has to express preferences on the policies or composition of Union institutions.

Most brutally put, second-order theory implies European elections do not have much to do with the institution that is, in fact, being elected. Indeed, it has been taken to mean that any electoral link between the citizen and Union institutions is accidental and not systematic. Voting can neither be interpreted as a judgement on rival programmes for a forthcoming EP (albeit filtered through media debate rather than a close reading of manifestoes) nor as an appraisal of the relative performance of parties in an outgoing EP. As such, European elections seem to deliver neither *ex ante* nor *ex post* representation. Those who are nominally representatives at European level are independent of voters, rather than linked to them.

Moreover, the difficulty of prising European elections free from national issues can be directly attributed to the split-level pattern of the EU's party system. As long as it is national parties whose names appear on ballot sheets, European elections have, as seen, the paradoxical effect of introducing a further quasi-general election into the domestic political cycle: everyone votes at the same time within a single national constituency for the familiar range of national parties. This can make it hard to take European elections out of a national frame and use them, instead, to offer and register choice on Union issues.

Indeed, a common criticism of EU party formations is that they do not just fail to link voters and representatives on European issues, they also restrict competition at both the parliamentary and electoral levels. A 'grand coalition' pattern of voting in which the main parliamentary groups – the EPP-ED, PES and even the ELDR and Greens – link up across the political divide often seems to dominate the work of the Parliament. This is taken by some as evidence that contestation takes second place to the smooth management of parliamentary business (Rinsche and Welle, 1999). Thus the present President of the EP has argued that MEPs have yet to demonstrate to voters that preferring one set of candidates to another will change policy outcomes at the European level (ELDR, 1999).

Moreover, MEPs are arguably only free to focus on forming parliamentary coalitions which maximise the efficiency with which they can exercise their powers so long as there is little danger of their voting behaviour becoming an electoral issue. Not only, then, do restrictions on competition in the parliamentary and electoral arenas reinforce one another, they also cast doubt on the aforementioned indicators of successful party political development. It is hard to tell how far stability, cohesion, and defined dimensionality at the parliamentary level are only possible because choice and competition have yet to spill over into the cognitive mobilisation of a critical public opinion to which MEPs must, in turn, respond in their voting behaviour.

Indeed, present structures of party politics may even be a barrier to the further development of representation in the Union arena. As seen, James March and Johan Olsen argue that both representatives and represented need 'political capabilities' that are only likely to develop with use (March and Olsen, 1995). To the extent that the task of representing the public in the European arena is an idiosyncratic one that requires the steady development over time of specialised knowledge about the Union it may require representatives who are committed to making their careers in the EP. Yet, even the fourth (1994–9) and fifth (1999–2004) directly elected European Parliaments had majorities of members who had never served before (Corbett *et al.*, 1995). High turnover – and, indeed, periodic decapitation of the political leadership of some EP groups – can, in turn, be attributed to the decentralisation of powers to draw up electoral lists to national parties, which often have other objectives than the institutional continuity of European parliamentary parties. On the other hand, elections that continue to have a heavily domestic content cannot perform the developmental role (Held, 1996) of improving citizens' understanding of how best to use the EU's political system to achieve their needs and values.

Another criticism is that the development of the EU party system as an outgrowth of national party politics – with national parties continuing to dominate voter choice and EP party groups duplicating a conventional left–right focus – prevents the overall structure from adding any value to how citizens are represented at Union level. A third critique is that the apparent failure of the EU's party formations to provide more competition, choice or development in representative practices and capabilities is not just temporary or accidental. Rather, it suits established players in a way that makes change unlikely in the foreseeable future. If the goal-seeking behaviour of national parties can be used to explain the appearance of sophisticated parliamentary parties in the European arena, it can also help us understand the non-appearance of electoral parties.

Indeed, a disjunction between parties that are transnational for the purposes of co-operation in the European Parliament but not for European elections can be seen as optimal for national parties. On the one hand, it confirms their monopoly of electoral mobilisation, and seemingly allows them to run low-key depoliticised campaigns for the EP that reduce the risk of controversy spilling back into what is for them the primary arena, namely the domestic. On the other hand, present arrangements seemingly maximise the hold of national parties over their MEPs. As long as European elections are second order in nature, MEPs have no special incentive to follow the preferences of their electorate. Their chances of re-elections are conditioned by the domestic political cycle and not by any actions of their own. Yet, they do have reason to follow the preferences of their Selectorate. National parties reward or sanction their careers by deciding whether they are to be re-adopted as candidates for subsequent European Parliaments, or offered a route back into domestic politics (Andolfato, 1994). Competition to please domestic parties is further intensified by the use of closed lists in European elections in most Member States. Chances of political survival are not just dependent on being re-adopted, but on the order in which the party presents its candidates for election. Where it suits them, national parties clearly do have significant scope to instruct MEPs (Hix and Lord, 1996).

The power of national parties to block the entry of more transnational parties (Lord, 2001b) to the electoral arena requires clarification of what the alternatives are to the present arrangements for registering voter choice in European elections. One might be for citizens to have a direct choice between pan-European parties, though a more incremental development might be for national parties intending to join a group in the EP to indicate that affiliation on the ballot sheet alongside their domestic party name. Another possibility (mentioned by the European Council (2001) in the Laeken declaration establishing the Convention on the Future of Europe) would be for some EP seats – perhaps 10 or 20 per cent of the total – to be allocated in proportion to votes cast at Union level. This would create an incentive for parties to present themselves in a form that would allow votes to be aggregated across more than one Member State.

The key point is that each of these options would in some way require the co-operation of national parties in their own (partial) withdrawal from European elections. The creation of a bloc of seats to be allocated at Union level or even ballot paper descriptions that clarified links to EP party groups would require changes to the EU Treaties or national electoral procedures that can only be agreed by Member State governments dominated by national parties. Short of such changes, pan-European parties are likely to be deterred from competing directly with national parties in European elections. The minimum threshold needed to win just one seat in the EP varies from 1 to 17 per cent of the vote depending on the Member State. Pan-European parties without 'brand recognition' could well struggle to cross these hurdles in any significant way in any head-to-head competition with national parties.

In sum, then, the charge of cartelisation is that political parties substitute rent-seeking behaviour for the public interest in a properly functioning system of representative politics at Union level. That is to say, they prefer a predictable carve up of the policy outcomes of the European Parliament, avoidance of spill-back controversies to the domestic arena and a continued monopoly by established national parties on voter mobilisation to more open-ended forms of competition. This blunts expectations that better ways of linking voters to representative institutions at EU level will develop through the effects of political competition in rewarding and sanctioning party political behaviour in the European arena.

Yet, each of the foregoing critiques is questionable. Working as it were from the last back to the first, it is by no means clear that the EU's present pattern of party politics is the product of the anti-competitive behaviour of established actors. The difficulty with the cartelisation argument is that national parties neither seem eager to reap benefits from controlling MEPs nor do they appear capable of avoiding costs associated with their continued responsibility for European elections. Although national parties have the means to supervise their MEPs, survey evidence shows their attempts to do so vary from the patchy to the non-existent (Raunio, 2002). It may be counterproductive for national parties to issue instructions rather than trust their MEPs to use their judgement to negotiate their way into winning coalitions, given the smallness of most national delegations in relation to the Parliament as a whole and the fluidity of its alignments. Indeed, many MEPs claim that the direction of influence is often the other way round. On EU issues, it is often they who lead on the formation of positions adopted by their national parties. Their participation in EP committees means they enjoy asymmetries of information over their national parties on what are often highly technical issues. Moreover, they profit from slack in the domestic political environment: domestic political competition or media controversy is likely to be concentrated at any one time on a fairly narrow range of issues, with the result that national parties have no special incentive to deny their MEPs' discretion in their handling of others.

If the pay-offs to national parties of instructing MEPs are doubtful, what of the costs to national parties of continuing to be responsible for mobilisation in both domestic and European elections? European elections have often been destabilising of at least some of the national parties and party systems that fight them (Andeweg, 1995). They have been associated with party leadership changes, strains in multiparty coalitions, splits within parties and surges of support for anti-system parties. There is a basic structural reason why European elections can often produce unexpected results with destabilising consequences for domestic politics. Their role in introducing a general election of sorts into the domestic political cycle (see p. 84) is not anchored in an agreed understanding of the political choice that voters are being called upon to make. Is a European election a mid-term plebiscite on the performance of national governments? An occasional opportunity to vote 'with the heart' for parties that are most expressive of voter values, rather than 'with the head' for those that are most likely to affect outcomes? A means of expressing views on European integration or even of attempting to influence the legislative outputs of the EP? European elections are probably all of these things, at different times, and for different groups of people (Bréchon, 1999).

The destabilising potential of European elections suggests many national parties may fight European elections more through necessity than choice. As seen, a high proportion of voting remains habitual and 'brand recognition' remains important even where voters float freely between the alternatives. Any sudden substitution of pan-European for national parties as the means of structuring voter choice in European elections would thus risk further declines in turnout or an increase in random voting. Looked at this way, the continued availability of national parties for voter mobilisation is a service rather than a barrier to the entry of potentially more effective Euro-parties to the electoral arena.

Nor is it clear that the Euro-parties that have formed at elite level freeze competition within and between the Union's representative institutions. The need for consensus to exercise key powers of the Parliament under the absolute majority rule[9] or to pass resolutions that carry maximum weight with the Council and Commission does not preclude contestation at earlier stages of decision-making. A great deal of ideological differentiation is played out in committee debates, and is not, therefore, susceptible to statistical analysis of roll-calls. However, a possible indicator that disagreements are real enough is that many groups now appoint their own 'shadows' to the *rapporteurs* who are responsible for drafting reports on behalf of the committee as a whole (Neuhold, 2001, p. 13). Another is that their shared interest in coming together to form oversized majorities on final resolutions is preceded by ideological competition and adversarial behaviour in tabling or shooting down amendments to those resolutions (Kreppel, 2000, p. 134).

On top of this ideological contestation within the Parliament itself, the Euro-party system has the little noticed effect of reinforcing inter-institutional competition and checks and balances. Here it is essential to note that the role of parties at EU level is not monopolised by national parties of government. Indeed, the European Parliament even has a structural bias towards strong representation of national parties of opposition. This follows from the 'second-order' pattern of voting in European elections and its association with mid-term swings against national parties of government. The 1994–9 Parliament, accordingly, started life with a 39 : 61 per cent balance between government and opposition parties respectively. Likewise, in the case of the 1999–2004 Parliament, the centre right EPP became the largest single group for the first time since 1975, just as the unprecedented hold of the centre-left on parties of Government gave the PES access to 11 out of 15 places on the European Council, and to 13 out of 15 seats on various sectoral Councils of Ministers. In short, second-order elections mean that at least at the beginning of a Parliamentary term a Council of Ministers made up of national parties of government will face an EP with a preponderance of national parties of opposition.

What finally of the argument that representatives and voters are not linked on issues relevant to the functioning of the Union itself? The observation that European elections are often fought on domestic issues does not of itself justify the conclusion that they are irrelevant to the functioning of the Union without further demonstration that national and EU issues are neatly separable and that choices made in relation to one cannot in some sense function as proxies for the other. On the first point, many MEPs who took part in the survey for this book characterised the content of European elections as Union issues framed in domestic contexts. They also claimed a large part of their subsequent representative behaviour is played out at the interface of the two arenas and that success is defined by a capacity to draw connections between domestic and Union issues.

Nor is it clear why only pro or anti integration preferences, as opposed to 'left–right' ones, should be considered 'European issues'. Given the substantive content of the policies covered by the EU it would be extraordinary if representatives did not want to influence left–right outcomes. In any case, the EU political system does not so much suppress the supranational-intergovernmental cleavage as allow it to be addressed on a national-territorial basis through the Treaty formation process. For the EP to concentrate on pro-anti integration preferences, rather than left–right ones, would not improve representation. It would mean giving up a focus that corresponds to the Parliament's powers for one where another body, the European Council, makes the key choices. Indeed, the left–right character of the EP has led some to question how far there is a disconnect at all between the electoral and parliamentary levels of EU party politics. Herman Schmitt and Jacques Thomassen (2000) have shown that MEPs line up in the same order along a left–right dimension of political choice as those who vote for them.

This is an important finding but to my mind it is also one that allows us at last to identify what is deficient in party political representation at Union level. It is useful to begin by considering a couple of puzzles:

- It follows from the convergent nature of political competition that large numbers of voters will often feel that more than one group of representatives is equidistant from their preferences. A sensible basis for choosing might then be to judge who is more likely to deliver. That, in turn, might involve retrospective appraisals of past performance or prospective estimates of how each group of representative is likely to be strategically and institutionally positioned over the coming legislative term. What, of course, this puzzle does is to destroy any notion that voters can manage without active and informed judgements of the political system in which representative office is held. Left–right selections between national parties cannot serve as proxy choices in relation to the European.

- The same conclusion follows from the observation that voters may have good reasons to incline to the right in relation to one level of governance and to the left in relation to another. Indeed, experience of federal systems suggests this is quite common, and two characteristics of the EU make it likely in its case. First, the national and European levels differ in the methods they use for allocating left–right values. In the case of the Union, allocation is mainly a by-product of alternative approaches to regulation. Only rarely is it made explicit through financial transfers (Majone, 1996). Second, even where the latter do operate, actors may well stand to benefit from financial redistribution at one level of governance but lose from it at another. Thus a citizen of a relatively disadvantaged sociological group in a Member State that is a net contributor to the EU's budget could self-interestedly be of the left on domestic issues and of the right on European ones.

Yet these puzzles only scratch the surface of the problem. Like Schmitt and Thomassen, they equate representation with the aggregation of interests and preferences rather than the articulation of meanings, values and identities or the exercise of rights. Thus further reasons why represented and representatives need to interact on the specifics of each political system are, first, that left and right may acquire different meanings and appeal to different notions of identity in relation to each institutional order or level of government. Indeed, the construction and deliberation of those meanings and identities may require multiple iterations of the democratic process in the political system in which they are to be played out. Second, democracy as we have argued from the beginning is not distinctively defined by the satisfaction of wants at all, but by rights of control. Whilst (in spite of the foregoing the 'puzzles') the EU's party system could conceivably be rather good at satisfying wants by, as it were, borrowing preference orderings from the politics of its Member States, control of representatives presupposes a party system that links voters to the political system in a manner that allow the first to make active judgements on the second.

By way of footnote, if it is accepted that MEPs are neither closely instructed by national parties nor hugely pressured to anticipate change in electoral opinion, their behaviour will depend on the role conceptions they themselves bring to the task of representation. The evidence suggests that MEPs recognise a plurality of claims on their representative functions (Scully and Farrell, 2003). This is clearly brought out by Table 5.3 which reproduces relevant responses to a survey of MEPs conducted by

Table 5.3 MEP role conceptions

Roles: How important are the following aspects of your work?	*Average on scale 1–5*
Legislating	4.4
Parliamentary oversight	4.2
Social group representation	3.9
Developing strategies for European policies	3.77
Social mediation	3.22
Representing individual citizens	2.97
How important is it for you to represent the following?	
All people in Europe	3.55
All people in my Member State	3.92
All the people who voted for my party	3.72
All the people in my constituency	3.88
My national party	3.65
My EP party group	3.42
A specific group in society	2.59

Source: Based on *MEP Survey 2000* by S. Hix and R. Scully for the European Parliament Research Group. Details on www. lse.ac.uk/depts/eprg.

Simon Hix. Indeed, Hix *et al.* (1999) are surely right that the EP is a mosaic of different representative practices. Not only do MEPs bring national norms of representation with them. But their behaviour is structured by cross-country differences in electoral and party systems. Thus even in the case of the EP, how citizens are represented at Union level depends on where they live.

Conclusion: the EU as compounded representation?

This chapter has begun the task of analysing the presence, voice and weight of different actor types in Union decisions. It shows there is much to be said for the notion that the EU compounds (Benz and Esslinger, 2000) or piles different modes of representation on top of one another. However, this leaves the following unanswered questions.

1. Are the various strands of representation given equal importance? Probably not. The territorial representation of Member States is almost universal across all Union decisions. Only for particular decisions is ideological representation through the EP given equal weight with territorial

representation of Member States, as we will argue further in Chapter 7. Interest representation through policy networks depends on patterns of interdependence and histories of mobilisation that are specific to policies and sectors. Regions differ markedly in how motivated they are to organise at Union level.

2. On what principles are the different strands of representation compounded? Compounding requires high levels of consensus within and between each mode of representation. Thus Co-decision requires the agreement of both the territorial representation in the Council and the ideological representation in the EP. This, in turn, requires approval of at least 71 per cent of the bloc vote held by Member States, and, in practice, of a similar proportion of MEPs if the Parliament is to secure the absolute majority of its Members (and not just of those voting) needed for it to contribute to outcomes by passing amendments of its own. However even consensus within and between the Council and EP will not be enough, where the delivery of objectives also requires a high level of agreement between representatives of immediately affected interests .

3. What do present arrangements for Compounded Representation mean for the Democratic Audit tests with which we started the chapter? Probably that the tests associated with modified consociationalism (*EUDA Tests 3 & 4*) are better met than those connected to concurrent consent (*EUDA Tests 9 & 10*). The following paragraphs explain.

How far does the distribution of executive and legislative office in the EU ensure the inclusive and proportional representation of national democracies (EUDA Test 3)? The distribution of both legislative and executive office is inclusive of representatives of each national democracy, though, in the allocation of Council votes and EP seats, there is room for improvement in the present trade-off between parity of representation of states and proportional representation of populations.

How far do representatives of national democracies shape and control Union decisions they consider of vital importance (EUDA Test 4)? The rule that the 'Council decides' means that national governments retain a high level of collective control over Union decisions. Although their individual control may be diluted by majority voting in the Council and Co-decision with the Parliament, the former is used sparingly in practice and majorities of the latter are usually inclusive of nationalities as much as of ideologies. Indeed, national governments shape as well as control (*EUDA Test 4*). As we will see in Chapter 6, they shape agendas, even where the Commmission has the formal right of initiative.

How far is the designation of executive and legislative positions by Member States matched by opportunities for citizens directly to elect representatives of their own at Union level (EUDA Test 9)? Opportunities for citizens to elect office holders directly at Union level are limited to those who hold office in just one part of one branch of government (the legislative branch). Executive power is shared between appointed office holders (Commissioners) and those elected at another level of government (national governments). Legislative office is divided between the Council and the one institution that is directly elected at Union level (the European Parliament).

How far do individuals and groups have means of aggregating and deliberating preferences at EU level (if need be, independently of their national governments) (EUDA Test 10)? Ideological representation through the EP, interest representation through assorted channels and even regional representation provide various means of aggregating and deliberating preferences at EU level independently of governments. But the first is constrained by shortcomings in the EP's electoral connection, the second by inequalities, and the third is but patchily developed.

6
Accountability (The Commission)

Introduction to chapters on accountability

If to be representative is to 'stand in for' citizens, to be accountable is to owe them 'accounts' or justifications on the basis of which office holders may be rewarded or sanctioned (Keohane, 2001). To be responsible, in such a way is, in the view of some, democracy's core meaning. As seen, one classic interpretation holds that it is not the satisfaction of wants, or in contemporary terms the aggregation of preferences, that distinguishes democracy from other forms of rule, but its character as a system of rights and duties organised around political responsibility (Plamenatz, 1973, pp. 180–4): a right on the part of the ruled to join with other members of a community to hold rulers responsible, and an obligation on the part of rulers to accept responsibility by accounting for their actions. In addition, many political thinkers have been pessimistic about claims that the people can realistically govern themselves in mass societies, except in so far as they can periodically use elections to hold those who do in fact rule to account (Schumpeter, 1943).

Yet, it is possible to put accountability at the core of democracy without being at all complacent about the ease of delivering it in practice. On the one hand, it is notoriously difficult to institutionalise without perverse and unintended consequences (Macintyre, 1981). On the other hand, it is always complex and often elusive. For example, the chapters that follow will need to employ four distinctions to reach a full assessment of the accountability of Union institutions. The simplest of these is between *ex ante* and *ex post* accountability of decisions before and after they are taken. The remaining three are as follows:

Vertical and horizontal accountability. Under hierarchical or vertical forms of accountability all public administrators are within the control of a political leadership; that political leadership is then responsible to elected representatives who are accountable to the people. A quite different mode of accountability is, however, possible between institutions and individuals that have few or any powers to appoint or dismiss one another. In a system of horizontal accountability actors have to give accounts not so much on pains of loss of office but of diminished co-operation of others in the delivery of their goals. This distinction is important to our analysis on two counts. First, national experience accustoms many citizens of the Union to vertical forms of accountability. Yet the Union itself is, arguably, more suited to horizontal forms of accountability, given its divided system of government. Second, the distinction offers a temporal dimension. Just as we opened the last chapter by noting the challenge of making European Union (EU) institutions representative at a moment when the politics of mass representation are themselves becoming more difficult, choices about the public control of Union institutions are arguably being made in a context of a shifting balance between vertical and horizontal forms of accountability occasioned by the emergence of new forms of governance. These trends have been described as being towards a 'multicentric form of accountability to different institutions, for different purposes, to different degrees and in terms of different, though mutually complementary standards' (Spiro, 1969, p. 98).

Internal and external accountability. Much accountability is not to 'others'. Rather it is an internal process by which actors and institutions enforce democratically agreed standards on themselves. Indeed internal and external accountability are interdependent. Just as the system of external accountability to others would be overloaded if it could not rely on modes of self-enforcement, that of internal accountability presupposes an overarching democratic process by which self-enforced standards can be negotiated, agreed, policed and converted back into externally enforced standards in the event of lapses. This distinction poses a number of questions for accountability in the EU arena: how far does internal accountability require all those who participate in the making of Union decisions to observe norms of political or administrative behaviour agreed at EU level? Has the Union yet found a satisfactory means of relating the internal and external strands of accountability one to the other, and so on?

Output and input accountability. Decision-makers are often required to account for their actions in terms of their consequences. Where, however, causation is complex or unstable, and any one decision is the product of 'many hands', it may be difficult to attribute consequences to particular actions, or, as March and Olsen put it, to discover 'blameworthy agents'. Under such conditions 'making someone accountable' is always an 'act of injustice' (March and Olsen, 1995). An alternative that requires no attribution of consequences to individuals or institutions is just to ask whether each player acted appropriately – according to the rules and roles assigned to them – in the inputs they made to decisions. This distinction poses a predicament to the EU. The fact that most of its decisions mix inputs from several of its institutions and from national and European authorities suggests outcomes will be hard to attribute and that actors should, accordingly, be required to account for the appropriateness of their inputs to decisions. On the other hand, public justifications for Union policy often rest on claims to output legitimacy through superior performance. This surely entitles the public to expect Union institutions to account for whether their policies have had the beneficial consequences by which they were 'sold' in the first place.

The foregoing distinctions will be used to apply the following Democratic Audit (see pp. 28–9) tests that concern accountability.

How far are those who hold office or make decisions in EU institutions accountable to representatives of national democracies who are, in turn, responsible to their national publics and parliaments (EUDA Test 5)?

How far are those who hold office or make decisions in EU institutions accountable to elected representatives of citizens at Union level (EUDA Test 11)?

The accountability of the Commission will be appraised in the remainder of this chapter; that of the Council in Chapter 7; and that of the European Central Bank in Chapter 8 (which will overlap with an appraisal of Democracy and Constitutionalism in the EU).

Three models of Commission accountability

The value of a detailed democratic assessment of the Commission might be questioned on a number of contrasting grounds. First, that as an un-elected body, it so clearly fails the most basic test of democracy as to make further evaluation superfluous. Second, that to test the Commission for democratic standards is to misunderstand its purpose and justification as an independent institution capable of producing those desirable outcomes that happen to be 'incentive incompatible' with majoritarian democratic procedures (Majone, 2001). Third, that the Commission is, in any case, only marginal to the democratic performance of the Union, since, for the most part, it is only a proposer and not a maker of decisions.

In answer to the first objection, democracy requires only that public institutions be controllable by elected representatives, not that all should themselves be elected (Mill, 1972 [1861]). Whether the Commission satisfies that condition is a question a Democratic Audit is eminently suited to answer. As for the second objection, those who have thought most deeply about it acknowledge there may be little alternative to strengthening the democratic control of the Commission as it assumes 'discretionary' powers. All they ask is that new means be found of undertaking those of its functions that are not discretionary and where, instead, there is an agreed and justifiable case for impartial administration at arms length from standard democratic procedures (Majone and Everson, 2001, p. 167).

As for the third objection, it is undermined by a failure to understand how agenda-setting operates as an independent source of political power. The Commission's exclusive right of initiative under pillar one means that it can keep the gates closed on the consideration of new initiatives even where the *status quo* is undesirable to many citizens or their representatives. If it does decide to make a proposal, the rules for amending a Commission draft mean it can influence where the bargaining is likely to end up by determining the point from which it starts. Moreover, in cases where preferences are not already fully formed, it can influence ways in which problems are constructed, attention is organised, and actors mobilised into the European arena for their consideration.

Yet, assessment of the Commission is unlikely to prove easy. A certain elusiveness about what it does – neatly summarised in Laura Cram's description (1994) of it as a 'multi-organisation' – creates ambiguity as to how far it can be held responsible for any one aspect of the EU's performance. It is most commonly thought of as the EU's executive. In reality, it shares executive power, since its main role is to supervise the implementation of Union law, rather than to implement it for itself. On the other hand, it is a key actor in the EU's legislative power. It drafts pillar one legislation, it makes the key decisions on which the European Parliament (EP) amendments are most likely to succeed and it has a presence at every stage of co-decision that goes well beyond the formal specification of its powers in the Treaties. It even has a quasi-judicial role to the extent it is responsible for investigating infringements of the Treaties and, if necessary, bringing actions in the European Court of Justice (ECJ). On top of all that, it acts as an international negotiator for the Union in matters where it has internal competence, a role it usually performs in co-operation with the Presidency of the Council. In short, the Commission has a share in almost every branch and function of Union governance without having control of any. An additional complication is that the mix between its roles varies from one part of the Commission to the next (Nugent, 2001).

It may even be difficult to form a view of what democratic standards are relevant to the Commission by putting it in the one category it is often assumed to occupy without ambiguity, namely that of a bureaucracy, and then drawing lessons from the wider literature on the public control of administrative bodies. The notion that the Commission should concentrate on the classic bureaucratic role of impartially administering decisions (Christiansen, 1997) taken by elected politicians collides with at least two other views of its proper functions: that it should be a source of policy entrepreneurship in the interests of one particular cause, namely that of European integration itself; and, second, that it should have representative functions, whether on behalf of those who are disadvantaged by intergovernmental bargaining, or of a European interest that is likely to be neglected by all other actors in the system with their *foci* on single geographical areas and individual policy sectors. Belief in this representative role is to be found in the Commission's White Paper on Governance which argues that the 'Community method ensures fair treatment of all Member States from the largest to the smallest' and that the Method operates as a 'double filter': first, the Commission has to be convinced there is a general 'European interest' that would justify action; then elected actors 'come together' at the 'level of the Council and European Parliament' to form the Union's legislature' (European Commission, 2001d, p. 8).

The data set of documents compiled for this survey reveal three views of how the Commission should itself be held democratically accountable. They are as follows:

The Commission should primarily be accountable to Member States. The argument here is that since the Commission employs powers that have been delegated by Member States it should primarily be accountable to them. The UK Government in particular has used the Future of Europe debate to argue that the Commission should be more accountable to the European Council, which should, for example, set its annual programme (UK Government, 2000).

The Commission should be accountable to both Member States and the European Parliament. Statements of this view are found in the Commission and EP documents, though also in contributions from some national governments. An example is the Commission's interim report on its own internal reform which states that 'in its relationship with the Council and the European Parliament, the European Commission is at the service of the European citizenry, translating into action the objectives defined on citizens' behalf by representatives in the Council and the European Parliament' (European Commission, 2000a, p. 7). For defenders of such dual responsibility it does not follow from the exercise by the Commission of powers once delegated from Member States that it is only to the latter it should be accountable. As seen, Member States can be held to have voluntarily limited their own sovereignty in favour of a new institutional order, one feature of which is an inter-institutional balance that would not be well served by close supervision of the Commission by the (European) Council. Indeed, accountability of the Commission to the (European) Council and EP is sometimes presented as providing just two of the links in a network of horizontal relationships in which *all* Union institutions should be able to extract accounts from one another by using rewards and sanctions that are both evenly distributed and entrenched in a separation of powers system.

Whatever its obligations to Member States and the European Parliament, the Commission should also be directly accountable to citizens: The White Paper on Governance emphasises that the Commission cannot just be accountable to Member States and the EP, since it has obligations to any individual or group with a right to good administration. It goes on to argue that the obligations in question have been accumulated through ECJ judgements, rulings of the Ombudsman, the Charter of Fundamental Rights of the EU and standards of individual treatment laid down in the Treaties and secondary legislation of the Union (European Commission, 2001d). In other documents used in this survey, the Commission uses the rhetoric of 'twin pillar democracy in Europe' not to connote national and European parliaments, but to distinguish all representative institutions on the one hand from the direct 'involvement of citizens in devising and implementing decisions that affect them' on the other (European Commission, 2000d, p. 4).

Of all the Union institutions, the Commission has most consistently argued that the EU should mix indirect and direct forms of democracy. This may be self-serving to the extent it would maximise the number of 'principals' between which the Commission could manoeuvre without becoming fully beholden to any, and justify policy-making through the direct engagement of the Commission with groups and individuals of Civil Society. Yet, the Commission's case for participatory decision-making is also made with an eye to change in society and its implications for the accountability of public institutions. It has argued that the standards by which it is held to account should themselves be negotiated on a continuous basis with representatives of civil society who should, in turn, be mutually accountable to one another: all stakeholders in Union policies should be required to 'demonstrate the coherence of their constructions' (European Commission, 2001e, p. 276). If the second of our standards seeks to substitute horizontal accountability of Commission, EP and Council to one another for vertical Commission accountability to Member States 'principals', this solution seeks lines of accountability that reach beyond the political system altogether, or as the Commission's one-time Forward Studies Unit (FSU) puts it, 'to break the cartels of representation that currently exert a covert stranglehold on key stages of the policy process' (*op. cit.*, p. 273).

Having distinguished three notions of how the Commission should be accountable and to whom, we need to appraise how far each standard is satisfied in practice. We begin by examining what evidence there is for the effective public control of the Commission by elected governments of the Member States.

Control by elected governments of Member States

There are various ways in which the Commission is exposed to the control of national governments (Pollack, 1997a, pp. 118–19; Kassim and Menon, 2003, pp. 131–2). In a political system where the legal base for each action is closely scrutinised by all institutions (not least the Commission itself) it matters that it is the Member States which specify each area of competence through their negotiation of the Treaties. Individually and collectively they can also influence the direction of the Commission by how they choose to exercise their powers to appoint its College and Presidency every five years. Moreover, the Commission depends on the Member States for resources and co-operation. Although the Union benefits from a system of 'own resources' its budget still needs to be agreed every five years by unanimous consent of member governments, which micromanage the deployment of resources to the extent that the Union institutions cannot move expenditures between seven closely specified ceilings. The agreement of member governments is also needed for any increase in the staffing of the Commission. A dysfunctional relationship with any one Member State will likewise cause problems for the Commission in terms of implementation on the ground and provision of information needed for effective policy-making.

Some of the foregoing controls are individual and others are collective. Some – such as a refusal to agree to changes to the Treaties or to budget ceilings, or a veto on specific candidates for the Commission Presidency, or even various forms of non co-operation – can be exercised by individual Members. Others – such as a revision of the existing Treaty powers of the Commission – require their unanimous agreement. Indeed, in the absence of consensus on the budget the Commission can continue to spend resources, albeit within existing ceilings. A further crucial distinction is between *ex ante* and *ex post* opportunities to control the Commission. Rules for Treaty formation provide strong *ex ante* control to the extent unanimous agreement of Member States is needed to confer a power on the Commission, but only weak *ex post* control to the extent that Member States likewise need to be unanimous if any of the Commission's powers is to be recalled or redefined. A third point is that none of these controls is without cost to Member States. These may be costs of monitoring the Commission or those connected to reverse dependencies of Member States on the Commission. Amongst the latter are needs Member States themselves feel for a credible enforcement mechanism at European level, and for a body that will save them transaction costs in policy initiation and bargaining (Majone, 1996, p. 69).

Mark Pollack (1997a) has elegantly formulated the possibilities and limits of control of the Commission by national governments. He observes that the points in the foregoing paragraph combine to create a margin in which the Commission can expect the costs of control to exceed the pay-offs to Member States of exercising it, and beyond which Member States are likely to challenge the Commission. The result, he concludes, is that there are good structural reasons why the Commission will always be somewhere in between a runaway bureaucracy and a subservient one (Pollack, 1998, p. 218).

An indicator of whether Member States are prepared for the Commission to have a wide or narrow margin of discretionary choice is the resources they commit to monitoring it. Both of the key powers of the Commission – its right of initiative under pillar one and its oversight of implementation – are subject to 'stakeholder' participation and monitoring through the following system of committees, known as Comitology.

Consultative committees are formed at the Commission's own initiative, usually from business and professional interests, or organisations of civil society.

Expert committees have a mixed composition of national civil servants and technical experts designated by governments. Together with the consultative committees, they form the two kinds of *advisory committee* with which the Commission works when it is preparing legislation. However, as Neil Nugent points out (2001, pp. 245–6) expert committees are the more powerful for two reasons: first, the Commission is usually obliged to consult them before initiating legislation; and, second, their membership overlaps with the national officials who will eventually consider the same proposals in Council working groups.

Management and regulatory committees. Whereas consultative and expert committees are mainly involved with the Commission when it draws up legislation, management and regulatory committees oversee its contribution to the implementation of Union law. Management and regulatory committees are chaired by the Commission, but otherwise comprise officials from each Member State. If a qualified majority of a Management Committee disagrees with an implementing measure proposed by the Commission it can appeal to the Council which can substitute an implementing measure of its own (again by Qualified Majority Voting [QMV]). In the case of Regulatory Committees the onus is reversed. The Commission can only proceed with an implementing measure with the agreement of a qualified majority of the committee. If it fails to gain a majority on the committee, the matter is passed to the Council for decision. Armed with the differing opinions of both Commission and the regulatory committee, the Council can approve the Commission's proposal, reject it or substitute its own preferred approach. Throughout, the Council decides by Qualified Majority. Regulatory Committees – which are procedurally the stricter form of supervision – are more commonly used than Management Committees.

The Member States also employ a gamut of devices in the body of legislation to limit the Commission's discretion. These include sunset clauses, obligations to review and evaluate measures, and even encouragements to third party actors to sound 'fire alarms' that may relieve Member States from some of the direct costs of monitoring. Also worth noting are estimates of the personnel that national administrations are prepared to commit to the task of supervision. Wolfgang Wessels (1997) estimates that up to 40 per cent of senior national officials now spend some of their time on EU business. Although much of this work is with Council Working groups, participation in the latter overlaps, as seen, with oversight of the Commission.

What, however, is less clear than the effort Member States put into monitoring the Commission is the control they get out of it. A primary source of ambiguity is that management and regulatory committees hardly ever use their powers to appeal to the full Council in the case of disagreement with the Commission. Is this a sign of their success in forcing 'the Commission to take objections seriously and search for consensual solutions?' (Scharpf, 2001, p. 8). Or does it suggest that the participation of national officials in EU decision-making just compounds the problem of unsupervised administrative power by encouraging a *copinage téchnocratique* (Wessels, 1998, p. 214; Radaelli, 1999; Trondal,

2001, p. 39) in which national civil servants may nominally be designated to oversee the Commission on behalf of elected national governments yet settle down to common problem-solving with Commission officials in a process that is opaque to the public and its representatives at either level of government ?

These are not easy questions to answer, since the distinction between acting as 'national representatives' and transferring loyalties to the shared process may itself be elusive. Jarle Trondal's (2001) survey shows how national officials who participate in EU committees often identify with both levels of governance. In addition, there is often 'slack' in their environment. They are not always fully instructed or without scope to reverse the direction of influence by feeding EU-level discussions back into the framing of national preferences that form the basis of any guidance they are themselves given.

Regardless of how far it is achieved in practice, there are objections to attempting national supervision as the only means of democratic control over the Commission. First, are the familiar arguments against concentrating power in the hands of national governments. Second is the objection that to make the Commission the agent of the Council without clarifying that is, indeed, the nature of the relationship risks the public viewing the Commission as a prime mover when it is mainly the handmaiden of the Council. Governments could even have perverse incentives to profit from that misperception by transferring blame and dumping problems into the European arena. The result would then be a loss and not a gain to democratic accountability.

Control by the European Parliament

The following are amongst means of control presently available to the EP. It can dismiss the Commission. Its approval is needed for the appointment of new Commissions and thus by implication for the replacement of any dismissed College. It can appoint special commissions of enquiry and ask written and oral questions of the Commission. Its approval is needed for the discharge of the annual accounts of the Commission. Its legislative and financial powers can be used to deny the Commission a number of its goals. Each of these is now examined in turn.

Ex ante accountability: the EP's power to confirm the Commission in office

Although each President and College of Commissioners is appointed by the Member States, they can only take office after a vote of approval by the EP. To ensure this power would normally be exercised by a freshly elected Parliament, the Treaty on European Union (TEU) (1992) aligned the terms of Commissions and Parliaments, so that the first would (normally) take office some six months after the second. From 1994–5, the EP sought to maximise use of the procedure to extract accounts of how an incoming Commission intended to use its powers by turning 'investiture' into a three-stage obstacle source over which any new Commission would have to pass. First, a vote was taken on the nominee for the Presidency of the Commission. Second, other nominee Commissioners were 'heard' by the Parliamentary committee corresponding to their anticipated portfolios. Third, a vote was taken on the overall composition and programme of the incoming executive (Hix and Lord, 1996).

Yet, Helmut Kohl probably went a little far in predicting after the Maastricht European Council that the EP's new power to confirm the Commission would be 'a matter of great political significance' (Kohl, 1992, p. 1126). In spite of its ingenuity, the procedure only gives the EP a limited controlling power over the appointment of the Commission. In the end, the Parliament only has a 'take it or leave it' choice over a President and College designated by Member States. Absence of the 'positive power' to pick and choose means that Commissions are not representative executives in the sense of being 'equilibrium governments' so aligned in their composition, portfolio distribution and policy programme with representatives' preferences as to beat all possible alternatives in any parliamentary vote (Laver and Shepsle, 1996).

Nor is it even clear that it is easy for the Parliament to use the investiture procedure as a 'negative' or 'veto power' on the Presidency or College of Commissioners. One problem is that the EP's bargaining hand is crucially shaped by what would happen in the event of a 'non-decision' or, in other words, a failure to agree with Member States on the appointment of a Commission. The legal position is that the old Commission would continue in office, though only as a caretaker or trustee.[10] Such a 'lame-duck' Commission could suit some Member States more than the EP. A second difficulty is that national leaders may try to organise their own support base in the EP if confronted by any risk of being denied the Commission of their choice. Ambitions of executive formation could thus compromise the high levels of independence hitherto enjoyed by the EP.

Case studies of the designation of the Santer and Prodi Commissions in 1994–5 and 1999 respectively underscore the foregoing themes. The independence with which MEPs can hope to exercise a veto on the appointment of a College or Presidency was called into question by the vote on Santer's own appointment in July 1994. A study of MEPs who voted for Santer against the wishes of their party group, reveals that most came from national parties of government. Up to 45 members seem to have been persuaded to switch their votes, a figure that exceeded Santer's majority of 21 (Hix and Lord, 1996). Likewise Santer had little difficulty 'calling the EP's bluff' at a later stage in the procedure when, on the evidence of its committee hearings, the Parliament criticised five out of the twenty nominations to the 1995–9 Commission. He correctly calculated that even if none of the nominations were withdrawn by the Member States making them, the EP would still vote for the overall Commission. In fact he secured a large majority – 418 in favour, 103 against and 59 abstentions – without doing much to respond to MEPs' hints that he should at least change the remits and distributions of responsibility between Commissioners.

The formation of the 1999 Commission likewise showed how limited is the scope for MEPs to engage in pro-active 'executive shaping'. First, President Prodi successfully resisted suggestions from the largest group in the EP that he should use his own powers over the formation of the College – recently expanded by the Amsterdam Treaty – to press for a Commission that reflected the 'centre-right' outcome of the 1999 EP elections (*Le Monde*, 14 July 1999). Second, he forced the EP to back down from its claim that his Commission was being appointed twice (for the remainder of the term of the Santer Commission and to a five-year term of its own) and that it would, therefore, need to be invested twice, by refusing to take office on such a basis. Third, the EP was itself more circumspect than it had been in 1994–5 in its judgement of individual nominations. Only one – the Belgian nominee Philippe Busquin – was criticised on the somewhat 'local' grounds that he was insufficiently bilingual to represent both sides of his country in the Commission.

Assuming that in both cases, a majority of the EP had a preference for an effective Commission, neither in 1994–5 nor in 1999 was it in a strong position to withstand a stalemate on the appointment of the Commission. In the first instance it had been difficult even to agree to an appointment to the Presidency at a time when a heavy agenda of pro-integration business awaited implementation. In the second, the Commission Presidency had for several months been in the hands of a College that had itself resigned.

Table 6.1 uses the survey carried out for this research to summarise MEPs own assessments of the investiture procedure. On average they rate it quite highly as a means of testing the suitability of Commissioners for office, but see it as affording only weak leverage over the composition of

Table 6.1 *Ex ante* accountability. MEPs' assessment of their influence under the investiture procedure. (Reflecting on your own experience of the EP's role in confirming the 1999–2004 Commission, please use the scales provided (0–10) to assess the usefulness of the procedure.)

Procedure	*Average*	*Standard deviation*
Influencing the composition of the Commission	3.63	2.39
Influencing the assignment of responsibilities between Commissioners	3.13	2.60
Influencing likely policy programmes and legislative proposals over the life of the Commission	5.04	2.85
Testing the suitability of individual Commissioners for office	6.93	1.39

the College and only moderate influence on its policy programme. However, the standard deviations in the last column of the table indicate wide differences in the evaluations reached by individual MEPs.

In addition to the structural constraints discussed earlier, a common complaint amongst MEPs is that opportunities to use parliamentary hearings to 'pin Commissioners down by means of coherent and logically developed cross-examination' are lost as 'everyone attempts to get in on the act'.[11] A contrary complaint is that at other times the leading party groups try to 'fix' the hearings rather than let them develop into open-ended enquiries into fitness for office. One MEP who participated in this survey even complained that in 1999 'an appalling cross-party deal' was hatched to let one candidate Commissioner off the hook on a matter of importance.[12] A slightly more upbeat assessment, however, is that the very act of 'hearing' all nominee Commissioners 'obliges each to spell out the value added that he or she can bring to the College'. Indeed, the same respondent argued that it alerts EP committees to 'frictions ahead in the way in which responsibilities are apportioned in the Commission'[13] and this feeds into subsequent scrutiny over the course of a parliament.

The most positive appraisals of the procedure relate to its effect on the policy intentions, rather than the composition, of incoming Commissions. As one respondent puts it,

> The whole exercise sharpened up the Commission's thinking on policy development: it seemed to come up with some decent policy proposals as a result, and it is a useful learning exercise in the development of

> mutual understanding between Commissioners and the parliamentary committees with which they have to deal.[14]

Another interviewee who thought that the EP's influence on the composition of the Commission was a marginal one of anticipation only – 'we might have a bit of influence where governments do not put up candidates who they fear would run into diffulties before parliamentary committees' – was much more positive about the 'impact of the investiture procedure on "programmatic content" ':

> The Commission prepares its programme in dialogue with the EP. The President of the Commission goes round the leaders of the groups. Meanwhile, the confirmation procedure is going on in the background.[15]

The last point implies that the Investiture procedure does not give the EP as much of an executive-shaping role as confirm that its main relationship with the Commission is a legislative one after all. One of the main developments between 1994–5 and 1999 was that second time round the EP now required each nominee to the College of Commissioners to fill in a twenty-page questionnaire, the replies to which it made public (European Parliament, 1999d,e). Several questions probed individual fitness for office. Others reflected opportunities to turn the hearings with nominated Commissioners into the first stage in the development of a legislative relationship. Given that each Committee leads for the EP in its specialist area – and the composition of each is substantially new at the beginning of each Parliament – the hearings can be used to inform the Commission of the likely preferences and behaviour of MEPs in the legislative process. This is useful to both sides. It is useful for the EP to have its own preferences embedded in initial proposals given that it is procedurally difficult for the Council to amend Commission texts. For its part, anticipation of the EP's preferences allows the Commission to maximise the number of measures passed at first reading, and to strengthen its defences against the Council. Where there is agreement between the EP and the Commission, the EP can use its amendment powers to steer a text back in that direction after the Council has made its own changes. Indeed there is a chance it will defend the position all the way to Conciliation where the Commission has no formal powers. Cutting across these various considerations is that statements made by Commissioners to specialist parliamentary committees at the moment of investiture become performance indicators over the remainder of the five-year term and thus grounds for *ex ante* accountability.

Ex post accountability: the EP's power to dismiss the Commission

It is useful to begin by clarifying what is the EP's power to dismiss the Commission and what it is not. It should not, for example, be confused with the power of national parliaments to break governments. A power of dismissal that is intended for use whenever an alternative executive is more likely to satisfy the partisan preferences of a majority of the legislature has to be distinguished from one that is only designed to sanction cases of mal-administration. The EP's power of censure falls into the second category, as is suggested both by its name (censure) and the fact that it requires a 'double' majority (two-thirds of MEPs voting and an absolute majority of the Parliament itself, i.e. 314 out of 626), not a 'simple one'. Moreover, the survey for this study confirms that most MEPs would themselves oppose the application of partisan forms of dismissal to executive–legislature relations in the EU. The following response is typical:

> The double majority is a justifiable constraint. In most political systems the power of the legislature to remove the executive is balanced by the power of the executive to dissolve the legislature, thus requiring it to justify any decision or threat to vote down the government of the day. This is not possible within the EU political system, but the double majority is a good substitute. It means that the executive can only be removed by a cross-party coalition. You would need at least the support of the two main groups. Thus it is a constraint on the use of dismissal for unilateral party advantage in much the same way as the threat to dissolve can be used as a constraint.[16]

Indeed this may even understate the procedural difficulty in using the power of censure as a partisan means of altering the political balance of the Commission. Bearing in mind that censure can only be used to remove the entire College and not individual Commissioners, any two-thirds majority would almost certainly have to embrace MEPs from much the same party families as the Commissioners who would be victim to any 'mass cull': the PES, EPP, ELDR and possibly the Greens. Although some of those party groups might at any one time reasonably hope to be better represented in a replacement Commission, there would also be losers from within the coalition necessary for the censure.

Until the resignation of the Santer Commission in March 1999 many doubted the power of censure was even a useful discipline against mal-administration. The Parliament was considered too dependent on a strong Commission, and too closely aligned with it in battles over the supranational or intergovernmental shape of European integration, to emerge as a fierce and independent critic prepared to wield the ultimate sanction of dismissal.

Indeed, censure appeared to be a 'nuclear option' made unusable by the drastic consequences of its own employment (Clergerie, 1995). Not only were MEPs assumed to have little interest in plunging the Union into an inter-institutional crisis. It was also thought to be a constraint that the College of Commissioners could only be dismissed as a whole, without any discrimination of individual responsibility for underperformance or wrongdoing. The injustice of such indiscriminate dismissal was thought likely to sharpen the determination of pockets of MEPs from different nationalities or party families to protect 'their Commissioners' from disgrace by withholding the two-thirds majority needed for censure.

How far these various constraints are still felt to be relevant is illustrated by answers to a series of questions (Table 6.2) in the survey carried out for this research. Reluctance to damage the reputation of the Union or the EP's own relationship with the Commission are thought to be less significant as constraints than pressures from governments to lay off the Commission or the unwillingness of specific groups of MEPs to pass censures mainly directed at Commissioners from their own political family. One participant in this survey argued that effective pursuit of wrongdoing in the Santer Commission was at one stage hampered by 'national parties phoning MEPs to ask them to dessist from embarrassing their Commissioner'. PES members came under significant pressure from the

Table 6.2 *Ex post* accountability. MEPs' assessments of their powers to censure the Commission. (On a scale of 0–10 please assess how far the following constrain the EP's ability to censure the Commission?)

MEPs' assessment	*Average*	*Standard deviation*
The need for a double majority	5.6	2.69
The belief that the Commission is an ally of the Parliament	5.28	1.98
Reluctance to damage the reputation of the EU	4.85	2.67
National governments may inform MEPs of their reluctance to see a change of Commission	6.31	2.56
MEPs are reluctant to vote for censures critical of Commissioners from their own party families	7.06	2.08

French and Spanish Socialist Parties.[17] The Committee of experts set up to examine the charges against the Santer Commission concluded in robust language that the party political affiliations between Commissioners and groups of MEPs was 'deforming' the Parliament's power of censure (second report of Committee of Independent Experts, p. 22). At one point the leader of the largest party group is even reported to have urged members to support 'our Commission'.[18]

EP data lists only five censure motions as having been formally tabled since 1979. Three fell into the period 1990–2, were tabled by small groups and defeated by overwhelming majorities (European Parliament, 1999g). Yet, in contrast to the conventional wisdom that censure offered few opportunities for executive control, insiders noted a tendency well before the first successful use of censure in 1999 for the Commission to respond even to remote threats of parliamentary discontent developing into censure motions. Richard Corbett, Francis Jacobs and Michael Shackleton cite the following example:

> In December 1989 and January 1990 ... the Socialist group considered a proposal from one of its members to table a censure motion. Although this found little support, and was decisively turned down in the Group, it did provoke a flurry of extra meetings between Commissioners and Socialist Group leaders and greater attention being paid to the 'social dimension' of the Commission's work programme then being prepared. (1995, p. 247)

Instances of such sensitivity were also confirmed by responses to this study. A possible explanation is that the censure procedure is easy to initiate even if it is hard to conclude. The support of only 10 per cent of MEPs is needed to table a censure and have it debated by the Parliament. The Commission then has to divert resources to fighting off a censure that may, in the meantime, damage its reputation. The result is that it may accommodate grievance even at a relatively low level of discontent, notwithstanding the difficulties the EP would also face in fully prosecuting a censure. The following is the view of one observer from within the Commission:

> Defending a motion of censure soaks up resources. It is a distraction from the Commission's routine work. It is potentially debilitating of the Commission's credibility. And it can snowball – no one can predict where it might end or control its consequences. All of this when only 60 MEPs are needed to set a censure motion in action.[19]

The TEU (1992) strengthened the power of censure as an indirect consequence of the requirement that an incoming Commission could only take office after a vote of approval by the EP. This reduced the danger of Member States responding to a parliamentary censure by merely re-appointing the same Commission and increased the power of the EP to stipulate conditions for any replacement. It effectively raised the procedural hurdle for a replacement College from a third to a half of MEPs voting, the former being the blocking minority needed to protect a replacement Commission from a second motion of censure, the latter being the majority now needed to confirm a Commission in office. Conversely, the role of the Parliament in the resignation of the Santer Commision may have had some positive spill-back for its admittedly still limited powers to shape incoming Commissions under the Investiture Procedure. The incentive to align the composition and programme of the Commission with parliamentary opinion could only be improved by a reversal in the conventional wisdom that the EP would never force the dismissal or resignation of a Commission. Thus the inclusion of a Green (Michaele Schreyer) in the Prodi Commission (1999–) has been seen as a move to increase its protection against censure by giving it a wider base of support in the EP than its predecessor.[20]

In 1997, the EP demonstrated how it could use 'the ultimate deterrent' of dismissal to reinforce other modes of accountability. It passed an indicative motion of censure while also appointing a special committee of enquiry to look into the handling of the Bovine Spongiform Encephalopathy (BSE) crisis. It would later claim that the 'suspended death sentence' over the Commission yielded significant concessions, including new legislation on food hygiene, a transfer of responsibility for food safety from one Commission Directorates-General (DG) to another, and, as a consequence of the last, a reduction in conflicts between producer and consumer interests in the administration of food policy (Westlake, 1997; Shackleton, 1998).

On the other hand, the BSE episode also illustrates how the power of the EP to censure the Commission can only provide an incomplete system of accountability in a political system where executive power is dispersed and the consequences of policy failures take time to develop. The EP's special committee of enquiry was clear that 'primary responsibility' lay with the British Government and 'secondary responsibility with an *earlier* Commission' (Reimer Böge MEP, European Parliament, Verbatim Report of Proceedings, 18 February 1997). While, however, managing to pass an indicative censure on the *sitting* Commission, the EP was unable even to get the British Agriculture Minister to appear before its enquiry

(Lord, 1998a, p. 89). In an interview for this study, a former President of the Parliament re-iterated the problem: the Commission was the only body that the EP could hold politically responsible for the handling of BSE, not the body that was causally responsible for the problem.[21] However, a Commission-based observer feels the BSE case also illustrated how the power of dismissal continued to be limited by the absence of a killer instinct on the part of a Parliament grown accustomed to compromise in its dealings with other Union institutions.

> The EP missed a golden opportunity to censure the Commission on BSE. It had the scientific evidence and had proved wrongdoing. It pulled back because of a culture of accommodation: provided that the Commission has offered some concessions, the reflex of the EP's leadership is always to consider that the reasonable thing to do is settle.[22]

A larger challenge to the view that the Parliament's power of censure does not amount to much in practice was, of course, the resignation of the Santer Commission in March 1999. This occurred immediately after a meeting of the EP's party groups leaders – the Conference of Presidents – indicated a double majority of MEPs was prepared to vote for dismissal. Yet the 1999 experience has left the EP with two differing views of how best to approach censures. Some MEPs believe the procedure was improved by the insertion of a quasi-judicial phase in which a committee of 'wise persons' from outside the Parliament was appointed to investigate allegations against members of the Commission. This made the procedure even less majoritarian in the sense of being exercised more from some points on the political spectrum than others. The game was changed from one of calculation of party advantage or, in other words, of who was likely to win or lose from replacing the Commission, to an adjudication of whether standards of public administration had been violated (Lord and Beetham, 2001). The quasi-judicial stage may also have made it easier to form the necessary majority for a justified censure. Whereas the Parliament floundered before the appointment of the committee of wise-persons, the latter, depending on its outcome, would help resolve matters one way or another by raising the costs to MEPs of either defending the indefensible or witch-hunting for partisan reasons. A contrasting interpretation is that the 1999 censure was an abdication and not a triumph. According to this view elected representatives should judge for themselves whether an executive merits dismissal, since only they can, in turn, be responsible to the public for the proper use of any power of censure.

Both the Santer resignation (1997) and the conditional vote of censure on BSE (1997) illustrate how a case for censure needs to be built up through the use of other procedures: in the first case, the rule that the Commission's accounts for each financial year can only be 'discharged' by the EP declaring itself satisfied that moneys have been properly spent; in the second, the power of the Parliament to appoint special committees of enquiry. This raises the question of how far the EP really has succeeded in developing 'seamless ladders of escalation' from day-to-day forms of scrutiny through more middle-range investigative procedures (such as budgetary discharge and special committees of enquiry) to a full censure of the Commission. Taking the example of special committees of enquiry, a total of ten have been established by the Parliament since 1979, though only three since the procedure was formalised by the TEU in 1992. A possible explanation for this paradoxical decline in their use since their formal authorisation is that when the Treaty provision came to be operationalised by inter-institutional agreement the Council fought a rearguard action to prevent committees of enquiry upsetting the balance between the institutions. The Council was concerned, in other words, that a Commission which was too fearful of being investigated by the Parliament might become more watchful of its relations with the latter than with Member States. It thus put limits on the powers of disclosure available to committees of enquiry (Lequesne and Rivaud, 2001, pp. 871–2), thus somewhat reducing their procedural attraction to MEPs. As Tony Blair has put it, 'we cannot simply see the Commission as an executive accountable to the Parliament. The Commission also has a crucial partnership with the Council of Ministers which we must not weaken' (UK Government, 2002).

Amongst other problems with the censure procedure are that it (formally) only allows the EP to enforce collective and not individual responsibility on Commissioners. This is consistent with the principle that initiatives of the Commission should be adopted and defended by the College as a whole. It also – as several respondents to this survey were eager to point out – precludes games in which particular partisan interests in the EP attempt to gun down individual Commissioners. Yet, in the view of the chair of the committee of wise persons which investigated the allegations against the Santer Commission, it may actively encourage an element of political irresponsibility: it may tempt individual Commissioners to court levels of under-performance or transgression that are not enough to motivate a collective censure even if they might have been sufficiently egregious to have provoked an individual censure had that option been available to the EP.[23] One senior MEP who does not share the preference of many of her colleagues to continue with the present system of collective responsibility goes so far as to argue that the EP should unilaterally adopt a procedure for the individual censure of Commissioners, that is, without Treaty authorisation. In her view the lesson of 1998–9 was that collective censure puts the EP into a dither that may last for 'several months' between the acquisition of sufficient evidence against individuals and the development of sufficient motivation to censure the Commission as a whole. Meanwhile, the Presidency of the Commission, for its part, gets 'sucked into a defence of the indefensible that ends up dragging down the good as well as the bad'.[24]

The so-called *Lex Prodi* attempts to deal with this difficulty. In response to the role of just one or two Commissioners in bringing down the whole Santer Commission, President Prodi asked those appointed to his Commission to promise they would resign if requested to do so for good reason. The Commission as a whole could then be meaningfully held responsible to the EP for the President's judgement in requesting resignations or otherwise. It is also worth noting that proposals for the internal reform of the Commission have included attempts to specify standards for the conduct of individual Commissioners (European Commission, 1999c).

Another difficulty is that even though the censure procedure can be used to turn the heat on the College of Commissioners, it may not be an effective means of controlling the wider bureaucracy (Page and Woulters, 1994). It is Secretary Generals and not Commissioners who are in charge of DG. Trends in modern public administration cast further doubt on how far threats to dismiss the College of Commissioners can be used to deliver more day-to-day forms of accountability at lower levels. As seen, decision-making in the EU often seems to be an example of how decentred and 'networked' forms of governance are replacing politically directed administrative hierarchies. A great deal of administration and initiative has passed into the hands of specialist policy communities formed at the intersection of national and European bureaucracies, and at the interface of the three main Union institutions. In effect each institution delegates much of the management of each issue to the experts in its own institution, who then network extensively with their counterparts in the other bodies (Peterson, 1995a; Kohler-Koch, 1996). All of this is corrosive of hierarchical approaches to public control exercised through threats of dismissal against a politically appointed leadership such as the Commission. The specialists to whom so much day-to-day control is delegated may not only be anxious to resist those demands of accountability from the political leadership of their institution that go against the consensus of their own policy community. They may also be in a position to do so, first, on account of asymmetries of information (they just understand the problem better than those who purport to control them) and, second, because only they can deliver the collaboration of other network participants which is so important to the solution of co-ordination problems faced by all.

Whether there are means of exercising public control of a decentred and networked form of governance may thus require us to look beyond the ultimate power of the EP to dismiss the Commission's political leadership. The rest of this chapter examines two possibilities: first, EP controls over legislative approvals and financial resources needed by actors at a lower level of governance than the College of Commssioners; and, second, direct relationships of accountability between participants in decentred and networked patterns of governance and the wider public.

Control by granting and withholding resources

Although appointment and dismissal are widely conceived as the main instruments by which parliaments can control executives, a great deal of day-to-day control depends on the power of representative bodies to grant or withhold specific resources needed for the exercise of power, rather than the conferral or denial of power itself. The 'power of the purse' is an obvious example, though we will also consider ways in which the EP can link scrutiny and control of existing policies to decisions to give legislative authority to new ones.

Whilst it can often only make minor changes to the Union's overall budget, the EP has scope to use it as an instrument of public control. It has exploited the Union's financial rules to develop an activist approach to parliamentary scrutiny. It has used the 'rule of unity' – that income and expenditure is best monitored where it is included in a single budget – to resist the funding of Common Foreign and Security Policy (CFSP) and Justice and Home Affairs (JHA) from outside the Commission's budget and thus from outside its own purview (European Parliament, 2000e, p. 26). It has used the 'rule of specification' – that each budget line should have a specific purpose – to object to proposals that the Commission should be allowed to decide for itself on transfers between chapters in the budget, and to insist that when a budget line is suspended the money should be held in reserve until the 'budgetary authority' (i.e. the Parliament and not the Commission) decides what to do with it (European Parliament, 2001g).

In addition, the EP has exercised control by

- Using its amending powers to alter the purposes and conditions under which money can be spent (Corbett, 1995, p. 235), and not just the quantum of budget lines.
- Voting for some allocations to be held in reserve. This allows it to exercise continuing control, since the funds can only be released on a further application by the Commission to the EP.
- Establishing links between the approval of forthcoming budgets and the discharge of previous ones. Amongst demands that the EP has recently linked to the discharge of Commission accounts are that errors in expenditures should be reduced from 5 to 2 per cent of the total and that the Commission should come up with an action plan to narrow the gap between commitments and expenditures. The EP has taken the view that failures to spend budget lines are just as much a drift in the Commission's agency away from the original intentions of the elected budgetary authority as any decision to spend funds in ways different to those originally specified by the Parliament. It has also made it clear that criticism of particular programmes in previous discharge procedures could be grounds for scaling back their allocations in future budgets (European Parliament, 2001g). A difficulty, however, faced by the EP in asserting these various principles of public control is that it is Member States who make 83 per cent of the final disbursements under the EU's budget with the Commission only acting as overseer. In the vote on the discharge of the 1999 budget (taken in 2001) the EP, accordingly, attempted to grapple with this problem by suggesting a system of naming and shaming that would analyse the number of criticisms made by the Court of Auditors, both by Member State and by DG of the Commission itself (European Parliament, 2001h).

Still, the discharge procedure has to be rated as a key instrument of public control, not least because it was the persistence of the EP in questioning irregularities in the 1996 accounts that triggered the investigations behind the resignation of the Santer Commission in March 1999.

Another resource a parliament can grant or withhold is legislative authority. In the case of the EU this is an important instrument of control, first because its Parliament uses its legislative powers with high degrees of freedom from executive domination and, second, because rule-making is the main business of a polity that has a comparatively small budget as a percentage of its GNP. A Commission official interviewed for this study claims that relationship building with the EP lies at the heart of successful management of a DG's legislative planning:

> We are in day-to-day contact. We talk to MEPs on relevant committees to build up relations, follow them, make an analysis of what they say in debates, and construct a full profile of the things that interest them, their hobby horses, the peculiar angles they have on particular problems. When the Presidency of the Council presents its work programme for each 6 months, it is particularly useful to watch MEP reactions. One example is a proposal that we are currently framing on hygiene. This is something that we have been planning to do any way since last July, but we decided to accelerate it when we realised that it was likely to be well received in the EP.[25]

Inside observers of the Parliament (Corbett *et al.*, 2003, pp. 41–55) claim a positive feedback loop between the Parliament's scrutiny role and its legislative powers, with the following components:

1. MEPs make extensive use of powers to ask written and oral questions which are then published with their answers in the Official Journal (OJ) of the European Union. Whilst these can be directed at either Commission or Council, around 90 per cent seem to be asked of the former. Although, MEPs use questions to play many and varied 'political games', many questions correspond to their membership of specialist committees which lead in the exercise of the Parliament's legislative powers, and, with which the Commission, as seen, has an incentive to maintain an effective relationship. Face-to-face questioning of the Commission in the committees can also be insistent. Corbett *et al.* (2003, p. 371) mention how one committee put the case of an unpaid fine by the Greek Government on the agenda of each of its meetings until it got sufficiently 'under the skin' of the Commission to get action.
2. The EP claims that it now uses three 'annual events' to make 'comprehensive assessments' of the Commission: the budget, the discharge procedure and the preparation of the Commission's annual legislative programme (European Parliament, 2001j). In an interview for this survey, the present President of the Parliament argued that the aim was to build each specialist committee of the Parliament into the preparation of the Commission's annual programme.[26] Another example of stocktaking is that the Petitions Committee now analyses patterns of complaint to the Parliament about Union policies and procedures

and then makes them available to the specialist committees responsible for deciding new legislation.[27]

3. Although the EP is not represented on Comitology committees, it may influence their supervision of the Commission by specifying the controls on implementation listed in the enabling legislation. These include time limits, spending limits, reporting requirements, consultation requirements such as public hearings, rule-making requirements and appeals procedures.

Regardless of overall levels of parliamentary control of the Commission, several participants in this survey shared the view that it works better 'in relation to some DG's than others, and some EP Committees than others'.[28] It is, however, also clear they consider themselves much better placed to exercise public control over the Commission than the Council. Table 6.3 shows how on a scale out of ten MEPs rate their overall ability to

Table 6.3 MEPs' overall assessment of their powers to control the Commission and Council

	Average perception of difficulty on scale 0–10	*SD*
How far are the following obstacles to making the Commission/ Council accountable to the EP? (Scale 0–10)		
The Commission is not very transparent	5.40	3.22
It is always possible for the Commission to blame someone else	3.71	2.40
There is no individual responsibility of Commissioners	5.38	3.30
The power to censure the Commission is difficult to exercise (see also table 6.2)	5.82	3.09
The Council is not very transparent	8.53	2.32
The Council can always blame someone else for decisions	6.47	3.01
Council members consider themselves accountable to national parliaments rather than the EP	7.93	1.97
Willingness to explain decisions to the EP varies with who holds the Council Presidency	6.58	
Comitology allows the Council to escape the scrutiny of the EP	5.64	2.37

Table 6.3 Continued

	Average perception of difficulty on scale 0–10	*SD*
Pillarisation allows the Council to escape the scrutiny of the EP in CFSP	6.33	2.35
Pillarisation allows the Council to escape the scrutiny of the EP in JHA	6.91	1.51
Taken Overall, how far is the EP able to influence the Commission/Council? (Scale 0–10)	*Average perception of EP influence*	*SD*
Commission	5.78	2.20
Council	3.23	1.59

influence the Commission and Council at 5.78 and just 3.23 respectively. The Commission was seen as largely blocked by existing procedures in any scope to escape responsibility by blaming others. On the other hand, MEPs are disagreed amongst themselves in how far they feel the Commission is adequately transparent. The average perception that opacity remains a difficulty is 5.4 on a scale of 0 to 10 with standard deviation of 3.22.

Control by stakeholders, the role of consultation and transparency

If policy networks are corrosive of hierarchical or vertical lines of accountability of administrative actors to political leaderships, they may open up new horizontal lines of accountability between network members who come from different institutions, who have the specialist knowledge to test the credibility of 'accounts' and the capacity to sanction poor policy justifications by withholding their co-operation. Adrienne Héritier explains (1997, p. 110): 'because decision-making involves a consensus among different actors who monitor one another suspiciously, every step in policy development implies a high degree of mutual control among knowledgeable actors'.

However, in claiming that its obligations of democratic accountability are not exclusively to representative institutions, the Commission does more than imply policy networks that can be an effective means of extracting accounts. As seen, it claims it should – and can – be held directly accountable to individuals for certain standards of accountability. Prominent amongst these are consultation and transparency, which we now examine as test cases of what has been termed a 'procedural' approach to the control of administrators. Since such standards can be expected of any component within a decentred and networked public administration their enforcement is a further alternative to modes of accountability directed only at the political leadership of the Commission. They are also standards that require Commission-based actors to account for the appropriateness rather than the consequences of their actions.

Consultation

The Commission analyses the origins of its proposals under pillar one into the following (overlapping) categories.

- Thirty-five per cent are required to meet the Union's international commitments;
- Twenty-five to thirty-five per cent are amendments needed to bring existing Union laws up to date with technological and social change;
- Twenty per cent respond to specific requests for the Commission to table legislative proposals made by the European Council, the Council of Ministers or Member States. The European Council alone made 80 such requests between 1995 and 1998. Moreover, the Commission claims, that it is especially attentive to requests to legislate if they are either contained in a resolution passed by a large majority of the EP or they are a response to concerns that either the Council or EP expressed in passing previous measures;
- Ten per cent are required to enact policies that have already been stipulated in the Treaties or by existing legislation;
- Less than ten per cent are initiatives based on a 'unilateral' Commission's assessment of the 'Union interest' (European Commission, 1999a).

In short, the Commission contests the view that its monopoly of initiative under pillar one is used to conjure up policies that have not already been substantially discussed with others in various processes. Yet, quite apart from the 10 per cent of proposals which it admits are fully on its own initiative, the rest still leave the Commission with substantial choice over the means by which goals are to be realised. Here we have already noted three points. First, procedural restrictions on amendments to its texts mean that when it makes a proposal (or even where it fails do so) the Commission has agenda-setting powers to structure – and restrict – the choices available to others. Second, governments have protected themselves against that effect by requiring the Commission to discuss their initiatives with committees on which they are represented. Third, the Commission's own answer to the question of how others – private groups and individuals – can influence agenda-setting is that it is responsible for developing procedures that ensure all those who want to express a view have the opportunity to do so.

At one level, the Commission rates its own record of consultation highly: 'the Commission incorporates external consultation into the development of almost all its policy areas' (European Commission, 2002a, p. 3). Yet, it also admits to difficulties which overlap with the pitfalls of basing Union policy on interest representation discussed in the last chapter. One senior official who participated in this survey argues that the Commission often finds it hard to know who to consult before it launches a policy and, then, as the policy develops, it runs into the opposite problem that 'stakeholders' are all too organised along lines that introduce rigidity to both the policy and patterns of access:

> There is a chicken and egg problem. Some sectors only become organised in a manner that allows for structured consultation as a consequence of decisions. But what then of the requirement that we should consult *before* decisions are taken? Repeat decision making can solve this problem only for another to crop up: areas where the Union has been active in policy-making for a long time may become too settled. Patterns of who is included in consultation reproduce themselves.[29]

As this suggests, the Commission struggles to establish principles and procedures that offer consultation without privilege or even capture and dependence. It has tried to deal with this difficulty by employing 'open processes' of consultation (mainly Green and White Papers) only to find that these pose a problem of their own: they 'tend to lead to a large number of comments, which often can be difficult, even impossible, to process' (European Commission, 2002a, pp. 7–8). The further difficulty of knowing when consultation has exhausted all those with a legitimate interest in inclusion was lucidly summarised in the following contribution to this survey: consultation with civil society usually involves a very structured public sector in dialogue with the muddle of civil society.

You never quite know whether you have identified all the relevant interests and the right ones to talk to.[30]

Then, of course, there is the danger of replacing representative institutions with fragmented forms of sectoral interest consultation whose participants have neither the incentive nor the means to consider the external costs or other cumulative unintended consequences of their individual discussions. The Commission admits that problems of fragmentation inherent in discussing policy formation with sectoral interests have been compounded by failure even to base each consultation on a consistent set of principles uniformly applied across different parts of the Commission. 'Each of the Departments has had its own mechanisms and methods for consulting its respective sectoral interest groups' (European Commission, 2002a, p. 3). Failure to co-ordinate the results of previous consultations into joined-up policy-making across Sections and DGs was likewise lamented by another contributor to this survey: 'We have a system of consultation that is completely mad. Horizontal linkages between consultations in different sectors and on different issues hardly exist at all, and early stages in many consultations are hidden from view.'[31]

A final problem is that the Commission cannot in any case fully control the quality of any consultation process. As it puts it, the 'commitment to principles cannot be unilateral, both sides have a role in applying them effectively' (ibid., p. 9). This, in turn, raises the thorny question of whether those who are consulted should themselves be required to be representative and accountable. It may not be easy to insist on such principles where the Commission cannot pick and choose who to consult but must, instead, include all those whose co-operation is needed for effective policy delivery (Peterson, 1995a).

Transparency

Apart from a commitment to openness in the Amsterdam Treaty, transparency is often assumed to have a special place in any assessment of the EU, since in contrast to many other attributes of democracy, it would not appear to be particularly difficult for the Union to provide immediately. Adrienne Héritier (1999) argues that the Commission has identified transparency as one of a number of sources of 'substitute legitimation' that might be employed pending conditions more propitious to a fuller development of representative democracy in the European arena. The Commission may also have an incentive to embrace transparency as a form of institutional self-protection. It often sees itself as more a victim of 'responsibility without power' than a wielder of 'power without responsibility' (Lord, 2001, p. 655). Transparency would at least make it more difficult for Member States to dump insoluble or unpopular policies on to the Commission, often without sufficient resourcing (Peterson, 1995b).

Amongst indications of the Commission's current thinking on transparency are the following:

- (Overlapping with the last topic) consultation requires a transparent policy cycle in which all interested parties know when and how to organise themselves to influence the development of Union policy (European Commission, 2000a).
- All Commission officials should show transparency to one another and not just to the public (ibid). A good deal of accountability has in the first instance to be internal to bureaucracies themselves – and to take place between colleagues and peer agencies – if external overseers are not to be overloaded.
- The use of scientific expertise in policy-making should be transparent. The public should be able to find out which scientific committees contribute to which elements of the policy process, on what criteria scientific advice is considered or set aside, and, in some cases, even what that advice is (European Commission, 2001c).
- Not only should existing policies be more extensively reviewed, all affected should know what are the procedures for evaluation, and when and how they can contribute to them (ibid).
- Networked and decentred forms of governance need not create transparency problems, since each component of a complex public administration can be made to account for the 'adequacy of its procedures aimed at openness' (European Commission, 1997, p. 20). An early paper on internal reform of the Commission thus suggested publicly available audit-trails – or records of who participated at each stage of a decision and with what effect – would be one way of reconciling transparency with complexity (European Commission, 2000a).
- Old-fashioned bureaucratic foibles, rather than new forms of governance, are still behind significant failures of transparency: 'the complex and extended chain of approvals required in the Commission for the simplest of items has become almost legendary. It might have originated in a desire for carefulness, but it has evolved in a way that diminishes and obscures responsibility' (ibid., p. 7)

An important case study in the problems raised by transparency was provided by a decision at Amsterdam (1997) to delegate to the Commission the task of drawing up a regulation on public rights of access to documents across the range of Union institutions. Although the measure was initially thought to be straightforward it proved difficult to negotiate between the institutions and required two readings in the European Parliament instead of the anticipated one. The main difficulties arose in defining what should be legitimate exceptions to a general rule in favour of transparency and who should, then, decide their application. The following are three examples:

1. *What level of access should be given to documents submitted to the institutions by third parties?* Where these contribute to decisions, the public should, arguably be in a position to verify the claims contained within them. Yet, they can in certain circumstances be construed as containing information 'belonging' to the third party. In others, the possibility of disclosure could make parties to a decision less willing to exchange information (European Commission, 2000c, p. 5).

2. *Should there be space to think?* A second issue was at what point do documents become definitive positions of the institutions in which they are produced, as opposed to preliminary attempts by a few individuals' brainstorm ideas. To the extent any transparency regime discourages creativity and 'space to think'[32] it can have perverse and unintended consequences (March and Olsen, 1995, pp. 143–6). The Commission noted that most national systems limit disclosure to documents that have been authoritatively adopted, though in some, documents that are suited to being archived are also disclosed even if they have not issued in a decision (European Commission, 2000c, p. 4).

3. *What should happen where transparency conflicts with other rights of individuals?* Then, most obviously of all, the Commission had to find some way of dealing with conflicts of rights, notably where the public right to transparency clashes with rights of individuals to personal data protection. It noted that disclosure in some systems can only occur if all names of individuals are first taken out of documents, but then went on to point out that, though desirable, this would put the institutions under considerable administrative strain (ibid., p. 5).

Conclusion to the assessment of the Commission

Paul Magnette has argued that the 'European Commission is one of the most controlled executives in the world. Situated between the Council and the Parliament, subject to the jurisdiction of the ECJ, watched over by the Ombudsman, the Court of Auditors and a series of ad hoc bodies, it is surrounded by mechanisms of control' (Paul Magnette, 2003, p. 51).

This chapter has confirmed just how far the Commission is surrounded by multiple mechanisms of control exercised by different actors. Indeed, a view held by several MEPs is that in developing adequate control of the Commission they may only have weakened it to the benefit of still less accountable national officials operating within the framework of the Council.

> Although, I think we ought to be unforgiving in chasing up the Commission – it has to be said that the fine job that the EP has done in the last 24 months in bringing the Commission to account has had the perverse effect of increasing the freedom of those who are the truly politically irresponsible forces in the EU: the various national officials based on the Council. The Council of Ministers has been laughing all the way to the bank in the last 24 months: the national officials who run the Council – with little political responsibility to the EP, to national parliaments or even to ministers – have just ridden rough shod while the EP and Commission slag it out.[33]

We cannot however conclude that both the Democratic Audit tests associated with accountability (see p. 132) are satisfied in relation to the Commission unless we can also show that the 'multiple principals' who survey that body are themselves publicly controlled. Are national governments adequately accountable to their national democracies for any control they exercise over the Commission, and are MEPs really 'representatives of citizens' in the exercise of their controlling powers? The last chapter considered the second question. The next chapter will assess the first.

7
Accountability (The Council)

Introduction

In this chapter we continue our appraisal of how accountable the key institutions of the EU are with an assessment of the Council. Much has already been said about the Council. Chapter 5 asked how far it provides nationally elected governments with proportional and inclusive representation in the Union's decisions. Chapter 6 considered its contribution to the accountability of the Commission. But neither asked how it is itself brought to account for its various roles in the Union. The importance of this cannot be understated: if members of the Council are to be 'Guardians', they must themselves be guarded.

The Council of Ministers is a complex body. It meets as a 'political formation' by bringing together Ministers from the elected governments of Member States. However, far from being a unitary body, it meets as a series of sectoral Councils that roughly correspond to demarcations between departments and ministerial portfolios to be found in most Member States. This mosaic of ministerial meetings is, in turn, serviced by a significant technocracy. There are now 250 working groups of the Council, staffed by national officials.

These groups are linked to the full Council by a series of powerful committees, also composed of national civil servants. The best known are the Committees of Permanent Representatives (Coreper 1 and 2) (Bostock, 2002). Recent years have, however, seen a growth in other preparatory committees: the Economic and Finance committee in matters of macro- and micro-economic policy co-ordination; the Political committee on Common Foreign and Security Policy (CFSP) questions; the military committee on ESDP matters; and the K.4 committee on JHA issues (Maurer, 2003a).

This further element of complexity reflects attempts by Member governments to put the Council at the centre of recent trends to proliferate new forms of policy-making 'beyond the Community Method'. Another consequence of the same development is that powers have also been delegated from the Council to new administrative agencies (such as Europol for collaboration between the police forces of the Member States and Eurojust for co-operation between prosecuting magistrates) and even to individuals (such as the Secretary General of the Council in his role as Mr CFSP).

Not only do the working groups, Coreper and other preparatory committees have a significant role in framing and filtering the choices of the political leaders, they also take many decisions in the name of their Ministers. Some estimates put the number of decisions taken at official level as high as 80 per cent (Wallace and Hayes-Renshaw, 1997, p. 40). What is, of course, more difficult to measure is how far this allows national officials to constitute themselves as a 'run-away bureaucracy' at European level, or how far, to the contrary, they only deal with one another as loyal servants of their political principals.

Much of the work of Ministers and officials is to rhythms set by meetings of the heads of Government in the European Council. It should not however be assumed that the direction of influence is always 'top-down'. European Councils are often short and over-loaded. Their members are also aware it may be 'a mistake for princes to meet to discuss what their envoys have not already decided'. As Fiona Hayes-Renshaw and Helen Wallace argue (1997, p. 159), there has long been a debate as to whether the European Council should be considered a part of the Council of Ministers. It occasionally convenes as such in order to make decisions with the formal powers of the Council, and to the extent that Foreign and Finance Ministers are in attendance, its composition overlaps with the two most powerful sectoral Councils (General Affairs (GAC) and Ecofin). Yet, the Treaty is ambivalent about the European Council's status, treating it as a formal institution only of the European Union and not of the European Community, while charging it with the 'political leadership' of the whole (ibid., pp. 160–2).

The unclear relationship to the European Council, and the various delegations of powers within and away from the Council, means that the Council is a body of uncertain external boundaries, as well as internal complexity. Added to this is a certain ambivalence as to whether its participants are merely representatives of particular Member States, or actors with a measure of shared responsibility for what is after all an institution of the Union as a whole (Hallstein, 1970, p. 77). If it promises to be a sometimes elusive object of assessment, specification of what democratic standards the Council should meet is more straightforward. Building on the Democratic Audit tests of accountability discussed on p. 132, that associated with modified consociationalism (*EUDA Test 5*) requires the Council to be accountable to national parliaments and electorates. Indeed, it is that which distinguishes 'modified' from original conceptions of consociationalism. The Audit test associated with 'concurrent consent' (*EUDA Test 11*), on the other hand, implies a more horizontal form of accountability in which the Council is checked and balanced by the Parliament elected at the level of the EU's political system itself.

National elections

National governments enjoy the decision rights of the Council by indirect election. Some have speculated that one way of better connecting the Union to the citizen would be to internalise choices about integration into domestic cleavage structures, so that they can be registered through national elections. Yet, Table 7.1 shows that in the few countries where data is available EU issues are not salient in national elections. Although it is difficult to compare the importance of Union issues to domestic electoral choice across Member States since those polling organisations rarely probe the question in the same way, there would

Table 7.1 The salience of EU issues in National General Elections

	Question put	*Percentage*	*Rank relative to other issues*
Sweden 1998	Voters who on an open-ended question mentioned the EU as an issue important to their party choice	6	7
UK 2001	Most important issue		
	British Membership of the Euro	7.9	3
	Britain's relations with the EU	3.7	5
France 2002 Presidential	In the Presidential elections, which among the following themes were important to you?		
	The European Construction	13	14
	The Introduction of the Euro	4	17

Sources
France: SOFRES poll for RTL, TV1 and Le Monde, 10–11 April 2002, $n = 1000$.
Sweden: Swedish Electoral Studies Programme (Holmberg, 2001).
UK: British Election Survey (2001)/NOP, $n = 2352$.

still seem to be a general pattern: even where European issues have divided public opinion and to some degree changed pre-existing cleavage structures, it is still relatively rare for them to shape voter choice. Take the example of the UK. Although an EU issue ranked third in a survey of the 2001 election (thanks to the need to decide membership of the single currency), it was only important for 7.9 per cent of voters.

Behind this finding lie structural constraints on the use of national elections to register voter preferences in relation to two political arenas. For the most part citizens only receive one vote in such elections. A vote used to register views on Union policies cannot be used to express preferences on domestic issues or *vice versa*. Indeed, there is a risk that using national elections to provide representation in relation to two very different political systems may reduce the representative qualities of domestic institutions, rather than increase those of the Union. In some Member States, the prospect of Union issues entering domestic controversy seems to have contributed to a drift towards cartel parties (Katz and Mair, 1995), whose main concern is to manage issues between themselves, rather than compete freely. This is, first, because Union issues may threaten the cohesion of parties that have developed around domestic issues; second, because opportunities to appoint to office and influence the policy outputs of two, and not just one, political system (the national and European) can now be used to sustain any cartel of *status quo* parties in the domestic arena; and, third, because the involvement of governing parties in striking compromises in the Council of Ministers with counterparts from a technicolour range of parties narrows options they might otherwise have used to differentiate themselves domestically.

National parliaments

It may be rare for the work of the Council of Ministers to be affected by national elections. But that need not stop representatives elected to national parliaments from scrutinising the work of the Council. A number of factors underscore the importance of giving significant attention to national parliaments in a Democratic Audit of the EU:

- We cannot reach a definitive assessment of whether Union decisions are sufficiently exposed to parliamentary representation and control until we have also reviewed the contributions of national parliaments. Whilst the EP is the only parliament elected at the level of the EU's political system, it is only one of many parliaments with a capacity to influence Union decisions.

- As seen, the classic definition of the democratic deficit views the problem as a dispossession of national parliaments. Powers which previously required parliamentary approval in the domestic arena can now be exercised by executive discretion at Union level (Dimitrakopoulos, 2001, p. 406). The Finnish Parliament has even adopted this interpretation of the deficit as the basis for its scrutiny by requiring its government to give it an opportunity to express an opinion on any matter that would have been laid before it had Finland not joined the EU.[34]
- National parliaments are, on one influential reading of the problem, heavily implicated in the democratic dilemmas facing Member societies of the EU. Fritz Scharpf (1999) puts the problem as follows. Member States struggle in many policy areas to satisfy the output conditions of democracy, namely capacity to deliver the preferences of their electorates. The Union, on the other hand, has profound difficulties meeting the input conditions: shared identity, first-order elections, fully developed political parties or other form of democratic intermediation, common language, media and public space. It follows that the democratic deficit is a problem that can only be managed, rather than solved, but, in Scharpf's view, one way of doing that would be to create a better match between use of Union institutions for satisfying the output conditions of democracy and use of national democratic institutions for meeting its input conditions (Scharpf, 1996, p. 31). That would suggest a role for national parliaments in scrutinising Union decisions and making them visible to national electorates.

It is useful to start by noting opposed notions of what role national parliaments ought to play. Some see the controlling roles of the EP and national parliaments as additive and complementary, with the implication those bodies should collaborate and divide their labours, in order to maximise the total quantum of parliamentary control in the European arena. One notion of a desirable division of labour is that the EP should scrutinise the Council as a collective decision-making body while national parliaments concentrate all their energies on holding their governments to account for their individual contributions (European Parliament, 1997). Another is that national parliaments should concentrate on matters where the Council decides by unanimity (Treaty change, CFSP and Justice and Home Affairs (JHA)) and the EP on those where it decides by majority.

In contrast, others argue that national parliaments have delegated powers to the overall complex of Union institutions, all of which they need to monitor if they are to ensure none overstep the terms of their agency. They may even need to be especially watchful of the EP, given its history as an energetic 'agency-shaper' and enthusiast for supranational solutions. The idea of a division of labour can be criticised from the EP end too.[35] As one member of its Constitutional Affairs Committee has put it, 'the EP is the Parliament' of the European *Union*.[36] It has a responsibility to scrutinise all three pillars, given that any meaningful public control may need to include the external effects of decisions taken under one pillar on the other two.

As this discussion suggests any national parliament faces an opportunity structure in relation to Union decision-making at one end of which it is doubly constrained: the only government over which it has powers can be outvoted in a Council that only co-determines outcomes with the EP. At the other extreme (Treaty changes and the second and third pillars) it can exercise whatever control it can extract from its relationship with a government that is a 'veto player' on a Council that decides matters alone. It is also worth noting that national parliaments may be called upon to scrutinise a variety of outputs, ranging from EU legislation to more discretionary executive actions in areas such as CFSP, JHA and forms of economic co-ordination associated with Monetary Union (The Stability Pact and the Open Method of Co-ordination).

Most national parliaments have become more active on EU matters since the early 1990s. All Parliaments now (more or less) have a European Affairs Committee (EAC). Indeed, the formation or strengthening of those committees was a concession many extracted in exchange for ratification of the Treaty on European Union (TEU) or for agreement to accession. Even the French National Assembly and Senate – which had already exhausted a meagre constitutional limit on the number of parliamentary committees to just six long before they developed an appetite for monitoring EU decisions – have been able to appoint *'délégations'* on European questions (Assemblée Nationale, 2002). In addition all national parliaments participate in the Conference of Presidents of European Union Parliaments (COSAC). This permits an exchange of views – and sometimes even of 'best practice' – on the roles of different kinds of parliament on EU questions.

The scrutiny role of national parliaments is acknowledged in a legally binding protocol to the Amsterdam Treaty. This requires they receive draft legislation, Commission White and Green Papers and Communications, and all documents related to the 'creation of an area of Freedom and Justice' (mainly JHA). It further states that a legislative proposal can only be placed on the Council's agenda six weeks after the text has been sent to national parliaments.

Yet, COSAC complains that 'some Parliaments still do not receive all documents to which they are entitled within the stated period' (COSAC, 2001b). A converse difficulty is that scrutiny by national parliaments may be hampered by a surfeit of unstructured information as much as by paucity. Even the most committed only have the time and resources for in-depth scrutiny of 100 of the 1500 or so Union dossiers they receive per year. The key to effectiveness is thus a filtering mechanism based on a precise understanding of the significance of each document so that no decisions end up being made at Union level on which national parliamentarians would have liked to express their preferences and, conversely, no time is wasted on those where they have no strong views.

Some governments see advantage in structuring the information flow to their parliaments, though they differ both in the explanations they are obliged to provide and those they are prepared to volunteer. Denmark provides an example of the significant demands to explain and inform that can be put on governments. All EU documents forwarded to the Folketing must include analysis of any impact on domestic law, the economy and employment, public finance, environment and equal rights of men and women. Any views received from non-governmental organisations must also be summarised (Folketinget, 2002, p. 12). In contrast, the significant formal powers of the Austrian Parliament on EU questions are weakened in practice by the absence of any obligation on the Government to submit explanatory memoranda. The result is that it passes only half as many resolutions as its Swedish and Finnish counterparts (Hegeland and Neuhold, 2002).

Yet, failure by governments to collaborate in presenting information to parliaments may be counterproductive. Alternative means of obtaining the information are available, and governments that do not volunteer themselves as the principal conduit may lose the opportunity to present 'national impact assessments' or to advocate their own preferred outcomes. Before 1991, the French National Assembly compensated for parsimonious disclosure by its own government by obtaining documents from the EP, with the result that it was often better informed on wider policy development in the Community than on French government objectives (Dimitrakopoulos, 2001, p. 410).

National parliaments also differ in what they can do if they are dissatisfied with flows of information from their governments. In the cases of all three countries that joined in the last enlargement (Austria, Finland and Sweden) the right to participate – and thus receive information – on the preparation of EU decisions is written into the national constitution or will soon be so (Hegeland and Neuhold, 2002, p. 2). The Finnish

Parliament can hold the Prime Minister personally responsible for forwarding all Commission proposals as soon they are translated, and all Council agendas as soon as they are agreed by Coreper.

Above all, national parliaments differ in their powers to act on their scrutiny of EU decisions. It is common for Member States to enter scrutiny reserves where their national parliaments need more time to form a position. This means all have some power of delay, though there is a risk of the procedure being used strategically to achieve the bargaining preferences of governments, rather than sincerely to protect the purview of parliaments. Nor is it always clear what say (let alone control) national parliaments have in decisions to lift reserves that are supposedly entered in their name (European Convention, 2002b, p. 5).

The key difference, however, is that only some national parliaments can issue instructions their governments are more or less obliged to follow. As shown in Table 7.2, the Danish and Austrian parliaments can issue legally binding mandates on all Union questions, and the Finnish and Swedish Parliaments politically binding ones. The Dutch and German Parliaments have partial mandating powers, confined in the former case to pillar three decisions, and, in the latter, to those involving the competence of the Länder. The German constitution now requires the Government to take account of the views of the Bundesrat where the Länder have partial competence, and to negotiate from a common position where they have exclusive competence.

But what happens if governments depart from their instructions? In none of the six cases (Austria, Denmark, Finland, Germany, Netherlands and Sweden) has it been possible to put an absolute prohibition on 'deviations' from mandates. Yet, significant 'commitment technologies' are available to national parliaments that want to develop them. The Danish Folketing 'goes public' with its mandates by announcing them to a press conference after each meeting of the EAC. This increases the costs to the reputation and trustworthiness of Ministers of any deviation. The Danish, Finnish and Swedish Parliaments have all developed procedures which allow them to participate in judgements their governments make of where it is best to be flexible in negotiations. The Danish government must return to the EAC for fresh instructions if it feels unable to keep to the mandate. Swedish Ministers are expected to remain in continuous contact with the Chair of the EAC, who will, in turn, telephone the leading committee member from each of the other political parties to consult on any proposed deviation from the parliament's original position.[37]

All three Parliaments likewise have monitoring mechanisms. Minutes and voting records of Council meetings are used to check that the

Table 7.2 National parliaments and the EU

	Special arrangements for contacts with MEPs	*Power to mandate?*	*Relative[1] powers where Denmark = 10*
Austria	MEPs may attend EAC of either chamber with speaking (but not voting) rights	Yes, legally binding	8.0
Belgium	MEPs may attend and vote in committees of the Chamber	—	2.7
Denmark	—	Yes, legally binding	10.0
Finland	—	Yes, politically binding	8.8
France	MEP have speaking (but not voting) rights		4.0
Germany	MEPs may attend EAC of Bundesrat with speaking (but not voting) rights	Federal Govt must co-ordinate position with State Govts where latter have competence	6.7
Greece	A joint committee of the national parliament and MEPs in which both have the same rights	—	1.3
Ireland	—	—	3.3
Italy	MEPs may attend EAC of either chamber with speaking (but not voting) rights	—	3.7
Luxembourg	—	—	2.3
Netherlands	MEPs may attend EAC of either chamber with speaking (but not voting) rights, even where positions are discussed with Ministers	Tweede Kamer can mandate on JHA matters	6.0
Portugal	—	—	2.0
Spain	MEPs may attend EAC of the Senate with speaking (but not voting) rights	—	1.7
Sweden		Yes, politically binding	8.3
UK		—	5.3

1. This scale is based on an idea developed by Olivier Rozenberg (2002).

government has kept to its commitments. Reports have to be submitted after each Council of Ministers. In the case of the Swedish Riksdag, for example, the 'Government has to submit a written report of the position that it has taken within 5 days of each Council meeting, explaining what positions it has backed and why'.[38] Where the Government departs from a mandate, the Riksdag EAC reserves the right to take a vote on whether the deviation was justified and all MPs can pick up on any embarrassment of the government through 'interpellations' or votes of no confidence in the full parliament (Hegeland and Neuhold, 2002, p. 6). The case of the German Länder illustrates a further possibility: representatives of bodies other than national parliaments can monitor the behaviour of governments by being directly incorporated into national delegations to Council meetings. Indeed, the Convention has discussed the generalisation of this practice with Council delegations from all Member States (European Convention, 2002c, p. 9).

At the other extreme to those with mandating powers, the Greek, Portuguese, Spanish and, until recently, the Irish Parliaments, are generally classified as having few powers. In between are a series of parliaments which, in the words of a report prepared for the Convention, have 'more or less effective systems for allowing national parliaments to express their views on a legislative proposal, while leaving their respective governments free to decide whether to take them into account' (European Convention, 2002a, p. 6). On one interpretation, that is not much different from the relationship between the legislative and executive on non-EU decisions. As Jean Blondel puts it (1990, pp. 241–2) parliaments in most European political systems 'participate' in – rather than 'exercise' – legislative powers. Indeed, during interviews for this study, officials from the Belgium Parliament, vigorously argued the case for a relationship limited to participation rather than instruction. In their view, mandating is a form of 'reactive' behaviour. It presupposes an agenda that has already been set at Union level, on which instructions can be given. By accepting it as a model, national parliaments risk neglecting opportunities to develop as more pro-active policy shapers, perhaps through inter-parliamentary networking between themselves, about which more in a while.[39]

How might the foregoing differences be summarised in an overall assessment? Using indices developed in two other studies (Bergman, 1997; Maurer and Wessels, 2001) Olivier Rozenberg (2002) has constructed a 'scorecard' in which a maximum of 10 points is assigned to the Danish Parliament and the powers of the other national parliaments are then ranked by comparison. Its results are shown in the final column of Table 7.2.

It is, however, insufficient for a democratic audit to enumerate differences between the powers of national parliaments on EU questions. It is also necessary to analyse the causes of those differences, if responsibility for deficiencies is to be attributed and an assessment reached of whether they are corrigible. The paragraphs that follow argue that the influence of national parliaments on Union issues is a cumulative product of factors that operate at three levels of analysis: first, at the level of individual institutions, the energy and performance of national parliaments themselves; second, at the level of national political systems, the structure of executive–legislature relationships in each Member State; third, at the level of the Union, the role of the EU's own political system in shaping constraints and opportunities for national parliamentary influence. Whereas, of course, the first two factors vary across Member States, the third is common to them all.

Determinant of influence 1: national parliaments themselves

National parliaments vary in the energy and commitment they give to the scrutiny of EU issues. The Scandinavian parliaments provide benchmarks of how far national parliaments are able to use scrutiny to form 'legislative partnerships' with their governments on Union questions (Arter, 1996). They typically have line-by-line discussions with Ministers of Council agendas for the coming week. As Tapio Raunio observes (2002, p. 188) only those whose EACs meet weekly are likely to be engaged in line-by-line scrutiny of Union business. Another indicator of commitment is the proportion of each national parliament involved in Union matters. To the extent expertise is central to scrutiny it is likely to be superior where it is delivered through collaboration between EACs and other specialist committees of national parliaments. The Danish Parliament has appointed a European Councillor to encourage the range of its Standing Committees to draft opinions on Union matters (Folketinget, 2002, p. 10). The *délégations* in the French Senate and Assembly are constructed to ensure overlapping membership with all other committees. The EAC of the Swedish Parliament is likewise composed of one member from each of its other committees.

Variations in the time and resources committed to Union matters would seem to be linked to how far the EU is contentious in Member States, and in what way. Scrutiny is more active where at least a section of elite opinion is sceptical (Raunio and Wiberg, 1999), and less so where there is a 'permissive consensus' on issues of European integration. An example of how scepticism (in the proper sense of the word) can motivate wariness is provided by the following response to the survey undertaken for this study:

> Our EAC is especially vigilant about the growth of 'soft law' in several Councils. Its worry is that the Council and other Union institutions use soft law as an alternative to gaining explicit authorisation – under duly ratified Treaty changes – for an expansion of competence.[40]

Some of these differences can be linked to another: although scrutiny by the EP can support that at other levels, and national parliaments discover things in their own scrutiny of interest to others, national parliaments vary in how well they are organised for inter-parliamentary collaboration and in their preferences for what form it should take. This time it is often those with pro-integration public opinions that are most likely to formalise contacts with the EP. Belgian and Greek MEPs can attend the committees of their national parliaments. Eleven out of fifty members of the *EU-Ausschuss* of the German *Bundestag* are MEPs.

Differences in the value national parliamentarians place on contacts with the EP are not just linked to pro-anti integration preferences. They also reflect hardheaded 'choices of arena' or calculations of how best to influence policy outcomes. For national parliaments that have few powers on EU matters – and for many individual MPs from countries where opposition means exclusion from influence – contacts with MEPs may be the only means of influencing Union legislation. Where, in contrast, a national parliament already enjoys a 'legislative partnership' on EU matters with its own government, contacts with MEPs have to be more guarded. The protection of bargaining hands requires that discussions in Scandinavian EACs are closed to the public, let alone to MEPs whose institution is a potential rival to the Council in the shaping of Union legislation. The willingness of governments to inform MPs of positions they and other members of the Council are likely to support would be curtailed by any risk of that information being used by MEPs to push the Council closer to its bottom line on individual amendments or in Conciliation Committees.

A possible solution is for MEPs to have restricted access to national parliamentary committee meetings dealing with 'preparations for Council of Ministers meetings' as is the case in the Dutch Parliament. Nor does the problem arise at all where it is national parliaments who make contact with MEPs, rather than *vice versa*. This they can do by exercising their entitlement to send representatives with speaking right to EP committees. Nor, finally, are bilateral contacts between the EP and individual national parliaments the only possible form of interparliamentary collaboration. Although COSAC has received decidedly 'mixed reviews' several parliamentarians argue that its multilateral approach of promoting horizontal contacts between national parliaments as well as vertical ones with the EP is the right one and that its potential has only just begun to be exploited.

Determinant of influence 2: domestic political systems

Whether a parliament is weak or strong on European issues may have as much to do with its general strength in its domestic political system as the energies and preferences of its members on issues of European integration. The political systems of the Member States cover the spectrum from those with parliaments that dominate governments through those with balanced or variable relationships to governments that dominate parliaments (Pennings, 2000). Executive-dominated parliaments lack control of their own agenda and business (Döring, 1995) in ways that complicate scrutiny of EU matters. For example, the British House of Commons, arguably, combines one of the most painstaking with one of the most inconsequential of EU scrutiny procedures. Although its Scrutiny Committee has been praised for its identification of matters of concern to MPs, scrutiny can be taken no further than an adjournment debate on the floor of the House. Apart from being cursory, ill-attended and at inhospitable times (after 10.30 p.m.), the Government, which controls parliamentary business, usually only makes space for about 12 such debates a year. Most of those debates end without a vote and, in any case, the government majority is always available to defeat a challenge. How the matter is handled in the Council thereafter is a matter of executive discretion (Giddings and Drewry, 1996).

Unpacking further factors that affect degrees to which parliaments are dominated by their governments, national parliamentary control of EU policy is likely to be higher in Member States that often have minority or coalition governments, and in those which have committee-based parliaments. The Danish model has evolved through 30 years' experience of having to find some institutional means of deciding how to use national decision rights in the Council of Ministers in a Member State where, as David Arter puts it, Governments are typically so much in the minority that it is 'opposition parties ... that in practice make decisions' (1999, pp. 119–20). Yet, even where governments are in a majority, active scrutiny of EU matters may be more likely where the majority is drawn from more than one party. Parties to a governing coalition often rely on their supporters in parliamentary committees to monitor Ministers from other parties.

A strong committee-based parliament may be needed to overcome the asymmetries of information and expertise between domestic legislatures and their governments which alone have direct access to EU negotiations. Gaps in understanding can only be minimised by small sections of MPs devoting sustained attention to the acquisition of specialist knowledge of EU affairs (Raunio and Wiberg, 2000). Likewise, the sifting of an estimated 1500 EU texts a year requires that some MPs devote disproportionate time to performing the task on behalf of the parliament as a whole. The development of strong parliamentary committees may, however, be constrained in executive-dominated systems (Blondel, 1990). The EACs of executive-dominated parliaments are more likely to be controlled by the party disciplines of ruling parties than *vice versa*.

Any link between their influence on EU issues and their general strength in domestic political systems casts doubt on the fashionable notion that there is a body of transferable 'best practice' between national parliaments that might be used to solve the EU's overall 'democratic deficit'. Although often described as a 'model' the Danish system may be better classified as an 'idiosyncracy' once it is considered how far a parliamentary 'mandate giver' that cannot itself be controlled by the executive 'mandate taker' depends on the near permanence of minority government in Denmark. The Danish case may also suggest that mandating works best where it is grafted on to a consensus culture of domestic politics. A calculation (based on a sample of 79 Council meetings) that the Danish Government meets at least some parliamentary opposition to its proposed negotiating position in 58 per cent of cases, falls to just 5 per cent once only objections from mainstream parties are considered.[41]

On the other hand, the relationship between the power of national parliaments on EU issues and their general strength in domestic political systems is inexact. The Italian Parliament has not developed a powerful scrutiny of Union questions, although it was until recently one of the most likely to dominate governments in domestic politics. Conversely, the Finnish Parliament has claimed an effective scrutiny of EU issues from within a system in which the executive is generally strong in relation to the legislature.

What accounts for these variations? One possibility is that the factors reviewed in this and the last subsection interact. In other words, national parliamentary assertion on EU issues is a joint product of the level of Euroscepticism in domestic politics and the powers of a parliament in its national political system (Johanssen and Raunio, 2001; Rozenberg, 2002).

Second, it is, as Wolfgang Wessels points out, easy to miscalculate the prospects for the Europeanisation of any national-level institution by forgetting that adaptation may not be required of the whole body so much as of its selective parts or practices that deal with the Union. In systems where the party politics or parliamentary procedures of EU questions form something of a microclimate of their own it is more likely they will partially escape the general pattern of executive–legislature relations. Third, opportunities to use Treaty ratifications to ratchet up their rights of participation in EU decision-making may favour national parliaments from late entrants able to imitate what is available elsewhere. They may also depend on somewhat chancy conjunctures. Thus the Austrian Parliament owes its powers on EU questions to the fact that it was the Greens who were pivotal to agreement of the accession Treaties (Fitzmaurice, 1996); and the Irish Parliament to the tales of the unexpected associated with the rejection of the Nice Treaty and the need to persuade the public to vote differently in a second referendum.

Determinant of influence 3: the EU political system

What finally are the constraints common to all national parliaments posed by the shape of the EU's political system? Perhaps the most important of all is that the closed nature of Council meetings raises the costs to national parliaments of monitoring the behaviour of their governments. An important change, however, is that results of Council votes are now made public, as are explanations of votes by Member States (Council of the European Union, 2000, pp. 13–14).

Another constraint is that there may be limits to how far national parliamentary rights can be loaded on to the EU decision-making without it losing its problem-solving capacity. That some parliaments mandate their governments may depend on others not doing so. This argument needs, however, to be treated with caution, since there is little evidence that the Member States whose parliaments have the strongest mandating power are obstacles to consensus in the Council. Thus Denmark was only the sixth most frequent 'naysayer' between 1994 and 1998, casting 'no' votes in just 5.0 per cent of Council roll calls and abstaining in a further 0.8 per cent (Matilla and Lane, 2001, p. 43). A Folketing official even doubts there is a single instance where the powers of the Danish Parliament have prevented the Council from taking a decision.[42]

One reason why mandating by national parliaments may not lead to high levels of negative voting on the Council is that Qualified Majority Voting (QMV) creates a balance of constraints. Since by binding their governments too tightly they risk a policy outcome that is even further from their preferences than if they had issued no mandate at all, national parliaments often indicate a range in which it is acceptable to settle, rather than issue precise instructions.[43] One respondent to this Audit even claimed the Danish parliament had adapted to QMV by concentrating its scrutiny on cases where its government was most likely to be pivotal in the Council.[44] This response, however, hints at constraint as much as opportunity, since it underscores how far influence will be a product of how preferences are distributed between other Member States, and not just of feelings within national parliaments themselves. A national parliament seeking to base its instruction to its own government on the voting behaviour of others may also find the latter difficult to predict. One participant in this survey argues that the nearest the Swedish Government has come to falling out with its EAC was when it told the latter that there was no point in voting against a measure, although it turned out Germany and the UK were also opposed.[45]

So, is national parliamentary control unambiguously easier where the Council decides by unanimity? National parliamentary disquiet with scrutiny of CFSP and JHA would suggest not. The following is the assessment of the House of Lords:

> Our involvement in the formation of the CFSP is negligible. As a Parliament we are informed after the event and there has been no occasion whatsoever since our arrangements for scrutiny of both pillars were set up on which we have been consulted about any CFSP document or decision before it was finalised. (House of Lords, 1996)

Another systemic constraint common to all national parliaments is the EU's extended policy cycle. In practice, national parliaments may want to operate both 'up' and 'down' stream to the single intervention point (the publication of a draft text) created for them by the Amsterdam protocol. To the extent Member States have already bargained with one another through the committees the Commission consults prior to drafting legislation, many documents forwarded to national parliaments already represent a compromise that governments may want collectively to defend against individual attempts at parliamentary scrutiny. A representative of the Irish Dail to COSAC has complained that texts often have an air of having already 'been passed by governments' before they are forwarded to their national parliaments (COSAC, 2001a, p. 33).

National parliaments have responded by attempting to penetrate more deeply into the agenda-setting stage of Union decision-making.

Since 1999 the Danish Folketing has held public hearings on Green and White Papers which are increasingly used by the Commission for consultation and then drafted resolutions, on the strength of the hearings, for forwarding to the Commission (Folketinget, 2002, p. 10). The Finnish Parliament has sought to participate in the preparation of decisions before they reach full meetings of Ministers by requiring its reports be taken into consideration by national officials attending Council working groups or COREPER.[46] Above all, growing awareness that the Commission develops much of its programme in response to the political leadership of the European Council offers opportunities to national parliaments which are prepared to extend their scrutiny to how their Prime Ministers or Presidents contribute to Union decision-making.

However, these innovations cannot solve the converse problem that the EU's complex multi-stage decision-making may drift substantially from options on which national parliaments have had an opportunity to express opinions. In spite of a reputation for slowness, Union legislation can sometimes move too quickly for effective intervention by national parliaments. When asked what was the single greatest constraint on effective national parliamentary supervision, one respondent to this survey replied 'time':

> Changes may be made to a draft at COREPER just one day before it comes up for decision on the Council itself. Neither we nor even the civil servants will have had a chance to read the text and reflect on its full implications. Ministers who come to the EAC will often say that even they are in the dark. For example, the text on the arrest warrant which went for decision at the 20 December meeting was only available in French beforehand, and the last minute compromise it contained was everything.[47]

Growing use of informal trialogues – small group meetings between the Presidency, the Commission official responsible for the legislation, and the EP rapporteur – to thrash out compromises can mean that closure in EU law-making comes quickly, not least because of resource limits on how many texts the Council and EP can allow to go the full round of second stage amendments and conciliation committees.

It may only be possible to overcome this problem by giving national parliaments rights of participation towards the end of the legislative cycle, and not just in between the publication of a Commission draft and the agreement of a Common Position of the Council. One Member of the Convention has suggested that a certain number of national parliaments should have the right to table 'reasoned amendments' that would have to be considered in a Conciliation Committee of the EP and the Council (European Convention, 2002d).

Conclusion to section on national parliaments

A commonly expressed view is that European integration has been responsible for the second of a two-stage process of parliamentary abasement: first, executives rose to prominence within domestic political systems and came, in many cases, to control, rather than be controlled by, their legislatures; second, executives started to act together in the European arena, making national parliamentary control still more elusive. Not only is it inherently difficult for national parliaments to monitor the behaviour of their governments in a distant political system where they have no permanent presence or means of observing the Council in action. Moreover the EU's segmental polity has powerfully reinforced the hollowing out of the democratic state. The vertical model of accountability of political leaderships collectively responsible for all executive actions to parliaments and publics on which so many European political systems have traditionally been based is challenged within the state but also beyond it in so far as participation in the EU means a 'peeling away' from the disciplines of collective responsibility as individual government ministers, officials and departments become involved in Sectoral Councils of Ministers, Council working groups and dense forms of co-operation between counterpart agencies of Member States (Dehousse, 1997).

A very different assessment is that innovations by national parliaments in response to European integration have been one of the few counter-trends to a general weakening of legislatures relative to executives. Not only has the need for governments to secure ratification of a seemingly iterative flow of Treaty changes provided parliaments with leverage to extract new powers of pre-legislative scrutiny, those concessions have in some instances spilled back to domestic legislative practice (Hix and Raunio, 2000). This more benign interpretation does not, however, imply present arrangements are optimal. Criticisms that the EU's political system could be better configured to allow for national parliamentary influence are implicit in suggestions for change submitted to the Convention. Apart from the key demand that the Council should meet in public, five others are worth highlighting.

1. Proposals for their structured participation in discussion of the Commission's annual programme imply national parliaments could

be given earlier and more systematic influence over the Union's policy agenda (European Convention, 2002d; Stuart *et al.*, 2003).

2. Proposals to involve national parliamentarians in key appointments – maybe of the President of the Commission – imply that democratic authorisation of the Union's political leadership should include representatives of national parties of opposition and not be monopolised by governments.
3. Proposals that national parliaments should be able to issue early warnings or even ex-post challenges on questions of subsidiarity (European Convention, 2002a) imply that governments should not be alone in policing boundaries between the national and Union levels of governance, since they are themselves amongst the principal beneficiaries of transfers of power to the European arena.
4. Suggestions that more 'framework' legislation should be adopted at Union level imply that excessive use is currently made of Regulations rather than Directives. Indeed, the Commission's annual reports on Law-making (European Commission, 1999a) show the ratio of the first to the second is around 10 : 1. Directives do not entirely pre-empt the legislative role of national parliaments, which are able to participate in the choice of means by which an agreed objective are to be achieved. Greater reliance on Framework legislation would not so much involve a shift in legislative powers from the Council of Ministers and the European Parliament to national parliaments as from Comitology Committees to domestic legislatures.
5. Proposals for minimum standards set out in a Charter of national parliamentary rights have been made along the lines of the following statement from the President of the Spanish Cortes:

> the national parliament–Government relationship should be subject to certain minimum rules guaranteeing the possibility of parliamentary intervention in the decision-making of the Council. These should guarantee that national parliaments can control governments during the period of a legislative proposal. The code of conduct should have ECJ judicial protection. (COSAC, 2002)

Given that democracy is 'rule by others', a case can even be made that minimum standards are not just needed by those who might otherwise be poorly represented through national parliaments, but by those whose national parliaments already have significant powers on Union issues. Governments that are inadequately accountable to their own national parliaments are, after all, able to participate in the making of law binding on all Member publics. Here, however, we come up against a central tension in the national parliamentary route to the democratisation of the Union. Minimum enforceable standards may not always be easy to reconcile with the mantra that it is for each Member State to define the role of its parliament(s) on EU issues. Democratisation of the Union through the EP might paradoxically be the best means of securing the diversity and autonomy of national parliaments. It avoids the issue of whether the latter should be subject to minimum standards if they are to contribute to the quality of a shared rule extending to societies other than their own.

Indeed, it is important to acknowledge a number of other institutional and normative limitations to attempts to democratise the Union through its national parliaments.

- As long as national parliaments have different powers and capabilities, reliance on them to the exclusion of a role for the EP in key policies risks political inequality: how well citizens are represented on Union issues will depend on where they live.
- Except where they develop networks of inter-parliamentary communication, national parliaments are not the most obvious fora for deliberation at the level of the Union's political system itself. Indeed, Burke's famous question to the electors of Bristol might be asked of national parliaments with mandating powers on Union issues: 'What sort of reason is it in which the determination precedes the discussion, in which one set of men deliberate and another decide, and where those who form the conclusion are perhaps three hundred miles distant from those who hear the arguments?' (Burke (1975) [1774], p. 175).
- National Parliaments share neither the EP's permanent focus on the European arena nor its organisation for the acquisition of the skills needed to monitor a highly complex political system (though some are remarkably successful in turning a minority of their members into specialists on Union issues). This matters since asymmetries of information are a principal means by which modern executives get to dominate legislatures (Krehbiel, 1991). As one participant in this survey who self-consciously described herself as an MEP from a new Member State described the EU: 'It is an institutional system that you really do need to experience directly if you are to understand it. I have often found that those who visit for even 2–3 days have a grasp that is not shared by others.'[48] Indeed, there may even be an opportunity cost to national parliaments in monitoring the EU: time spent scrutinising Union law-making may be time that cannot be given to domestic scrutiny.

- No national parliament can exercise collective control over the Council. The EP rightly observes 'neither the Council nor the European Council can incur ultimate political censure, since no vote of confidence is possible either in national parliaments or the European Parliament' (European Parliament, 1997, p. 5). Yet, there is a crucial difference between the EP and national parliaments. The first, as we will see, arguably has some important powers to check and balance the Council in everyday policy-making and, whatever controlling powers this confers, it is exercised over the Council as a collective decision-making body. Since, in contrast, national parliaments only control individual governments, they are constrained by *faits accomplis* emerging from bargaining relationships and decision-rules of which they can influence but a part.

Checks and balances? The European Parliament and the Council

If there are limits to how far the Council can be made accountable through the relationship of its individual members to their national parliaments, does the Union compensate for these in arrangements for the Council to be accountable as a body to the EP? According to one perspective, the Council has to be more assiduous than it used to be in cultivating its contacts with the EP.

> [Recent changes] have led to an explosion in contacts between Parliament and Council at all levels. Working group chairs are now regular visitors to MEPs' offices as well as to committee meetings. Similarly, the Permanent Representatives and their Deputies from Coreper are figures that have emerged from the shadows and become familiar interlocutors. Indeed such is the level of contact with the Council that the Commission often feels that the Parliament prefers to deal directly with the Council and to make deals at its expense. They are not always wrong. (Corbett *et al.*, 2003, p. 364)

Yet, responses to this survey indicate MEPs are much less confident of their public control of the Council than the Commission. As shown in Table 6.3, MEPs on average rate their capacity to influence the Council at 3.23 on a scale of 0–10. MEPs find the Council less transparent than the Commission and better placed to evade responsibility by blaming someone else. When asked to indicate how far non-transparency and blame shifting were obstacles to accountability, MEPs answered 5.4 and 3.71 in the case of the Commission and 8.57 and 6.47 in that of the Council (all figures on a scale of 0–10). MEPs also feel individual Council Members see themselves as primarily responsible to their national parliaments, while Council Presidencies vary in their willingness to explain decisions to the EP. Given that MEPs are less confident of their powers to control the Council than the Commission, many are understandably nervous that legislative and executive powers may be drifting from the second to the first. But how justified is the pessimism of MEPs about their powers to control the Council? The following paragraphs investigate.

As seen, several of the EP's powers of scrutiny cover the operations of the Council and not just of the Commission. For example, its right to appoint special committees of enquiry that can investigate a range of institutions may be one of the few means of achieving public control in a political system of 'many hands'. Yet, the EP sees its scrutiny as structurally compromised by lack of Council transparency. What it would consider an adequate level of transparency is implicit in its calls for reform of the Council. It continues to press for a verbatim record of Council decisions to be published; for explanations of votes; and for the Council to meet in public wherever it acts in a budgetary or legislative capacity, even for it to be split into an executive and a legislative Council, in order to achieve a completely transparent demarcation between its functions (European Parliament, 2000a). Indeed, the Parliament has even accused Council Members of employing 'secret declarations' that affect the 'interpretation of otherwise publicly available texts' (European Parliament, 1997, pp. 13–14).

The capacity of the EP to check and balance the Council in the everyday operation of the EU's policy process is at its strongest in relation to pillar one decisions that require legislation using Co-decision. Given that the Commission frequently exercises its legislative initiative in response to what member governments perceive to be a need for Union-level lawmaking, it is by no means far-fetched to interpret Co-decision as conferring a power on the EP to deny the Council its legislation in a polity whose main business is rule-making. Council Members may accept significant EP amendments rather than 'return to go' in a lengthy legislative process that may have depended on unique windows of opportunity in domestic politics or on a complex 'log-roll' between themselves.

Yet, academics disagree in their analysis of how the EU's legislative process empowers the EP (Crombez *et al.*, 2000; Tsebelis and Garrett, 2000). All would probably agree with a study commissioned for the EP that 'full legislative power' requires a capacity 'to structure the agenda' at every stage of the process and not a mere '*pouvoir d'empêchement*' (European Parliament [Maurer], 1999a). However, one side of the debate argues that the Co-operation and Co-decision procedures directly confer 'agenda-setting' powers on the EP by allowing it to propose amendments that are 'procedurally easier for the Council to accept than reject' (Tsebelis, 1994). Others, in contrast, view any increase in the EP's ability to shape the EU's legislative agenda as the indirect consequence of veto powers conferred by the Co-operation and Co-decision procedures (Crombez, 1996).

Either way, two conclusions seem certain. The EP's power of amendment work by substituting a new winning coalition on the Council for that which prevailed when Member States first formed their common position (Tsebelis, 1994). Second, the EP's legislative powers amount to a form of 'bounded choice'. It can change outcomes but only within limits determined by the distribution of preferences within the other two institutions (Commission and the Council) and by the Union's decision rules (Kreppel, 2000). The Commission acts as the key gatekeeper. Only if it accepts the EP's amendments is it procedurally easier for the Council to accept than reject them. And there comes a point where either Commission or Council would prefer to risk a parliamentary veto than accept a Parliamentary amendment. Such a balance between Council and Parliament with their different claims to being representative bodies is precisely what would be expected of a standard of concurrent consent. But how does the balance work in practice? Attempts to measure it are problematic, yet instructive (See also Judge and Earnshaw, 2003, pp. 246–54). The following are the main alternatives:

The proportion of Treaty articles that allow the EP different degrees of legislative participation. Adapting an approach developed by Andreas Maurer (2003b), Table 7.3 classifies Treaty articles that allow powers to be exercised without the EP as 'parliamentary exclusion'; those which allow only for the EP to be consulted or informed as 'weak parliamentary inclusion'; and those which require its assent, Co-decision or Co-operation procedures as 'strong parliamentary inclusion'. Table 7.3 graphically illustrates the near complete exclusion of the EP from CFSP and JHA procedures (coming under the EU Treaties) but suggests, at first sight, that even pillar one remains only 'semi-parliamentary'. Yet, this measure needs to be read with care. First, it does not allow for variations in the frequency with which particular articles are used to in practice to introduce legislation. Thus Maurer calculates that between 1993 and 1997 Co-decision was used for 'nearly a quarter of legislation considered by

Table 7.3 Legislative inclusion/exclusion of the EP under Amsterdam

	Percentage of EC Treaty articles	*Percentage of EU Treaty articles*
EP's legislative status		
Stong inclusion (Assent + Co-operation + Co-decision)	28	6
Weak Inclusion (Consultation)	36	24
Exclusion	37	69

Source: Maurer, 2003b.

the Parliament' even though it was included in only 9.25 per cent of Treaty provisions (European Parliament [Maurer], 1999a). Second, a simple totting up of the frequency with which each procedure is mentioned in the Treaty says nothing about the relative importance of matters on which the EP is included or excluded from legislation. Under the first pillar, for example, the legislative exclusion of the EP is largely concentrated on just three policies: Agriculture, Fisheries and Customs policies (Maurer, 2003b, p. 234).

According to EP figures for the first two years (1999–2001) of Co-decision as defined by the Amsterdam Treaty, 23 per cent of measures were settled straightaway on first reading either because the Parliament proposed few changes or because the Commission and Council accepted most of the amendments it did make. At second reading, the Parliament then tabled a total of 569 amendments over the two years of which 21 per cent were accepted unchanged and 60 per cent settled on an EP/Council compromise (Judge and Earnshaw, 2003, pp. 250–1). These figures, however, make no allowance for varying degrees of importance between the amendments or for different 'degrees of acceptance' (Tsebelis and Kalandrakis, 2002, p. 186). Nor do they allow for cases where MEPs use their powers strategically to propose amendments that will fail in the short term but shape further Commission initiatives in the long (ibid., p. 204). Attempts have been made to fill these *lacunae*. Empirical evidence collected by Tsebelis and Kalandrakis suggests important and unimportant amendments seem equally likely to get through. Maurer's (2003b) work undercuts the further possibility that EP and Council always start off from close positions that makes agreement of parliamentary amendments deceptively easy. Whilst it is true that thirteen times as many measures introduced under Co-decision between 1993 and 2002 failed because of disagreement on the Council than on account of disagreement between the Council and the EP, 112 of the 348 Co-decisions concluded during that period 'went to the wire' in the sense of requiring a Conciliation committee to settle outstanding disagreements between the Council and EP.

Not only do the Council and Parliament seem to be part of a mixed-motive game of co-operation and conflict, the legislative process is increasingly organised for the early identification of which of the two tracks any measure is likely to follow. 'Trialogues' between the EP rapporteur, the Presidency of the Council and the Commission DG which framed the proposal now shadow it over the legislative cycle. Such 'legislative planning' is, however, open to a number of criticisms: first, that it prioritises speed and performance at the cost of scrutiny, reflection and amendment; second, that it encourages delegation to individuals on a scale that pre-empts the wider representative process in both Parliament and Council; and, third, that it substitutes inter-institutional collusion for mutual surveillance in the legislative process.

If one means by which the EP can check and balance the Council in the EU policy-process is through the exercise of legislative powers, another is through its financial powers. The annual budget begins with a proposal from the Commission, which the Council amends and sends to the Parliament. At the end of the day the EP can reject the budget outright. Most of its efforts, though, go into pressing for detailed changes according to procedures that differ for compulsory and non-compulsory expenditure. It has the final say on any amendments to the second. The Council has the final say on any changes to the first.

On closer examination, however, the EP's budgetary powers are constrained. They relate only to annual budgets that must, in turn, respect a five-year 'financial perspective' on which the Parliament is merely consulted prior to a decision by the Council. Together with other constraints, this has the following implications:

- The EP has no powers over the revenue component of the budget.
- The EP's powers of amendment are only procedurally strong in relation to the 54 per cent of the budget that goes on non-compulsory expenditure.
- Even then, the EP is only able to vary the non-compulsory expenditure up to a 'maximum rate of increase' which, for example, was just 3.2 per cent in 2001.
- The EP has to keep to no fewer than seven further ceilings, since the financial perspective also specifies maxima for each of the 'headings' into which the budget is divided (Laffan, 1997).

In recent years, the last factor has been a special cause of frustration to the Parliament. Although the overall Union budget has been in substantial surplus, the EP has had almost no room for manoeuvre, since the priorities for which it has sought extra resources – the reconstruction of the Balkans, various internal policies and administrative reform of the Commission – all fall under budgetary headings that are already up against their ceilings (Carlos Costa Neves MEP, Debates of the European Parliament, 11 December 2001). In each of the three budgets between 1999 and 2001 the European Parliament had to agree to raid the 'flexibility reserve' to achieve its objectives (European Parliament, 2001i), although it was itself a critic of that mechanism at the time of the inter-institutional agreement on the budget in 1999 (Terry Wynn MEP, Debates of the European Parliament, 11 December 2001).

EP amendments typically only increase the overall budget by around €1m or one per cent of the total. Since this roughly corresponds to what the Council normally shaves off the Commission's proposal in the first place, some MEPs have suggested that the budget process approaches an empty ritual: 'the Commission presents a proposal, the Council takes a slice off the proposed amount, the EP adds a bit more in, and we are supposed to come up with something wonderful in conciliation' (Kathalijne Buitenweg MEP, Debates of the European Parliament, 11 December 2001). The difficulty, as this quotation partially suggests, is that the Council may be able to use the advantage of moving before the EP in the budgetary procedure to anticipate the latter to the point at which the Parliament's impact amounts to little more than restoring cuts made in expectation of its own amendments.

However, the main obstacle to the EP operating as a check and balance on the Council may lie less in the configuration of its legislative or even financial powers than in shortcomings in their comprehensiveness of coverage and consistency of application. The EU has been portrayed as only 'semi-parliamentary' (Magnette, 1999) on the grounds that wide areas of Council decision-making go unchecked by any mechanism of parliamentary control at Union level. In addition, boundaries between forms or degree of check and balance sometimes appear more arbitrary than principled. The following are possible examples:

1. There are still cases where Council makes decisions by QMV but the EP is only consulted, even though departure from unanimity on the Council (and thus from circumstances most favourable to national parliamentary control) is usually recognised as requiring Co-decision with the EP. As the Finnish Parliament has put it, the 'democratic

deficit becomes most obvious where the Council takes decisions by QMV without the European Parliament being able to prevent the legislation coming into being' (quoted in European Parliament, 1997, p. 12).

2. What the Member States have conceded by allowing the EP to check and balance the Council through the operation of Co-decision they have partially taken back through the operation of comitology: 'Democratic control of legislative activities has improved... monitoring the implementation of this legislation, let alone the whole range of EU non-legislative activities is an even more difficult task' (ibid). Indeed, in the EP's view, comitology raises a number of concerns:
   - Comitology committees – in which the EP does not participate – allow administrators and 'experts' to exercise legislative powers that belong to the Parliament. Thus the EP has accused them of introducing measures that do not 'merely implement' but 'modify and supplement' essential aspects of legislative provisions (European Parliament 1998b, p. 6 and 2003a, p. 7). The difficulty, as the EP sees it, is that 'Increasingly, in an uncertain and complex world, policy is often made "on the hoof", and is characterised by flexibility and re-negotiation – in such a context, the supposed implementation of policy often actually constitutes the development and establishment of policy' (European Parliament, 1998b, p. 19).
   - Although the EP is the directly elected component of the primary legislature, there is no mechanism by which it can challenge comitology decisions as amounting to more than delegated legislation (European Parliament, 2003a, p. 7).
   - Comitology is not covered by the right of MEPs to ask questions of the Council and to receive answers that are in the public domain.
   - Comitology slips through the net of a wide range of mechanisms of parliamentary scrutiny, and not just those of the EP. Arrangements for the publication of Council votes that allow national parliaments to question their own administrations on their contributions to EU decision-making do not extend to any *de facto* legislation by regulatory or management committees. Moreover, whatever the powers of national parliaments over EU law-making, those powers stop at the moment that a measure is approved by the Council. They do not anticipate that significant decisions may be made at a later stage of defining implementing measures.
   - Key to accountability in any arrangement for delegated law-making is that affected actors should be able to alert the primary legislator to problems raised by secondary rules used in implementation. In the EP's view the non-transparency of comitology inhibits the sounding

of 'fire alarms'. It notes that equivalent committees in the US meet in public (European Parliament, 1998b, p. 21), while EU implementing committees do not even, in the EP's view, make sufficient of their documents public (European Parliament, 2003a, p. 8).

3. The EP complains about absence of full budgetary as well as of full legislative Co-decision. It is unclear how real is the difference between compulsory and non-compulsory and why that should justify conferring fewer powers on the EP over the first than the second. Some in the Parliament suspect that the distinction is, in practice, cover for 'cordoning off' the CAP from democratic control (European Parliament, 1997, p. 16). Given, as seen, the CAP is where the EP suffers from a high level of legislative exclusion, it would seem unconscionable that this should also be the main area where it cannot use the budget to request justifications for the main lines of policy development. In addition, the partitioning of the budget so that the largest single element of expenditure is where the EP participates least is hardly consistent with 'unified budgetary control' (ibid., pp. 7 and 16).
4. A number of procedures that do not conform to the 'Community method' have recently been introduced to the first pillar. Amongst them are forms of economic co-ordination related to Monetary Union: the Broad Economic Policy Guidelines (BEPG); mutual surveillance under the Stability and Growth Pact; and the Open Method of Co-ordination. These are clearly important to the allocation of economic and social values. Yet, the EP complains, there is no opportunity for *ex ante* scrutiny in the form of a public parliamentary debate in which the Council is required to justify its decisions before making them. The role of the EP is 'restricted to being informed by the Council of its final recommendations' (European Parliament, 1997, p. 15).
5. Above all, the Council describes a great many second and third pillar instruments as 'legislative acts' including joint actions, yet the EP is excluded from their determination. 'JHA legislation' raises a particular difficulty for the doctrine that only elected bodies should approve measures that could expose individual citizens to criminal sanctions (European Convention, 2002c, p. 4).

A special note on CFSP and JHA

The notion that CFSP and JHA are inadequately controlled at the Union level merits special attention. The Treaty only requires the Council to consult the EP on CFSP and JHA decisions and to report annually on the overall development of the two policies. Moreover, consultation means much less under pillars two and three than under pillar one (Fortescue, 1995, p. 23). Since the ECJ *Isoglucose* ruling does not apply to the second and third pillars, consultation offers the EP neither a power of delay, nor an assured opportunity that the Parliament will be given reasonable time to agree to a full and reasoned opinion. Indeed, the Council seems to decide for itself what form its obligation to consult should take and when it has been satisfied. Thus, the EP complained that the Council 'co-operated inadequately' on the initiative to catalyse the development of JHA by creating an Area of Freedom Security and Justice (AFSJ), that information was 'insufficient and late', and that the Council was then unwilling to take the Parliament's views into account (European Parliament, 2001a). Likewise on CFSP, the EP has complained that the only document on which it is consulted under the Treaties is the annual report setting out general choices. In its view it should be consulted on the preparation of each common strategy.

In addition to questioning the adequacy of parliamentary control at a stage rules and orientations are set, the EP argues that unaccountable forms of executive power are associated with patterns of delegation used to carry out CFSP and JHA. One pattern of delegation has been to set up a series of European-level agencies. In the case of JHA, these include Europol (police co-operation), Eurojust (prosecuting magistrates) and the Schengen Secretariat (Frontier management). Since each has a relatively modest staff seconded from nationally recruited professionals, the agencies are essentially co-ordinating mechanisms. Yet, there are occasions where they exercise significant discretionary powers. The Europol Director, for example, has been authorised by the Council to enter discussions with third countries on behalf of the Union (Official Journal of the European Communities 106, 13 April 2000). Above all, the agencies are key sites for the transposition of JHA orientations into policing on the ground. Eurojust has been authorised to initiate joint investigations and prosecutions in cases of cross-border crime, and to make joint recommendations to Member States on changes to criminal law in each country. Plans to create a joint Police training College – and to exchange 'best practice' – imply norms of policing may in the future be partially defined through collaborative processes at European level, rather than exclusively through agencies that are locally or nationally accountable. Amongst priorities the Council set for the College were 'training sessions for senior national police officers on the basis of common standards' (European Parliament, 2001c).

The EP repeatedly emphasises what it sees as gaps in accountability arising from the creation of CFSP and JHA agencies and office holders outside the Community framework. First, there are no executive figures whose mal-administration can occasion parliamentary censure, as would, for example, be the case if the High Representative for CFSP were a Vice President of the Commission rather than an appointee of the Council. Second, the agencies are not covered by general legislation on administrative standards in Union institutions such as the regulations on the processing of personal data (European Parliament, 2001d) and access to documents. This last is a significant consideration given that the Schengen computer contains the largest single database of personal information in Europe. Third, the exclusion of the ECJ from all of CFSP and much of JHA means that *lacunae* in responsibility to elected bodies are not compensated by judicial accountability or individual rights protections.

Control of CFSP and JHA agencies and office-holders is almost exclusively in the hands of the Council itself. Europol, for example, is given an annual work programme by the Council which also needs to approve its budget. The difficulty, of course, is that the JHA Council, consisting as it does of Internal Security Ministers, may share too many of the professional commitments of the law-enforcement agencies to develop critical perspectives of their work.

Continuing with the example of Europol, the EP's only supervisory right is one of receiving copies of the annual report to the Council. The following reveals the powers of supervision it feels it ought to have:

> In order for the EP to exercise democratic control, Europol must, as with the other European Institutions (e.g. the European Central Bank and the European Ombudsman) report on its activities in an annual exchange of views. In addition, the Director of Europol should appear before Parliament's competent committees when circumstances so require. Finally, the EP should have a say in the choice of the Director of Europol. (European Parliament, 2000b)

The Convention has likewise wrestled with problems of public control raised by Europol and Eurojust. Amongst options for improvement it has discussed are that the JHA agencies should be accountable to a special parliamentary committee (possibly a joint committee of the EP and national parliaments); or that there should be a High Representative for third pillar matters who can be accountable to the member governments as a group and be available to deal with the scrutiny requests of national and European parliamentarians (European Convention, 2002c, p. 5).

Another pattern of delegation used by both CFSP and JHA is one in which Member States effectively entrust tasks to one another.

For example, CFSP Joint Actions often involve the specification of individual national contributions. Likewise JHA increasingly envisages that law enforcement agencies accountable in one Member State may take actions that affect citizens of others. Mutual recognition of criminal judgements is being developed as a substitute for extradition procedures, and a Common Arrest Warrant has been agreed. Yet, the potential exposure of all Union citizens to standards of internal security and rights protection emanating from one Member State raises serious questions about leaving these to mutual recognition rather than common deliberation and standards.

To set against these concerns the EP has expressed at its exclusion from CFSP and JHA, are instances where inter-pillar linkages allow it indirect means of exercising some control. Several CFSP actions are funded out of the Commission's budget. Moreover, these are non-compulsory expenditures for which the EP is the budgetary authority. Less noticed in the literature is that the EP can likewise use its legislative powers to gain a measure of control. CFSP and JHA sometimes require the introduction of pillar one measures covered by Co-decision. A case study is the Money Laundering Directive which allowed the EP to press amendments on civic rights to confidentiality, on equal treatment of affected professions, and on what it considered the excessive discretion the original text allowed Member States in targeting links between money laundering and organised crime. The result was that the measure which had been predicted to pass at first reading went to two (European Parliament, 2001b).

Of particular importance is that the assent procedure allows the EP a measure of indirect control over CFSP. The Treaties provide that the EP has to give its assent to the admission of new states to the EU (Article 49) and to certain kinds of international agreement (Article 300). How easily this translates into European Parliamentary control of the Union's international dealings depends on a combination of factors, as follows:

- The Assent Procedure is a take it or leave it vote. The justification for this is straightforward: the EP's powers of assent are supposed to be analogous to those of parliaments within states to ratify international treaties. They can only vote on what has been agreed by third party states and international organisations. But it does mean that the EP cannot propose amendments of its own. If it is to have any 'agenda-setting powers' to structure the choice it is asked to approve, it has to be consulted during the negotiation of Treaties. To some measure the Council would seem to have recognised that its own interest in avoiding parliamentary rejections of international agreements are best served through briefing EP committees during the course of negotiations (Corbett *et al.*, 1995, pp. 214–15).

- An absolute majority of the EP's membership (and not just of those voting) is needed to give assent to the accession of new states to the Union. Only a simple majority is needed for it to assent to the various kinds of international agreement listed in Article 300. This mean that accession Treaties have to pass a more demanding hurdle of parliamentary approval. A possible justification for the difference in voting thresholds is that an accession Assent amounts to an agreement to terminate a foreign policy relationship and admit a state to the EU's own internal system of shared rule. In contrast, international agreements short of accession frequently need revision and renewal. This gives the EP repeat opportunities to use its powers of Assent (Corbett *et al.*, 1995), so softening the impact of the rule that it has no powers of amendment in relation to any one use of the Procedure.

Putting these elements together, the name of the game for MEPs seeking a measure of foreign policy influence is to make sure that the Union's dealings with outsiders are 'within the shadow of any veto' that the Parliament could one day exercise on attempts to formalise those relationships into a Treaty. Up to a point, the Council has scope to call the Parliament's bluff knowing that it would not lightly veto a Treaty that it itself values. On the other hand, there are some questions on which a threat of a parliamentary veto carries special credibility, notably human rights and democracy in third countries. Also worth mentioning is that the EP has developed signalling techniques that allow the Commission and Council to adjust third country relationships to future threats of failed assent procedures on an almost continuous basis. Apart from procedures for consulting the EP during the negotiation of Treaties that require assents, the Parliament regularly drafts reports on third states with whom it knows it is likely to be asked to assent to new or changed Treaties in the future. The appraisals reached, the amendments tabled, and the size and composition of majorities for and against those amendments in both committee and plenary, are all clues to how the Parliament could decide an assent vote.

However, indirect budgetary and legislative influence hardly amounts to systematic parliamentary control of CFSP and JHA. Indeed, inter-pillar spillovers may have the converse effect that the EP loses some of its controlling powers over pillar one on account of its weak hold over CFSP and JHA. Thus the Parliament has been anxious that plans for a

European Security and Defence Policy (ESDP) should be given an adequate parliamentary base. Given that it is intended ESDP should be used for crisis management and have access to the 'entire spectrum of civilian and military instruments' available to the Union (European Parliament, 2000c) *ex ante* scrutiny of military planning may be the last practical opportunity for elected representatives to scrutinise an initiative whose implications for other Union policies could unfold quickly in an emergency.

A further problem is that by making it hard to know what has been decided where and by whom the institutional complexity of CFSP and JHA raises the cost of monitoring by representative bodies and complicates the 'consistent operationalisation of control mechanisms' (Den Boer, 2001). Take the example of Schengen. As Andrew Duff puts it, Amsterdam 'glues' different parts of the original Schengen agreement on to 'the first and third pillars' (Duff, 1997, p. 53). It then allows the Council to decide on a case-by-case basis whether measures to implement the pre-Amsterdam Schengen acquis are to be treated as having a legal basis under pillar one or pillar three. On top of this, there are variable patterns of country participation in the EU's internal security policies. Title IV measures (on external borders, immigration and visas) are not binding on Denmark, Ireland or the UK. The UK and Ireland are outside Schengen. Although Denmark is inside Schengen, it is not obliged to adopt any implementing measures that use Title IV. All three countries are, however, able to opt in to measures to which they are not formally committed, though at different points in the policy process, and according to different decision rules and different distributions of institutional rights between full and *ad hoc* participants.

Justifications have, of course, been offered for existing arrangements for the accountability of CFSP and JHA. The following are amongst them:

1. CFSP and JHA cover policies in which the public interest requires secrecy. More meaningful perhaps than attempting to assess whether these policies strike an optimal trade-off between secrecy and accountability is to note that the trade-off itself is made problematic by any partial transition from national to cross-national policy frameworks. Countries that have combined secrecy with political responsibility in the management of internal and external security services have done so through intangibles of political culture (trust and a powerful internalisation of agreed norms that actors enforce on themselves). One concern is that it is only with time that these

conditions are likely to be reproduced at European level, and that, in the absence of more institutionalised scrutiny of CFSP and JHA, new forms of unaccountable power will develop in the meantime.

2. An argument sometimes used for high levels of executive independence in the case of foreign policy is that a policy that is external in its impact does not have the same implications as domestic policy for internal allocations of value. To this it can be objected that the designation of democracy and human rights as objectives for the CFSP is very much rooted in the internal values of EU societies. Aspects of foreign policy based on democracy and rights protection, arguably, belong as firmly in the representative branch of government as those requiring speed and secrecy belong to the executive. What it is to promote democracy and human rights is, after all, a matter of value, interpretation and deliberation. The credibility of such a policy is exposed to the charge that it is itself defined by inadequately democratic institutions.

Conclusion to chapters on accountability

Joe Weiler has remarked that 'critically there is no real sense in which the European political process allows the electorate to "throw the scoundrels out", to take what is often the only ultimate power left to the people which is to replace one set of governors by another' (1997b, p. 275). Such an approach to accountability is precluded by the whole nature of the EU as a dispersed system of power that often requires high levels of consensus between the elements. Many decisions are so inclusive of diverse actors (the Commission, the member governments, large majorities of the European Parliament, and even policy networks of more or less organised interests) that it is hard to attribute overall responsibility to any one body. Even if *per impossible* all those who had taken part in EU decisions over a number of years were to be removed from office at various levels and branches of government, the EU's consensus system would almost certainly require the appointment of 'replacement scoundrels' that resembled outgoing ones.

So what can be done? First, the EU can rely on input accountability where output accountability is hard to achieve: the difficulty of holding actors responsible for the consequences of policies that none can control on their own, does not preclude expecting each to account for how far their individual contributions conform to agreed norms. Second, the EU can mix and match horizontal and vertical modes of accountability: the difficulty in a non-majoritarian system of bringing all office-holders to account before a single electorate or body of representatives (vertical accountability) does not preclude different bodies of representative requiring accounts of one another before mixing their policy instruments to achieve objectives that none can deliver on their own in a divided system of government (horizontal accountability). Moreover, vertical accountability remains feasible for individual elements of the EU's political system – national governments to national parliaments and electorates, the Commission to the Parliament, and MEPs to their voters – provided it is only input and not output accountability that is expected. The foregoing points are thus intimately related. Bearing in mind this discussion of what is feasible in relation to EU institutions, the following paragraphs summarise what this chapter and the last imply for the Democratic Audit tests of accountability.

How far are those who hold office or make decisions in Union institutions accountable to representatives of national democracies who are, in turn, responsible to their national publics and parliaments (EUDA Test 5)? Most important decisions of the Union are, in any case, made by national governments that are elected representatives of national democracies. However, these vary greatly in how far they are, in turn, accountable to national parliaments, and few find that Union issues greatly affect their chances of re-election. Amongst those who hold office in Union institutions themselves, Commissioners are formally independent of national governments, though, in practice, they are closely scrutinised by them and heavily dependent on them for legislative approvals and policy delivery.

How far are those who hold office or make decisions in EU institutions accountable to elected representatives of citizens at Union level (EUDA Test 11)? The Commission as a whole can be dismissed by the European Parliament. MEPs use a variety of procedures to extract accounts from individual Commissioners and officials, who, in turn, have strong incentives to maintain a relationship of confidence with the Parliament. Co-decision allows the EP to check and balance the Council in some areas of law-making. However, there are many policies where the EP has few powers without it being obvious that national parliaments can compensate for absence of parliamentary scrutiny or control at Union level. Moreover, it is unclear how far MEP are themselves accountable for whatever controlling powers they exercise, given that their chances of re-election seem to depend less on their own performance than on the domestic political cycle (see Chapter 5).

8
Constitutionalism, Democracy and the European Union

Introduction

A key problem of democratic politics is that there may be grounds for placing limits on what are considered to be the normal democratic decision-rules of a political system. There are obvious reasons for wanting to define such grounds restrictively. Yet the problem cannot be avoided altogether for the simple reason that some values that are not explicitly democratic – the rule of law, rights and the protection of minorities – may need to be constitutionally guaranteed as a precondition for democracy itself (Dworkin, 1996; Habermas, 1996, pp. 84–104). Thus, as Yves Mény (2002, p. 4) puts it, 'an ideal democracy ... is neither a purely popular democracy nor a purely constitutionalist one, but rather a system able to realise a satisfactory equilibrium between them two'. In addition, certain public welfare decisions are not easily made incentive compatible with the pursuit of elected office. Even a suspicion that policies needing long-term commitment may not be honoured tomorrow may be enough to sap their credibility and effectiveness today. Such objectives may suffer from 'time-inconsistency' problems unless entrusted to those whose behaviour is unaffected by electoral cycles (Majone, 2001, p. 106).

All of this has a special relevance to the EU. Its multinational character, its size and remoteness as a political system mean there are particularly strong reasons for believing that democratic decision rules are only likely to be acceptable at the Union level if key values and rights are guaranteed against majoritarian forms of popular sovereignty (Katz, 2001). Indeed, the argument has been made that the constitutionalist elements of democracy are already more developed in the EU's political system than the populist ones. To cite Mény again: 'the European system ... is the most sophisticated machinery ever invented of constitutionalist democracy, but is still underdeveloped when it comes to its popular element' (2002, p. 6). The aim of this chapter is to test Mény's claim.

What, however, is a constitutionalist democracy? If we take 'constitutionalism' on its own to be the guarantee of particular rights or values by a political system, it is plain from what has already been said that a 'constitutionalist democracy' requires neither the rights nor the values nor the guarantees to be especially democratic. Rather, there are two approaches to constitutionalisation that can meaningfully be termed democratic. One is where the guarantee of a value is delegated to an independent non-democratic body by democratic means and can always be recalled by such, albeit under restrictive conditions such as super-majoritarian decision rules. A second is where a political system does not so much guarantee a value by delegating its delivery to one institution but does so by dividing powers between mutually constraining institutions at least some components of which are democratic. This distinction suggests that an assessment of constitutionalist democracy in the EU needs to include the European Central Bank (ECB), the European Court of Justice (ECJ) and the overall separation of powers in the Union's political system. The chapter examines each of these in turn, before appraising the Union against the following tests.

How far does the EU constitutionalise modified consociationalism or use its methods to constitutionalise other values (*EUDA Test 6*)?

How far does the EU constitutionalise concurrent consent or use its methods to constitutionalise other values (*EUDA Test 12*)?

The European Central Bank

The EU constitutionalises the delivery of its monetary policy by using its Treaties to delegate powers to an independent central bank. Since the Treaties can only be changed by an agreement of all Member States ratified by the parliaments or publics of each, ECB independence is constitutionally well entrenched. This arrangement has been defended as a safeguard to values that range from the neutrality of the democratic process, to individual property rights to forms of economic welfare that would otherwise be hard to achieve.

The ECB's decision-making body is its Governing Council. This consists of a permanent Executive of six central bankers (the ECB President, Vice President and four others) and a representative of each National Central Bank of states that are full members of Monetary Union (currently 12). All 18 Members of the General Council have one vote each. Although the Treaty allows them to take decisions by simple majority, in practice the General Council attempts to decide by consensus or at least without explicit resort to voting. The Executive members are appointed by 'common accord' of the European Council for a single term of eight years. They can neither be dismissed (except on application to the ECJ on the grounds of incapacity) nor re-appointed for a further term. Although there is some variation in how Member States appoint the national central bankers who participate in ECB decisions, all are subject to minimum conditions designed to ensure central bank independence. The Bank is self-financing through its open market procedures. It is also autonomous in its staffing and in its internal procedures. It is not, therefore, dependent on a political authority for regular authorisation of budgets, staffing levels or changes to rules of procedure.

Indeed, the ECB enjoys a remarkably high degree of independence in comparison with other central banks (European Parliament, 1998c). Jakob de Haan and Sylvester Eijffinger (2000, p. 396) use four indices to conclude that the ECB is the most independent monetary authority in the G7 area (in comparison, in other words, with Canada, Japan, the US and the UK). In addition, the ECB comes closer than most to enjoying monopoly control of monetary policy. The Treaty insulates it from actions of other public bodies that may in practice dilute a central bank's control of total money in circulation. It cannot be required to lend to Member States and only with great difficulty can it be obliged to follow external exchange rate targets.

In contrast to a supposition in some parts of the literature that there is an independence-accountability trade-off, arguments for independent central banking only preclude some but not all approaches to democratic politics. To see why it is important to identify what political values those arguments imply are promoted by putting monetary policy (to set the price of money and the supply) beyond normal arrangements for public control.

One suggestion is that independent central banking may facilitate the neutral operation of the democratic process itself. Empirical evidence (from across the OECD area) that governments in the past stimulated their economies prior to elections only to deflate them once safely returned to power (Nordhaus, 1975) suggests independent central banking may even improve the quality of public control by limiting scope for politicians to manipulate the conditions of their own re-election. A second value that may be served is the protection of minority entitlements. Where a majority owe debt or stand to gain from the reduction of interest payments that will have to be met out of future taxation, democratic politics may be a poor constraint on the use of 'surprise inflation' to erode the savings of a minority (Hibbs, 1977).

However, perhaps the main value claimed for independent central banking is improved economic and social welfare. The key argument here is the 'sound money paradigm' which postulates unemployment can only be reduced below its equilibrium for short periods (estimated at less than two years), needed for the correction of random errors (Lucas, 1981), for the separation of 'money illusion' from the effects of real economic change, or the adjustment of 'sticky' prices and wages. Otherwise, such attempts only embed a higher level of inflation in the system as the baseline for future rounds of price and wage fixing.

On the one hand, the 'sound money paradigm' seemed to underline just how far discretionary monetary policy allowed governments to cheat on voters through short-term conjuring tricks timed to coincide with elections. But it also implied that even honest governments would be unable to pursue optimal economic policies. Price and wage fixers would know that, however well-intentioned governments were now, they would have some incentive in the future to abandon their commitments to non-inflationary growth. That risk would then be priced into their calculations in a way that would make it impossible for governments to achieve a long-run optimum of non-inflationary growth even if they were sincere about pursuing it. Time-inconsistency problems would thus be intrinsic to monetary policy in democratic systems (Kydland and Prescott, 1977) without commitment technologies that reduced the probability of its abuse to zero (Barro and Gordon, 1983).

Implicit in all the above arguments is that any justification for independent central banking needs ultimately to be cashed out in terms of public welfare. Indeed, those who took office as the first Executive Council of the ECB went further in hearings before the European Parliament (EP). Without exception, they argued their powers could only be justified if interpreted as a delegation from the public (European Parliament, 1998c; see also European Central Bank, 2001, p. 55).

The foregoing points clarify why independent central banking presupposes certain approaches to public control at the same time as it excludes others:

1. If independent central bankers only have publicly delegated powers, the public or its representatives must have some means of revising or recalling that agency. This, in turn, presupposes they should have some continuous flow of 'accounts' for how that agency is used on the basis of which they can form informed views of whether it merits revision or recall.
2. If one aim of independent central banking is to 'safeguard against opportunistic behaviour by elected politicians' (Buiter, 1999, p. 187)

mechanisms of public control are needed to ensure that Central Bankers do not behave in the same way. These might plausibly take the form of requirements that Central Bankers should have to announce their decision-rules in advance and defend them as means of achieving public policy goals, rather than personal preferences.

3. If they are to be justifiable on the grounds that (in the long run) they improve the welfare for all, independent Central Banks should be required to demonstrate pareto improvement: that overall society is better off for having an independent central bank whose behaviour is ultimately neutral between groups and values in society.
4. If the momentous decision to put a key area of policy-making beyond normal democratic decision-rules is to be justified on account of the exceptional characteristics of monetary policy, it will be necessary to establish a system of control that limits independent central banking to the management of that area of policy. If the last point emphasises the need to ensure a central bank does not fall beneath the standards of its mandate, this point stresses the importance of it not straying beyond its mandate either.
5. Yet, if the aim is to prevent majorities using monetary policy for electoral or partisan advantage, each of the foregoing objectives will have to be achieved by forms of public control over a central bank that cannot be exercised from any one point on the political spectrum (Majone, 1996).

What scope is there to achieve these accountability objectives within the EU's monetary constitution? Taking the European Council, Council of Ministers and European Parliament to be the Union institutions that are indirectly or directly representative of the public, the following Treaty provisions are relevant to ECB accountability. The President, Vice President and other members of the Executive Board are, as seen, appointed by the European Council on a rolling-basis, and the EP is consulted on each appointment. The President of the Council may participate in meetings of the General Council and submit motions for it to deliberate (European Commission, 1992, A. 109b). The ECB has to submit an annual report to the European Council, Council of Ministers and EP. The President of the ECB must present the report in person to the Council and Parliament, and the latter may debate the Bank's performance in plenary session. At any other time, the EP can request the ECB to attend a public hearing before the 'relevant committee of the Parliament' (EMAC). In sum, the Treaty provisions on the ECB essentially anticipate what Majone calls accountability by reason-giving (1996).

One approach to assessing whether these arrangements are adequate has been to develop quantifiable indices of accountability and then compare the ECB with its 'peer group' of independent central banks in other liberal-democratic systems. De Haan and Eijffinger (2000), for example, have developed indices of accountability to complement those of independence reviewed above. They propose 13 accountability tests arranged under the headings of objectives, transparency and responsibility. Each test scores one point each. On the basis of a formal reading of the Treaties, they give the ECB an accountability score of just 4 out of 13. Although this rises to seven once the enquiry is broadened out from formal Treaty provisions to actual practice, it still compares badly with, say, the Bank of England on 11.

De Haan and Eijffinger identify the core weakness as absence of some mechanism for enforcing central bank responsibility through sanctions. That defect aside, they give the ECB a maximum score for simple objectives that facilitate assessment of its performance, and a middling score for transparency. The Treaty is restrictive in stipulating the ECB's objectives: it has a primary obligation to deliver price stability and only a secondary one to support other economic goals of the Union (European Commission, 1992 and 1997). The designation of one overriding objective reduces scope for the ECB to evade responsibility by claiming to have given priority to some goals over others, or by continuously renegotiating expectations of trade-offs between multiple objectives (March and Olsen, 1995, p. 159).

Use of comparative indices to suggest the ECB could be more accountable without ceasing to be independent can be complemented by the following theoretical arguments.

1. The Treaty could have allowed for temporary overrides of the ECB by an elected body where this would improve welfare without threatening the underlying principle of central bank independence (Lohmann, 1992).
2. All the advantages of central Bank independence could have been achieved by only giving the ECB a choice of means while retaining choice of ends in the hands of elected and accountable politicians. In the jargon, the ECB has 'goal independence' (the power to define what is meant by the Treaty mandate to deliver stable prices) when it only need have been given 'instrument independence' (free choice of means to deliver goals) (Rogoff, 1985). This allows it unnecessary powers over the purposes of economic policy: over when, for example, it is appropriate to turn from its primary objective of controlling

inflation to its secondary objective of supporting the other economic goals of the Union; over the value judgement of whether inflation targeting should be symmetric (it is equally bad to overshoot as undershoot) or asymmetric (only above target inflation is bad); and over the equally important question of whether policy should be reactive or pro-active. The advantage of having just one goal against which to measure the performance of the ECB is thus offset by allowing the Bank to define what is meant by satisfaction of that goal.

3. A final critique goes even further: in addition to retaining the power to set policy goals in the hands of elected politicians, the Treaty on European Union (TEU) could have made provision for the ECB to be given a performance contract. This could, for example have included a linear tax on inflation in excess of target (Walsh, 1995), a link between the personal salaries or bonuses of ECB Board Members and satisfaction of inflation targets, a procedure to follow in the event of failure to meet targets (such as writing a letter of explanation), or even provision for dismissal. Their defenders argue such contracts need not compromise central bank independence. Rewards and penalties follow from the mechanical operation of a pre-specified contract, rather than the caprices of an elected government. Indeed, the EU's super-majoritarian decision rules and its separation of powers system mean its institutions would have been particularly suited to the entrenchment of a contract with its Central Bank beyond political meddling. For example, a contract could have been subject to the Assent procedure. Any change would then have required a proposal from the Commission, a qualified majority of the Council and the agreement of the EP acting by an absolute majority of its membership.

When, however, other considerations of institutional feasibility are taken into account it becomes unclear how valid are all the foregoing arguments that the EU's monetary constitution rests on a suboptimal trade-off between accountability and independence. A difficulty with the override option is that any exceptional shocks that might justify a temporary repossession of monetary powers by the political authority would in all probability be asymmetric in character. They would, in other words, affect some euro-zone countries more than others. This could well involve a more than normal mismatch between the distribution of decision powers of the Council by voting weights, and interest in the outcome of the decision (de Sousa, 2001, p. 11).

A problem, on the other hand, with the contract proposal is that it would be difficult to operationalise within the EU's Federal system of

Central Banking. As seen, a majority of votes on the Governing Council is held by representatives of national central banks. So would the contract apply to the entire Governing Council even though any provision for the dismissal of national central bankers from the centre would terminate the federal character of European central banking and move it in a unitary direction? Or would the permanent Executive alone be rewarded or sanctioned even though it is only a minority of the General Council (Levitt and Lord, 2000, p. 227)?

Probably the most robust criticism, then, of the present accountability-independence trade-off in the EU's monetary constitution is the second that the ECB has unnecessary discretion over the definition of its own goals. Significantly, it is on this point that the *status quo* has been questioned both by Council Members and the EP. During his Presidency of Ecofin, French Finance Minister, Laurent Fabius proposed the Treaties should be changed to transfer decisions on policy goals from the ECB to the Council. The EP, as we will see in a moment, has sought to use its reporting powers to limit the discretion with which the ECB can define its own goals in practice.

The full impact of any flaw in arrangements for ECB accountability constitution can, however, only be understood in conjunction with a further feature of the EU's political system. In most political systems any independence-accountability trade-off will tend to soften over time: in the long run a central bank that fails to deliver on the needs and values of citizens will be exposed to constitutional revision of its statute and to the appointment to a Board of bankers whose preferences are more closely aligned to some social mean (Lohmann, 1998). Yet, the ECB's statute can only be amended by a process of Treaty change that requires the concurrent consent of all member governments (including those who are not a part of the single currency) and their parliaments or publics. This, in the view of some, means the ECB is protected from under-performance in terms of the felt preferences of society by the unusually high number of veto points that would be involved in any revision of its powers.

What, however, this critique ignores is that unanimous decision-rules need not be insuperable barriers to the removal of suboptimal arrangements, provided the correction of under-performance involves an efficiency gain for all and not merely a re-distributive benefit to some (Buchanan and Tullock, 1962). Rather, the problem may not be that the ECB's statute is hard to revise, but that the procedure for its revision makes it hard to isolate choices about the monetary constitution of Europe from a whole series of other matters. As Buiter puts it, the ECB was established under a Treaty that amounted to a 'take it or leave it vote on the entire contents of a document whose scope was only slightly less encyclopaedic than Larousse' (Buiter, 1999, p. 186). The theory of long-run convergence on accountability-independence optimum may therefore, in the EU's case, be hostage to cross-issue bargaining linkages with extraneous matters.

To summarise the argument so far, the EU's monetary constitution is simple to the extent ECB has just one overriding objective and is subject to just one mode of accountability (accountability by 'reason-giving'). Yet, it is complex to the degree the ECB owes duties of accountability to multiple principals. On the one hand, this is unsurprising given that independent central banking is intrinsically a system of divided government: a technocratic body has control of monetary policy and a political body of fiscal policy (taxing, borrowing and spending) in a situation in which both have an interest in the overall 'policy mix' partially determined by the actions of the other. On top of this, the EU's Treaty allows for an element of mutual scrutiny through reciprocal rights of attendance at key meetings. The Member State holding the Presidency can attend the Governing Council of the ECB on behalf of the Council, and the President of the Central Bank can attend sessions of Ecofin. As seen, the Treaty further requires the ECB to report to the EP, the Council of Ministers, the European Council and the Commission, and to give press conferences, which can be interpreted as an obligation to explain itself directly to the public and the markets.

The relationship with the EP has emerged as the most public platform for the ECB to be held accountable by 'reason-giving'. What is striking about the inclusion of a parliamentary dimension is that it was the one point on which the authors of the Treaty were prepared to break with an attempt to construct the ECB as a replica of the Bundesbank. In the Member States with the longest tradition of independent central banking in Western Europe (Germany and the Netherlands), parliamentary involvement had been seen as a threat to central bank independence second only to instruction by government. The President of the Dutch Central Bank was banned by law from even entering the parliament building in the Hague (European Parliament, 1998b). However, the EU's political system allows greater scope for parliamentary scrutiny of a Central Bank than those of its Member States. It is precisely because the EP is not an executive-dominated parliament that it can criticise the ECB without that being interpreted as pressure from a governing majority.

In deploying its scrutiny powers, the EP self-consciously bought into the critique that there is a suboptimal trade-off between Central Bank independence and accountability in the TEU. At a Public Hearing with

Monetary Economists in 1998 the EP was advised, first, that it should seek to make up for the unnecessary degree of goal independence accorded the ECB by at least pressuring it to justify its goals in public and, second, that even under the assumptions of the sound money paradigm, the choice between a short sharp shock or a long slow squeeze in returning an economy to a long-run equilibrium growth is a matter of taste or social preference and not technical expertise. It is thus one on which Central Bankers ought to consult elected representatives.[49]

On the strength of the hearings, the EP decided in the Randzio–Plath report (European Parliament, 1998b) to put a maximal interpretation on its Treaty rights and to deploy them cumulatively. It billed consultations on the appointment of the first executive board of the ECB as 'confirmation proceedings' (European Parliament, 1998a). Each nominee was required to return written answers to a standard questionnaire and appear in person before EMAC. A mechanism for requesting the withdrawal of nominees was also written into the EP's own rules of procedure (European Parliament Rules of Procedure, A. 36). During the 'confirmation hearings' the EP then reached an agreement with incoming ECB President, Wim Duisenberg, that regular hearings before EMAC would be held every three months.

Beginning with the 'confirmation proceedings' the aim was to press the ECB into ever closer specification of its targets, forecasts and policy rules, and for Members of European Parliament (MEP) then to use those statements as criteria to judge the ECB in each subsequent hearing or procedure. It was thus hoped that the ECB's relationship with the EP would be turned into a form of self-appraisal, made all the more devastating by the impossibility of dismissing it as a political interference, whose assumptions derived from anywhere but the practitioners of independent central banking themselves.

In addition, by boxing the ECB into its own pre-specified performance criteria, the EP expected to limit any scope for the Bank to obscure under-performance through vague objectives or retrospective redefinition of targets. It was, finally, made clear that grave or persistent failure by the ECB to live up to the performance standards it had set itself in parliamentary hearings could be grounds for the EP to use its Treaty right to request an unscheduled meeting with the ECB. Such a move, the EP evidently believed, would stand out as a 'summons' in public and market perception, and act as a powerful disincentive to under-performance in the first place.

With some exceptions, the ECB has willingly co-operated with the EP's operationalisation of its reporting obligations. This is *not* because the EP has either of two procedural powers by which independent central banks in other systems come under long-term pressure to adjust to social preferences expressed through representative structures (Lohmann, 1998). First, the terms of delegation to the ECB are not amendable by a majority of the EU's legislature, but by Treaty change. This means that while there are multiple veto holders on changes to the ECB's agency, the EP is not amongst them. Second, rolling appointments to the ECB's Governing Council do not require the formal confirmation of the EP. The European Council is only obliged to consult the EP on appointments of the President, Vice President and other members of the Executive Board, which, in any case, only currently comprises one-third of the ECB's Governing Council.

Rather the EP's 'monetary dialogue' with the ECB is supported by incentive structures inherent to central banking itself. Given that control of inflation is a 'credibility good' that is achieved at lower cost the more a monetary policy rule is internalised into the expectations of wage and price fixers, central bankers themselves have an interest in any system of accountability by reason-giving that allows them to clarify their intentions (Briault *et al.*, 1996, p. 9). Indeed, a new Central Bank without a proven track record of successful monetary management has a special interest in establishing its credibility. Yet, the ECB relationship with the EP is more than a matter of policy efficiency and public relations. The Bank's own pronouncements suggests it sees legitimation benefits that might be summarised in three propositions:

- Absence of legitimation by election, or even by a form of delegation that is revocable by democratic procedure (as opposed to intergovernmental negotiation), means that the only source of legitimation available to the ECB is its ability to justify its policies publicly.
- Justifying policies under cross-examination from elected representatives meets tests of public justification over and above any success in maintaining the credibility of financial markets.
- Of all representative bodies, the EP is the most likely to accept policy justifications in a form that respects the ECB's responsibility to set monetary policy for the Euro-zone as a whole (European Parliament, 1998a). Representatives of elected national governments or of national parliaments would be more likely to quiz it on the suitability of monetary policy for specific Member States, which is not its mandate. The EP, in contrast, is mainly organised into left–right ideological groupings without any single national perspective and, significantly, it is transnational party groups that take the lead in

questioning the ECB when it appears before EMAC. The bank puts the point thus:

> Given its independent status, the ECB cannot be held accountable by national governments or national parliaments. Instead it is accountable to the European public at large and to the European Parliament, a body with a European mandate and a direct democratic legitimacy. (European Central Bank, 2001, p. 56)

However, problems remain. In particular, the EP and ECB are less than fully agreed on what would amount to a satisfactory form of accountability by 'reason-giving' (Majone, 1996, p. 292). The EP has by no means been uniformly successful in pressing its own interpretation of reporting standards on the Bank. Differences remain between an 'account giver' (the ECB) anxious to maintain margins of ambivalence and an 'account receiver' (the EP) eager to narrow them (March and Olsen, 1995, p. 159). The main dispute has centred on what counts as transparency. The ECB has put a 16-year embargo on publication of its minutes, that being the maximum possible time that any Member of its General Council could conceivably still be a Central Banker. However, its argument that publication would complicate attempts to frame a monetary policy for the Euro-zone as a whole by exposing members of the General Council to pressures from different national audiences has drawn the riposte from EMAC that the range of opinions expressed at meetings could be released without attributing any views to individuals. In the EP's opinion, dissenting views need to be public knowledge to remove the alibi for misjudgement that no one could reasonably have foreseen what turned out to be mistakes at the time.[50]

In addition, the EP has pressed the ECB to publish a user-friendly version of the econometric model on which it bases its decisions (European Parliament, 2001e, p. 7). Behind this apparently oxymoronic request lies a serious point. As a former member of the Bank of England's Monetary Policy Committee puts it in his own critique of ECB transparency, meaningful accountability requires the ability to determine whether objectives have been achieved through luck or skill (Buiter, 1999, p. 195). De Haan and Eijffinger (2000, p. 400) likewise argue that where a central bank is left to define the meaning of price stability for itself it is all the more important that it should explain the steps and reasoning by which each of its decisions is made: this is a necessary safeguard against retrospective cover-ups of poor performance. In fact, the ECB has been somewhat slow even to publish its internal economic forecasts, let alone a detailed model of how it makes decisions. The first forecasts it published covered such a wide range as to be of doubtful value. Such reticence may at first have been understandable given that the introduction of the single currency is likely of itself to have changed economic behaviour in ways that cannot have been easy to predict. Yet, with the passage of time this alibi will disappear.

The foregoing difficulties suggest another: should the ECB's reporting obligations follow a logic of appropriateness or a logic of consequence, input or output measures of accountability? The difficulty with relying on the second is that there are limits to how far the ECB can reasonably be expected to have full control over outcomes. All systems with independent Central Banks amount to a division of powers in the making of economic policy: monetary policy is hived off to the Central Bank, but fiscal policy and market regulation remain with the political authority. In addition, precise control of outcomes is complicated by the ever-presence of shocks to economic policy, and by the complex causation and variable lags that dog its delivery. In contrast, the difficulty of adopting input measures of accountability that centre on the appropriateness of procedures for the making of decisions is that it requires the ECB to be a gold-fish bowl. It is the search for verifiable accounts of its internal procedures that produces demands for it to publish minutes, dissenting opinions and even econometric model others can simulate for themselves. Yet, to repeat, not to accommodate such pressures for input accountability is to leave little alternative to judging a body that does not fully control its performance by outcomes alone.

The European Court of Justice

Under the Treaties it is the ECJ which is responsible for ensuring the Union's 'law is observed'. The ECJ presently consists of 15 Judges and 9 Advocates-General appointed by common accord of the European Council. It has a Court of first instance, as well as a procedure for giving preliminary rulings on points of EU law referred to it by national courts. As seen in Chapter 3, the ECJ has established the principles that EU law takes direct effect in Member States (*Van Gend en Loos*, Case 26/62 ECR 1963) and that it is supreme over all kinds of national law (*Costa vs. Enel*, Case 6/64 ECR 1964). More recently it has added the principle of 'indirect effect' (*Von Colson*, Case 14/83 ECR 1984) which requires national courts to make their best endeavours to interpret national law in a manner that is consistent with European law. As Alec Stone Sweet and James Caporaso (1998, p. 103) put it, direct and indirect effect mean that 'national judges become agents of the Community order' even in a wide range of cases that are never referred to the ECJ.

The cumulative effect of these doctrines and procedures is that the ECJ is one of the most powerful of the Union's institutions. Its decisions are hard to reverse, since that would require the agreement of all Member States to a Treaty change. In addition, its decisions can have huge implications for ordinary lives and the allocations of values in Member Societies, as famously illustrated by the Grogan case in which the ECJ ruled that abortion was a service and that access to it was thus covered by rights of free movement (*Grogan* Case 159/90 ECR 1991).

Amongst questions all this raises are, first, how far does the entrenchment of the ECJ's powers and rulings contribute to constitutional democracy in the European arena? Second, how far is the ECJ itself exposed to public control in the exercise of its functions? The following are amongst arguments that the ECJ has contributed positively to the development of democracy in the European arena.

1. ECJ decisions have contributed to the democratisation of Union institutions in general and to principles of institutional balance needed for constitutional democracy in particular. A key example is the Isoglucose case in which the ECJ ruled that the Council could not approve legislation before it had received an opinion from the European Parliament since there was a 'fundamental principle... at Community level... that the people should take part in the exercise of power through the intermediary of a representative assembly' (*Isoglucose*, Case 138/79 ECR 1980).
2. The EU has developed a rights jurisprudence capable of nourishing democratic politics in the Union arena over and above the separate contributions of rights guaranteed at Union level. Although the ECJ has decided that it has no power to set aside Union legislation on grounds of conflict with fundamental rights (*Stork,* Case 1/58 ECR 1959) it has declared that it will interpret it to ensure conformity with 'fundamental rights in the Community order' (*Wachauf,* Case 5/88 ECR 1989).
3. In holding all power holders in the Union arena – national governments included – to their obligations under the Treaties the ECJ has also held them to the terms under which national parliaments or publics authorised transfers of power to the Union level.
4. The ECJ has applied 'rule of law' principles to the Union (Costa, 2001, p. 901) most obviously by insisting that all measures should be clearly attributable to a legal base in the Treaties and that 'each institution'

should act within the powers conferred on it (Arnull, 2002, p. 241). Once again, this helps ensure that the actions of the Union are those which have been democratically authorised by Treaty formation and ratification.

On the other hand, the role of the ECJ is open to the following criticisms on the grounds of democratic principle:

1. In the view of some, the ECJ has itself subverted the rule of law principle that all Union actions and institutions should comply with the terms by which they were democratically authorised. Nowhere else has it been accused of exceeding the terms of Treaty authorisation than in its definition of its own powers. As Anthony Arnull (2002, p. 243) puts it: 'for the institution charged with policing compliance with the principle of conferred powers to disregard the limits on its own powers would be unconscionable'.

2. The ECJ can itself be criticised as acting contrary to division of powers principles on the grounds that some of its rulings encroach on decisions that should, arguably, be left to legislators. Alec Stone Sweet explains the process by which the ECJ often assumes the role of legislator:

> As the ECJ interprets EC law, it gradually rewrites it. An EC directive may have meant one thing to the Commission, to the governments that have adopted the regulation in the Council, and to the national legislatures that transposed the directive into national law. As the directive is litigated and then interpreted by courts, however, it may come to mean something very different. (Stone Sweet, 2000, p. 184)

Indeed, Stone Sweet (ibid., p. 188) points out that in at least one of its decisions the ECJ 'enacted by judicial decision the main elements' of a directive that had been blocked by a Member State (the UK) using the legislative powers assigned to it under the Treaties.

3. Not only is the EU open to the charge of allowing excessive rule by judges it can also be criticised for failing to ensure the one condition that might make that form of rule acceptable: the neutrality of the judges. On the one hand, the ECJ is often perceived as a partisan for a particular cause, that of integration itself. As Caparaso and Stone Sweet put it: 'we view the Court as generally working to enhance its own autonomy, which is then exercised to promote the interests of transnational society and to facilitate the construction of supranational governance' (1998, p. 105).

On the other hand, it is unclear that the independence of the ECJ is as insulated as it could be from the influence of Member States. Unlike the Executive Board of the ECB where a single non-renewable term of eight years removes any personal incentives to anticipate the re-appointing behaviour of governments, ECJ Judges and Advocates-General are appointed for somewhat short renewable terms of six years. The Court does, though, resemble the ECB in shielding individuals from the pressures of 'their' governments by only making collective judgements. Personal contributions are not, in other words, attributed. However apart from this confidentiality restricting transparency and accountability by reducing publicly available information of how things could otherwise have been decided and by what margin (minority opinions), it does not extend to Advocates-General whose individual contributions are known to governments, in spite of their importance to outcomes of cases (Arnull, 2002, pp. 251–2). Nor can it be assumed independence will be safeguarded by the requirement of a 'common accord' of the European Council for the appointment of Judges and Advocates-General. Other members of the European Council would seem to do little to question the nominations any one government makes each time one of its incumbents completes a six-year term (Hix, 1999, p. 105).

4. Democratic disquiet at 'judge made law' might be partially assuaged were all citizens to have equal access to it. The empirical evidence does not suggest this condition holds. Apart from well-known procedural and resource constraints, data of cases brought in the ECJ shows that EU law is the most used by multinationals followed by lobbies that are organised at Union level (Stone Sweet and Brunell, 1998). This, of course, reinforces concern that the ECJ is inadequately checked and balanced by elected legislators at the level of the EU's political system itself, since a strong legislature is one way by which democratic politics can compensate for any danger that some individuals and sections of society are better resourced than others for access to rule by judges.

5. The very success of the ECJ in developing rights protections that the Member States find procedurally difficult to reverse (because they need to be unanimous to agree a Treaty change) may only have sharpened the determination of some Member States to develop new areas of policy outside the European Communities Treaties. Just as some of the boundaries between parliamentary and non-parliamentary forms of rule-making in the Union can be seen as arbitrary (Chapter 7), so can those between policies where the ECJ's jurisidiction is available for rights protection and those where it is not. The case of Justice and Home Affairs

(JHA) shows how the ECJ may be largely excluded where it is, arguably, most needed.

The question of how far the ECJ is subject to public control has been informed by a lively academic debate on the nature of the relationship between the Court and other centres of power in the EU's political system, including the elected governments of the Union. One assessment is that the EU's political system is configured in a way that favours a 'runaway' judiciary. Interpretation of the Treaty is delegated to a Court that knows its rulings will stand unless all Member States are unanimous in agreeing a Treaty change to reverse its decisions.

Other commentators argue this grossly exaggerates the autonomy of ECJ law-making and neglects nuance and balance in its relationship with elected governments, for the following reasons:

- The Court is subject to a number of informal dependencies on Member States that require it to win at least their passive acceptance for its rulings.
- The appointment of its judges on a rolling basis means that Member States can gradually change the judicial character of the ECJ.
- The ECJ only has imperfect information about the future composition of European Councils which will be responsible for future changes and will thus only venture rulings they feel are unlikely to be reversed under any circumstances.

Indeed, one author, drawing on the liberal intergovernmentalist position that the largest Member States can force the direction of Treaty change on their own by threatening alternative coalitions, predicts that ECJ rulings will remain close to the preferences of just two governments alone, France and Germany (Garrett, 1995).

All these positions are however open to the criticism that they reduce the ECJ's relationship with other institutions to a mixture of power relationships and functional considerations. As such they fail to comprehend the nature of the law as a body of principles that are to significant degrees self-limiting, since they have to be normatively defensible, internally coherent, and uniformly applied (Armstrong, 1998). This insight implies that like the ECB an important element in the control of the ECJ will be 'reason-giving' by a body which knows credibility is central to its own performance. Yet, as Giainne De Búrca points out, it would be a mistake to regard this as letting the ECJ off the hook. To the contrary it raises tough questions as to whether its judgements are always as well reasoned as they ought to be (De Búrca, 1998).

A well-divided system of government?

Much disquiet has been expressed at the division of powers in the European arena. For example, the Westendorp report (Council of Ministers, 1995) reported the following as the view of several of the representatives of heads of government designated to prepare options for the Amsterdam IGC.

> democratic accountability was being undermined by practices that make it hard for citizens to trace policies to treaties, legislation or implementing measures, and then determine the relative responsibility of any one institution for the measure in question.

As this quotation implies, present arrangements raise the following questions. Are divisions of power in the EU arena based on defensible democratic principles consistently applied? Are they comprehensible to citizens or their representatives who want to know who can be held responsible for what in the EU's political system? These are huge questions, so only a summary treatment of them can be attempted here. It is useful to distinguish two demarcations of power that raise rather different concerns: a horizontal division between the Union and its Member States; and a vertical one between the EU's own institutions. From previous chapters it is apparent there is no vertical division of powers between Union institutions that corresponds to the classic branches of government (executive, legislative or judicial). Nor is there a horizontal division between the EU and its Member States that can easily be summarised as a list of substantive policy responsibilities of the one but not the other. Rather the two layers of government contribute to almost all fields of public policy and where the Union operates it is almost never with financial, legal and administrative instruments that are exclusively its own. Member States and Union institutions mingle their means to produce outcomes.

Perhaps the closest the Union comes to a principled division of powers is in its use of 'subsidiarity' and 'proportionality' to guide relationships between the Union and its Member States, and in its use of 'institutional balance' as an ideal for relationships between Union institutions (at least in relation to the first pillar). These principles can be specified as follows:

- The Treaty definition of subsidiarity is that 'the Community shall take action only if and insofar as the objectives of the proposed action cannot be sufficiently achieved by the Member States and can, therefore, by reason of scale or effects of the proposed action be achieved by the Community' (A. 5).

- Proportionality is a 'least means' doctrine. If it can be shown that a value can be pursued at European level at less cost to the value of national autonomy then other means should be found of making Union policy until the same objection can no longer be sustained.
- 'Institutional balance' is often presented as the product of a highly original 'Community method'. If Community institutions cannot be held to conventional distinctions between branches of government (executive, legislative and judicial) they can be expected to follow a demarcation between proposing (the Commission) and deciding (the Council and, increasingly, the EP).

However, none of the above gets us as close as might at first appear to a clear division of powers. A common criticism of subsidiarity is that it is 'legally unclear and politically manipulable'.[51] For its part, the notion of an institutional balance based on a Commission with agenda-setting powers and a Council and EP with deciding powers has been substantially eroded in practice, as Chapter 6 demonstrates.

Indeed, wherever the Union divides powers, it soon mixes them up again. One EP report complains of 'a growing confusion of roles between the various bodies, leading, for example, to conferring Council of Ministers responsibilities on the European Council, Commission tasks on the Council of Ministers, and tasks which should be dealt with by COREPER on the specialist committees (the Political Committee or the K.4 Committee)'. All of this is, in the view of the report, further compounded by the 'insidious duplication of the institutions and procedures provided for in the Treaties by informal networks and meetings, thus undermining the system's practical efficiency, legal security and democratic control' (European Parliament, 1999c).

If demarcations between the Union institutions are blurred in practice, so are those between national and European levels public administration. The substantial participation of national officials in Union institutions (Council Working Groups and Comitology Committees) and the Europeanisation of large areas of domestic policy-making has been described as 'fusion' of the levels by Wolfgang Wessels and 'infranational' government by Joe Weiler. Up to a point this is just the EU's response to a problem common to all separation of power systems: if they are to provide 'joined-up government' they need to find means of reconnecting branches and levels of government without compromising the grounds on which powers were divided in the first place. As the Commission's White Paper on Governance puts it, in a 'multi-level system the real challenge is one of establishing criteria for how competence is shared not separated. Only a non-exclusive vision can secure the best interests of Citizens' (European Commission, 2001d, pp. 34–5).

Yet, even accepting foregoing constraints, there is room for improvement in present arrangements for the division of powers. The following are plausible suggestions largely taken from debates surrounding the Convention.

1. A single text could summarise who does what and how (European Convention 2002c, May 23–24 plenary). Although this would necessarily mean indicating the co-presence of both Union and national institutions in the delivery of most policies, that need not preclude some broad brush descriptions of their relative involvement (European Convention 2002c, April 15–16 plenary, p. 2). Indeed, it is extraordinary the Treaty does not spell out the principle – for the public to see – that tasks not explicitly allocated to the EU remain with Member States.
2. The difficulty of discovering and applying a general principle for assigning powers does not excuse imprecision in particular designations of competence. Gráinne de Búrca and Bruno de Witte (2002, p. 201) point out that the Treaties typically assign responsibilities to the Union without specifying 'what the relationship with national powers in that field should be'.
3. Whatever normative and functional criteria are used are almost certain to imply scope for allocations of competence to change over time. As is often remarked, subsidiarity presupposes a means of moving powers back down to national level: it is not just a principle for justifying their transfer upwards to European level. Yet difficulties with changing EU Treaties have combined with the *acquis communautaire* doctrine to produce rigidity.
4. Steps could be taken to improve mechanisms for policing divisions of power. If challenges to decisions are themselves to observe a separation of powers they should ideally be initiated by elected bodies but adjudicated by a judicial one. Both aspects are under-developed in the case of the EU. The Convention considered proposals that national parliaments should be able to issue 'early warnings' on subsidiarity grounds during the consideration of draft EU legislation, and that, once measures have been passed, they, and not just their governments, should be able to ask the ECJ to review them on grounds of competence. On the other hand, it is possible to question whether the ECJ should review questions of competence at all, given its own interest in the development of an EU legal order. A special Constitutional Court (Weiler, 1997a) or a competence court might be a better solution.

Conclusion

We began the chapter by noting that democratic systems often face the challenge of finding democratically defensible means of putting particular powers beyond the normal operation of the democratic system itself. If the EU has succeeded in developing democratically defensible means of constitutionalising particular institutions we would expect to find evidence for this in how far arrangements for the ECB, the ECJ and the overall separation of powers system in the Union satisfy the following Democratic Audit criteria with which we began the chapter:

How far does the EU constitutionalise modified consociationalism or use its methods to constitutionalise other values (*EUDA Test 6*)*?*
How far does the EU constitutionalise concurrent consent or use its methods to constitutionalise other values (*EUDA Test 12*)*?*

To the extent that the removal of national vetoes on constitutional change would itself require a constitutional change that could be vetoed by any Member State, the EU would seem to constitutionalise one precondition for consociationalism. The need for the unanimous consent of all national democracies to Treaty changes also provides some protection for the independence of the Commission and the ECB, the acquired jurisprudence of the ECJ, and those established powers of the EP which institutionalise elements of concurrent consent. At least one Member State can usually be relied upon to defend each of the foregoing ingredients of what has become an elaborate system of checks and balances. At this point, in other words, the two models of consensus politics overlap: consociational arrangements for changing the Treaties entrench mechanisms of concurrent consent in the day-to-day workings of the Union.

Yet the development of constitutionalist democracy in the EU arena is in other respects fragile or incomplete. As Simon Hix (1999, p. 128) puts it, 'The Judicial politics game has produced an incomplete constitution. For example, the EU does not have a bill of rights and who has *Kompetenz-Kompetenz* is unclear.' The ECJ has hitherto had to infer rights from a pastiche of sources such as Treaty provisions and the overlapping rights jurisprudence of Member States. Nor is it a Constitutional Court whose exclusive concern with constitutional questions insulates its rulings from any self-interest in the relative claims of the different bodies of law or levels of government with which it deals.

Complaints about the implications of Comitology for Co-decision, the de facto supervision of the Commission's initiatory powers by

Member States and the elusiveness of subsidiarity, all suggest that demarcations of powers that are formally constitutionalised by the Treaties are relatively easy to corrode in practice. Indeed, another possible gap is that the EU constitutionalises rights of States and not specifically of national democratic institutions. Thus, at the time of writing the only safeguard offered to national parliaments is the right to receive documents. Unless matters are changed by the Constitution proposed by the Convention, the policing of subsidiarity lies with national governments, who themselves exercise the powers transferred into the European arena, rather than with national parliaments, whose legislative powers are more likely to be circumscribed by European integration.

Whilst these difficulties point towards an insecure constitutionalisation, others suggest a problem of constitutionalisation insufficiently balanced by democratic counter-parties. The ECB has discretion over goals that could be defined by elected bodies without that compromising the technical independence of monetary policy. The ECJ often seems to act as a legislator within a political system that presents unusually high hurdles to any democratic override of rule by judges. Above all, neither of the elected components of the complex separation of powers system, the representatives of national governments in the Council and of transnational party ideologies in the EP, is well connected to its electorate on EU issues or in a manner that has yet made their own performance in Union institutions a matter for electoral judgement. In part this is a result of the division of powers system itself: incentives to participate and treat elections as first order are lower where all that is at stake at any one time is power in one institutional component, rather than that in the system as a whole.

9
Conclusion

The 'no democratic deficit thesis'

Recent comment on democracy and the EU has switched from alarmism to complacency. So fashionable has it become to question how far the EU suffers a democratic deficit that the literature will soon have as many versions of the 'no democratic deficit thesis' as it once had accounts of the deficit itself.

One approach uses the Principal–Agent analysis to question how far Union institutions ever drift from the control of the democratically elected governments of the Member States (Moravcsik, 2002). A second points to the Union as a sophisticated system of checks and balances and argues that at least the constitutional or protective features of democracy are met even if the more popular or participatory conditions are not (Mény, 2002, p. 6). A third assumes that one indicator of democracy is whether 'the voters get what they want' (Crombez, 2003, p. 103) and argues that the 'institutional set-up of the EU is not fundamentally undemocratic' (ibid., p. 114) on that score. Even the British Prime Minister seems to have endorsed the view that the EU's institutional *status quo* is an innovation in democracy beyond the state.

> These institutions based on the carefully balanced triangle of Commission, Council and Parliament, underpinned by the Court of Justice... represent a quantum leap in democratic governance on an international scale – the pooling of sovereignty in order to extend the reach of democratic action. (UK Government, 2002)

Each of these claims is an illuminating corrective to a previous counsel of despair. Each is flawed. Previous chapters of this Democratic Audit of the

EU show why. Attempts to use Principal–Agent analysis to finesse the democratic deficit typically ask the wrong question. Since national governments are themselves amongst the main beneficiaries of delegations of power to Union institutions the key question is not 'can governments control Union institutions?' but 'can citizens control all those, their national governments included, who combine to exercise the powers of the EU?' It is harder to give a positive answer to the second question than the first for the following reasons elaborated in previous chapters: poor citizen understanding of the Union's political system (Chapter 3), blind spots in the transparency of Union institutions that correspond to some of the main moments in the exercise of their powers (notably law-making behind closed doors in the case of the Council of Ministers) (Chapter 7), the uneven development of the powers of national parliaments on European issues (Chapter 7) and the difficulty of either internalising Union issues to any form of electoral politics (European or national) or of completely pulling off the argument that voter alignments on national issues can stand as proxies to those on European issues (Chapters 5 and 7).

If, then, the connection to the citizen and the popular and participatory ingredients of democracy are under-developed, should we be reassured by the claim that at least some aspects of 'constitutional democracy' are delivered through a sophisticated set of checks and balances that is in place? One difficulty is that the EU is only, in part, a system of divided government. Powers in significant areas of policy – the CFSP, JHA and macro-economic co-ordination – are largely concentrated on the Council with only patchy elements of parliamentary and judicial participation (Chapter 8). A second difficulty, as Mény himself observes, is that the constitutional and popular elements of democracy are interdependent to the point at which it is questionable whether it is meaningful to speak of the one being present without the other. Checks and balances on their own only deliver controlled government, not *publicly* controlled government. Then, of course, there is the Habermas argument (1997) that the democratic rights and popular sovereignty are 'co-original'.

What, finally, of the claim that aspects of the Union's institutions are at least as well configured as many others widely held to be democracies to the satisfaction of the output conditions of democracy? It is important not to 'straw-man' this argument since it is made with sophistication and nuance. For example, Crombez, who provides by far the best treatment of it, only claims there are features of the EU's political system that constrain any departure from median citizen preferences. He is careful to point out that Union institutions can 'prevent policy moving towards the median' (2003, p. 113) if it is not already there, and to say that it is the 'institutional setup', rather than citizen connections to it, that is not 'fundamentally undemocratic'. Yet regardless of such qualifications, this study has quarreled from the start with the core assumption of Crombez and other output perspectives. It has argued that democracy is not defined by the satisfaction of citizen wants *per se* but by rights and obligations of public control whose presence can only be verified by an investigation into inputs and process.

Democratic Auditing: the 'third way'?

More, however, than questioning individual claims on either side of the debate, the method of Democratic Auditing used in this book should make us sceptical of all sweeping generalisations for or against the existence of a democratic deficit. Instead it directs us to consider the democratic performance of the EU as something that will almost certainly vary against models of democracy, attributes of democracy and the institutional components of a political system. Let us now draw together some of the conclusions of previous chapters under these three heads.

Models of democracy

Although the question of whether democracy should be applied to the EU and on what model is, indeed, part of what makes the Union a contested polity, a principal finding of this study is that the range of contestation is narrower and simpler than it is normally assumed to be. Most prescriptions for a democratic EU imply a form of consensus democracy in a range between two models that I have labelled modified consociationalism and concurrent consent (Chapter 2).

In practice, the EU mixes and matches aspects of both the models. Questions of institutional design are initially settled by consociational methods (Chapter 4). Decisions within union institutions then combine both approaches. Concurrent consent is most evident where various outcomes (legislative, budgetary and to a lesser extent Commission formation) are co-determined by the Council and majorities of the EP (Chapters 5–7). Modified consociationalism is most developed where each national government retains significant control over Union decisions and national parliaments participate through their relationships with their own governments (Chapters 5 and 7).

Of course, combining aspects of both the models risks satisfying adherents of neither. Advocates of concurrent consent argue that large areas of Union decision-making remain outside the control of representatives directly elected at the level of the EU's political system itself. Some complain that the EP is excluded from everyday decisions in some policy areas (Chapter 7). Others directly confront consociationalism by questioning its core assumption that unconditional national vetoes on questions of institutional design are always desirable. Such vetoes, they argue, risk political inequality and institutionalise a form of minority rule where they are used to block change to policies that have become oppressive to all but a few veto holders (Chapter 4).

For their part, adherents of modified consociationalism might gibe at two constraints on national democratic institutions that hold no matter how the latter configure their dealings with the EU. They might be especially perplexed that these are paradoxes of consociationalism itself. They arise, in other words, from the very application of consociationalism to a political system like the EU. As just seen, the veto rights that are at the heart of consociationalism mean that once departures from its precepts are agreed to, they are difficult to reverse. Qualified majority voting, co-determination of outcomes between the EP and Council, and selective constitutionalisation of powers in the hands of independent bodies are all entrenched behind rules for Treaty change that cannot be reversed by any one national democracy. Second, consociationalism implies a normative standard of political equality – national democracies should be political equals – that is unlikely to be met where its own decision rules are employed by states whose power is as unequal as those of EU Member States. If we take liberal intergovernmentalism (LI) to be a plausible theory of how the politically unequal will bargain questions of institutional outcomes they must all (formally) agree, the prediction of LI that the main deals in European integration will be dominated by the two or three most powerful Member States is to say the least in some tension with the consociational value of political equality between national democracies (Chapter 4).

Whatever the tensions within and between the two models of consensus democracy my guess, however, is that the Union will continue to combine features of both. For reasons I discuss elsewhere (Lord and Magnette, 2004), many of its policy addressees have good reason to accept compromises between competing views of what is needed for the rightful exercise of Union power as more legitimate even than their own preferences for its legitimation. Far from being a 'cop out', this prediction begs a question of its own: does the Union combine the two standards according to defensible principles consistently applied?

Where the EU combines modified consociationalism and concurrent consent it uses the first to assign competences that can then be exercised in designated areas by the decision rules of the second. The important point is that this amounts to a sequence at each point of which the hurdle of consensus is set high. Imagine a Treaty change that empowers the EU to act by Co-decision. The initial Treaty change requires unanimity between a large and rising number of national governments, authorised by the democratic institutions of each Member State. Any secondary legislation then needs the agreement of Member States holding at least 71 per cent of the bloc vote on the Council and *de facto* of a similar supermajority of the EP. Informally the hurdles may be still higher and more numerous. As seen, the Council has a normative preference for unanimity even where majority voting is available to it. In addition, the informal politics of interest representation – the policy networks that come into play once the focus moves from the government to the governance of the Union – mean that the active co-operation of a large number of civil society actors may be needed for the delivery of policy goals.

The methods used to combine modified consociationalism and concurrent consent thus effectively require supermajorities across diverse institutions and processes each of which is formed on the basis of a different principle of representation (national–territorial in the case of the Council; cross-cutting political ideologies in the case of the EP and sectoral interests in the case of policy networks). The next section reflects on some of the implications of this 'compounding' of different approaches to consensus democracy.

Attributes of democracy

Cutting across its two standards of consensus democracy, the Audit proposed 12 tests of the Union's performance against specific attributes of democratic governance (citizenship, participation, authorisation, representation, accountability and so on). A crude summary of findings in the chapter which follow might be that at first sight elite-level patterns of actor involvement have some worthwhile representative qualities (Chapter 5). On the other hand, the accountability of its institutions is varied (Chapters 6–8), and they are poorly linked to the citizen. Chapter 3 highlighted just how problematic is democratic citizenship of the EU by almost any measure: identification, public understanding and participation. To the extent that they cast doubt on whether any control of Union institutions amounts to 'public' control (Chapters 3 and 5) weaknesses in linkages to citizens reinforce shortcomings in the accountability of Union institutions.

More insightful, though, than simply cataloguing these variations in performance is to attempt to analyse relationships between them. Chapter 2 argued it was important to distinguish compensated deficiencies (which arise through the delivery of other qualities of democratic rule or even non-democratic values widely shared by members of a political system) from those that amount to 'pure loss'. The following are examples of the first.

1. Difficulties in making the EU accountable are related to its development of forms of decision that always require high levels of consensus between representatives of Member States and often require the agreement of other actors too. The very involvement of so many different actor types in first pillar decisions may make it hard to attribute responsibility to any one individual or institution. On the other hand as seen on p. 195 any mechanism which removed EU decision-makers wholesale would almost certainly require any set of 'replacement rascals' to be like those who had been shown the door. Participants in decisions would still have to include representatives of all national governments, a majority of Commissioners and of the EP drawn (*de facto* or overtly) from the main party families, and networks inclusive of organised interests needed for the effective delivery of policy.

2. Poor linkage to citizens and weak forms of electoral accountability are likewise related to inclusive and consensual patterns of representation; and, indeed, to the EU's system of partially divided government. Consensus building dampens contestation. In place of a public space that continuously articulates clearly delineated alternatives, there is a sense in which the Union's highly inclusive practices creates a political system in which all mainstream actors are in 'government', leaving few to play a role of 'opposition'. Divided government, for its part, reduces incentives for electoral participation and for European elections fought on EU issues. Only one component of the EU's political system can be changed by those elections, and, however it is changed, a successor EP will always have to slot into the game of inter-institutional compromise vacated by its predecessor.

3. The difficulty of delivering political equality is related to competing standards of what equality should mean in the case of EU institutions. So long as the EU is pulled between the principles of parity representation of states (and therefore national democracies) and proportional representation of populations it cannot base the allocation of votes in the Council or seats in the EP on just one of these standards alone.

On the other hand, we have also discovered a number of trade-offs that can arguably be improved. Amongst them are the following:

- The relationship between the equal representation of citizens and of states remains less than linear (Chapter 5);
- Difficulties in achieving accountability based on 'outcomes' in a political system of many hands could be met by monitoring the appropriateness of inputs to decision-making (Chapter 6);
- Tensions between the empowerment of national parliaments on the one hand and the European Parliament on the other are no excuse for avoiding transparency improvements – such as requiring the Council of Ministers to legislate in public – that would facilitate all forms of parliamentary scrutiny (Chapter 7);
- The European Parliament could have greater say over the definition of the ECB's goals without the Bank losing its operational independence (Chapter 8);
- A role for an unelected Court of Justice in 'constitutionalising' certain individual rights need not preclude a role for a more democratically authorised legislator in deliberating and agreeing what rights should guide the Court's judgements (Chapter 8).

Time and place

The democratic performance of the EU does not just vary by attributes of democracy. It also varies across institutions and levels of Union governance, as follows.

- *By institution.* However much the main institutions of the Union interact to produce democratic qualities and defects, each has strengths and weaknesses that are distinctively its own. Examples include the closed nature of the Council (Chapter 7), the EP's poor electoral connection (Chapters 3 and 5), and doubts about equality of access to the ECJ (Chapter 8).
- *Across time.* Particular constellations of circumstance produce differences in how far the attention of actors is mobilised with the result that the same procedure for representation or public control may produce different results at different times. Thus, for example, the reversal in 1999 of conventional wisdom that the EP would never achieve the double majority for the censure of a Commission was facilitated by the media attention given to the report of the *Comité*

des Sages into allegations against members of the Santer Commission (Chapter 6).

- *Geographically.* Opportunities for democratic control depend crucially on how each Member State interfaces with the European arena. It is up to each Member to decide what procedures to use for the democratic ratifaction of Treaty change (Chapter 4), and what powers its national parliaments are to have over the behaviour of the national government on the Council of Ministers (Chapter 7). In addition, elections to the EP use national electoral systems to administer the poll and count the votes, and national party systems to structure voter choice (Chapters 3 and 5).

What is to be done?

Academic analysis is usually better suited to helping us think about the values and predicaments involved in prescription than to generating detailed recommendations themselves. In that spirit, a concluding thought is that this book has suggested a number of parameters that any prescription for a more democratic EU will find hard to ignore. Amongst them:

- The EU is likely to remain a dispersed and decentred political system made up of many levels and processes.
- Both well entrenched rights protections and consensus are likely to be preconditions for democratic politics in the European arena.
- There is unlikely to be full agreement in the near term on what model of democracy the EU should follow, even if the range of disagreement is likely to be limited to various forms of consensus democracy.
- Merely putting the institutional mechanisms of democratic politics in place cannot guarantee the connection of the EU's political system to the public. The development of a democratic citizenship, society, and public space on EU matters is likely to be slow and may lag any institutional construction.

What broad strategies of democratisation are possible within these parameters? It seems to me that prescriptions should centre on four themes.

1. Reduce the cost of monitoring (Crombez, 2003). Even within a dispersed and decentred system of accountability, a great deal more could be done to reduce the cost that each democratically elected body faces in monitoring the EU according to its chosen method. One improvement here might be to create a clearer distinction between the legislative and executive acts of the Council so that the first can be conducted in public. Another might be to create audit trails for over the life cycle of each Union decision, logging who participated when and who agreed to what.

2. *Make better use of the distinction between accountability based on logics of appropriateness and consequence.* As discussed in Chapters 6 and 7 the difficulties of attributing outcomes to individuals and even institutions in a complex system need not prevent actors being asked to account for their inputs to decisions.

3. *Create strategic nodes of public control.* The present position is that only a part of the EU's legislature is elected. No executive office is either directly or indirectly elected (unless the Commission is seen as a three-stage process of delegation from the people). Any wholesale departure from this would make the EU more majoritarian, but, as seen, that objection can hardly be sustained against selective departures since the elected office holders would still have to operate within a division of powers system in which the consent of many other bodies, including the Member Governments, would be needed. Indeed, the electoral process could itself be made consensual, as, for example, in schemes to appoint the Commission through an electoral college of the European and national parliaments, or, maybe more speculatively, through a points system accumulated by political families in proportion to votes in European and even national elections.

4. *Create room for challenge and spontaneity.* As Heidrun Abromeit has pointed out, consensus systems only limit aggregative, and not contestatory, approaches to public control. Devices such as Swiss-style referendums (which give the public rights to challenge decisions already taken) can be used as a backstop form of public control where consensus limits competitition between elites themselves. This suggestion acknowledges that public awareness and understanding of a political system does not develop in the 'abstract'. Publics have historically been mobilised into political arenas in response to 'concrete' experiences and problems, often involving angry reactions by some to decisions whose implications only become apparent once they have been made and implemented. Others have proposed limited opportunities (such as a legislative ballot) that would allow Union policy to be initiated and not just challenged by popular initiative. Either proposal could be procedurally defined to require some degree of consensus across Member States and social groups. The point is not that they need be alternatives to consensus, but that they should provide some alternative to elite

monopolies on consensus formation. Were they also timed to coincide with European elections – perhaps European elections widened in line with the previous point to include some impact on executive and not just legislative office – they could also encourage more voters to participate and established democratic actors (such as political parties) to differentiate themselves more clearly on European issues.

Notes

1. Interview, PES MEP, March 2001.
2. Various interviews, European Parliament, 2000–2.
3. I am grateful to Justus Schönlau for this point.
4. This calculation is taken from papers prepared for a meeting of the Constitutional Affairs Committee of the European Parliament on 7 November 2000 (fn. 1, p. 59).
5. Comment by N. Schmit, Luxembourg's personal representative on the IGC preparatory group, at a meeting of the European Parliament's Constitutional Affairs Committee, 12 October 2000.
6. Speech of the Vice President of the Catalonian Parliament to the Public Hearing on the prepartion of the Commission's White Paper on Governance, 16 March 2001, Author's notes.
7. Interview, European Commission, March 2001.
8. Author's notes from various meetings of the Constitutional Affairs Committee of the European Parliament during 2001.
9. The absolute majority rule requires the European Parliament to have a majority of its members and not just of those voting if it is to exercise certain of its powers under the Treaties. The following is an example of its impact: since there are 626 MEPs, a majority of Members is 314. If 500 vote, the minimum winning coalition under the absolute majority rule is 314 (62.8 per cent) to 186 (37.2 per cent). In fact, a lot of votes involve fewer MEPs with the result that the EP *de facto* requires supermajorities not unlike those of the Council of around 70 per cent.
10. Author's notes of advice of the European Parliament Legal Service to the Institutional Affairs Committee, October 1994.
11. Interview with ELDR MEP, January 2001.
12. Interview with ELDR MEP, November 2000.
13. Interview with ELDR MEP, January 2001.
14. Interview with ELDR MEP, November 2000.
15. Interview with PES MEP, January 2001.
16. Interview with PES MEP, January 2001.
17. Interview with ELDR MEP, February 2001.
18. Interview with PES MEP, March 2001.
19. Interview, European Commission, February 2001.
20. Interview with Green MEP, February 2001.
21. Interview with former President of the European Parliament, May 2001.
22. Interview, European Commission, February 2001.
23. Author's conversation with chair of the Comité des Sages, October 2002.
24. Interview with EPP MEP, January 2001.
25. Interview, European Commission, March 2001.
26. Interview with Pat Cox MEP, March 2001.
27. Interview with Green MEP, February 2001.
28. Interview with ELDR MEP, November 2000.

29. Interview, European Commission, November 2000.
30. Interview, European Commission, March 2001.
31. Interview, European Commission, January 2001.
32. Interview, European Commission, March 2001.
33. Interview with ELDR MEP, November 2000.
34. Interview, Finnish Parliament Official, 15 January 2002.
35. This view was repeatedly expressed in the interviews undertaken for this study with actors from the Scandinavian Parliaments.
36. Author's notes from meeting of Constitutional Affairs Committee of the European Parliament, October 2000.
37. Interview, Swedish Riksdag, 6 March 2002.
38. Interview, Swedish Riksdag, 3 March 2002.
39. Interviews, both Houses of Belgium Parliament, November 2000.
40. Interview, Swedish Riksdag, 3 March 2002.
41. Ibid.
42. Interview, Danish Folketing Official, 8 March 2003.
43. Interview, Swedish Riksdag, 3 March 2002.
44. Interview, Danish Folketing Official, 8 March 2003.
45. Interview, Swedish Riksdag, 3 March 2002.
46. Interview, Finnish Parliament Official, 15 January 2002.
47. Interview Swedish Riksdag, 5 March 2002.
48. Interview, PES MEP, February 2001.
49. Author's Notes at meeting of the Economic and Monetary Affairs Committee (EMAC) of the European Parliament, February 1998.
50. Interview with Member of EMAC, March 2002.
51. I am grateful to Uwe Leonardy for this comment.

Bibliography

Abromeit, H. (1998) *Democracy in Europe: Legitimising Politics in a Non-State Polity*, Oxford, Berghahn Books.

Ackerman, B. (1998) *We the People: Transformations*, Cambridge, Harvard University Press.

Almond, G. and Verba, S. (1963) *The Civic Culture. Political Attitudes and Democracy in Five Nations*, Princeton, Princeton University Press.

Andeweg, R. (1995) 'The Reshaping of National Party Systems', *West European Politics*, vol. 18, no. 3, pp. 58–78.

Andolfato, D. (1994) 'Les Euro-deputés en Question', *Revue Politique et Parlementaire*, no. 970.

Arblaster, A. (1987) *Democracy*, Milton Keynes, Open University.

Armstrong, K. (1998) 'Legal Integration: Theorizing the Legal Dimension of European Integration', *Journal of Common Market Studies*, vol. 36, no. 2, pp. 155–74.

Arnull, A. (2002) 'The Rule of Law in the European Union' in A. Arnull and D. Wincott (eds) *Accountability and Legitimacy in the European Union*, Oxford, Oxford University Press, pp. 239–56.

Arter, D. (1996) 'The Folketing and Denmark's European Policy: the Case of an Authorising Assembly' in P. Norton (ed.) *National Parliaments and the European Union*, London, Frank Cass, pp. 110–23.

Assemblée Nationale (2002) *La Délégation de L'Assemblée Nationale pour L'Union Européenne*, Paris, Assemblée Nationale.

Bardi, L. (1996) 'Transnational Trends in European Parties and the 1994 Elections of the European Parliament', *Party Politics*, vol. 2, no. 1, pp. 99–114.

Barnier, M. (2001) 'L'Urgence Européenne. Note Personnelle de Michel Barnier'

Barro, R. and Gordon, D. (1983) 'Rules, Discretion and Reputation in a Model of Monetary Policy', *Journal of Monetary Economics*, vol. 12, no. 2, pp. 101–21.

Bauman, Z. (1999) *In Search of Politics*, Cambridge, Polity.

Beetham, D. (1991) *The Legitimation of Power*, Basingstoke, Macmillan.

Beetham, D. (1994) *Defining and Measuring Democracy*, London, Sage/ECPR.

Beetham, D., Bracking, S., Kearton, I. and Weir, S. (2002) *International IDEA Handbook on Democracy Assessment*, The Hague, Kluwer Law International.

Bellamy, R. and Castiglione, D. (2000) 'The uses of democracy: reflections on the European democratic deficit' in E. Eriksen and J. Fossum, *Democracy in the European Union. Integrational Through Deliberation*, London, Routledge, pp. 65–84.

Bellamy, R. and Castiglione, D. (2002) 'Legitimizing the Euro-"Polity" and its "Regime", The Normative Turn in EU Studies', *European Journal of Political Theory*, vol. 2, no. 1, pp. 7–34.

Bellamy, R. and Warleigh, A. (1998) 'From an ethics of integration to an ethics of participation: citizenship and the future of the European Union', *Millennium*, no. 27, pp. 447–70.

Benz, A. and Esslinger, T. (2000) '*Compounded Representation in European Multilevel Governance*', Paper presented to conference, 'Linking European and National Governance', Mannheim Centre for European Social Research, 1–3 June 2000.

Bergman, T. (1997) 'National Parliaments and EU Affairs Committees: Notes on Empirical Varation and Competing Explanations', *Journal of European Public Policy*, vol. 4, no. 3, pp. 373–87.

Bergman, T. (2000) 'The European Union as the Next Step of Delegation and Accountability', *European Journal of Political Research*, vol. 37, no. 3, pp. 415–29.

Blondel, J. (1990) *Comparative Government, An Introduction*, London, Philip Allan.

Blondel, J., Sinnott, R. and Svensson, P. (1998) *People and Parliament in the European Union: Participation, Democracy and Legitimacy*, Oxford, Clarendon Press.

Boeden, M. (2001) 'Accountability Mechanisms and European Police Co-operation', Lecture at conference on Europol and Parliamentary Control, Dutch Senate, 7 June 2001.

Bogaards, M. and Crepaz, M. (2002) 'Consociational Interpretations of the European Union', *European Union Politics*, vol. 3, no. 3, pp. 357–76.

Bogdanor, V. (1986) 'The Future of the European Community: Two Models of Democracy', *Government and Opposition*, vol. 22, no. 2, pp. 344–70.

Bollen, K. (1980) 'Issues in the Comparative Measurement of Political Democracy', *American Sociological Review*, vol. 45, pp. 370–90.

Bostock, D. (2002) 'Coreper Revisited', *Journal of Common Market Studies*, vol. 40, no. 2, pp. 215–34.

Bréchon, P. (1999) 'L'Europe face au déficit démocratique', *Revue Politique et Parlementaire*, no. 1001, pp. 5–15.

Briault, C., Haldane, A. and King, M. (1996) *Independence and Accountability*, London, Bank of England, Working Paper, No. 49.

Buchanan, J. and Tullock G. (1962). *The Calculus of Consent: Logical Foundation of Constitutional Democracy*. Ann Arbor, Michigan, University of Michigan Press.

Buiter, W. (1999) 'Alice in Euroland', *Journal of Common Market Studies*, vol. 37, no. 2, pp. 181–209.

Búrca de, G. (1998) 'The Principle of Subsidiarity and the Court of Justice as an Institutional Actor', *Journal of Common Market Studies*, vol. 36, no. 2, pp. 155–74.

Búrca de, G. and de Witte, B. (2002) 'The Delimitation of Powers between the EU and its Member States' in A. Arnull and D. Wincott (eds) *Accountability and Legitimacy in the European Union*, Oxford, Oxford University Press.

Burke, E. (1975 [1774]) 'Speech to the Electors of Bristol' in B. Hill (ed.) *Edmund Burke on Government, Politics and Society*, London, Fontana.

Centre for Democratic Governance (2002) *Measuring Democracy and Good Governance*, Munich, Centre for Democratic Governance.

Christiansen, T. (1997) 'Tensions of European Governance. Politicized Bureaucracy and Multiple Accountability in the European Commission', *Journal of European Public Policy*, vol. 4, no. 1, pp. 73–90.

Christiansen, T., Jorgensen, K.-E, and Wiener, A. (2001). *The Social Construction of Europe*, London, Sage.

Chryssochoou, D. (1994) 'Democracy and Symbiosis in the European Union: Towards a Confederal Consociation?', *West European Politics*, vol. 17, no. 4, pp. 1–14.

Clergerie, J.-L (1995) 'L'improbable censure de la Commission Européenne', *Revue de Droit Public et de la Science Politique*, vol. 111, no. 2, pp. 205–20.

Committee of the Regions (1999) *Regional and Local Democracy in the European Union*. Brussels, Committee of the Regions.

Coppedge, M. and Reinicke, W. (1990) 'Measuring Polyarchy', *Studies in International and Comparative Development*, vol. 25, pp. 51–72.

Corbett, R. (1998) *The European Parliament's Role in Closer European Integration*, Basingstoke, Macmillan.

Corbett, R., Jacobs, F. and Shackleton, M. (1995) *The European Parliament*, London, Catermill.

Corbett, R., Jacobs, F. and Shackleton, M. (2003) 'The European Parliament at Fifty. A View from the Inside', *Journal of Common Market Studies*, vol. 41, no. 3, pp. 353–73.

COSAC (2001a) *Summary of Proceedings, XXIV COSAC*. Stockholm, 20–22 May 2001.

COSAC (2001b) Contribution from the XXIVth COSAC in Sweden to the European Council, 22 May 2001.

COSAC (2002) *'The Role of National Parliaments in the European Union'*, paper presented by Luisa Fernanda Rudi Ùbeda, President of the Congress of Deputies Spain. Madrid Conference of Speakers of the European Union 8–9 June 2002.

Costa, O., Jabko, N., Lequesne, C. and Magnette, P. (2001) 'La diffusion des mécanismes de contrôle dans l'Union européenne: vers une nouvelle forme de démocratie?', *Revue Française de Science Politique*, vol. 51, no. 6, pp. 859–67.

Costa, O. (2001) 'La Cour de Justice et le contrôle démoratique de l'Union européenne', *Revue Française de Science Politique*, vol. 51, no. 6, pp. 881–903.

Council of European Municipalities and Regions. 'Enhancing Democracy in the European Union. A Stronger Involvement for Local and Regional Government'.

Council of the European Union (1995) *Reflection Group's Report*, Brussels, Council of the European Union.

Council of the European Union (2000) *Council's Rules of Procedure*, Brussels, General Secretariat of the Council.

Council of the European Union (2001a) *Conclusions adopted by the Council* (Justice and Home Affairs), Brussels, 20 September 2001, SN 3926/6101.

Council of the European Union (2001b) *The Future of the European Union* (Laeken Declaration), Brussels, 15 December 2001.

Cram, L. (1994) 'The European Commission as a Multi-Organisation: Social Policy and IT Policy in the EU', *Journal of European Public Policy*, vol. 1, no. 2, pp. 195–217.

Crawford, G. (1997) 'Foreign Aid and Political Conditionality: Issues of Effectiveness and Consistency', *Democratization*, vol. 4, no. 3, pp. 69–108.

Crombez, C. (1996) 'Legislative Procedures in the European Community', *British Journal of Political Science*, vol. 26, no. 2, pp. 199–218.

Crombez, C. (2003) 'The Democratic Deficit in the European Union. Much Ado about Nothing', *European Union Politics*, vol. 4, no. 1, pp. 101–20.

Crombez, C., Steunenberg, B. and Corbett, R. (2000) 'Understanding the EU Legislative Process: Political Scientists' and Practitioners' Perspectives', *European Union Politics*, vol. 1, no. 3, pp. 363–83.

Curtin, D. (1993) 'The Constitutional Structure of the Union: A Europe of Bits and Pieces', *Common Market Law Review*, vol. 30, pp. 17–69.

Dahl, R. (1971) *Polyarchy: Participation and Opposition*, New Haven CT, Yale University Press.

Dahl, R. (1989) *On Democracy*, New Haven, Yale University Press.

Dehousse, R. (1995) *'Institutional Reform in the European Community: Are there Alternatives to the Majoritarian Avenue?'*. EUI Working Paper RSC 95/4. Florence, EUI.

Dehousse, R. (1997) 'European Integration and the Nation-State' in M. Rhodes, P. Heywood, and V. Wright (eds) *Developments in West European Politics*, London, Macmillan, pp. 37–57.

Dehousse, R. (1998) *The European Court of Justice: The Politics of Judicial Integration*, New York, St Martin's Press.

Delwit, P. (2000) 'Participation électorale et scrutin européen: une légitimité minimale' in G. Grünberg, P. Perrineau, and C. Ysmal, *Le Vote Des Quinze: Les elections européennes du 13 Juin 1999*, pp. 295–316.

Den Boer, M. (2001) 'Accountability Mechanisms and European Police Co-operation'. Lecture Organised by the Dutch Senate 7 June 2001, Unpublished Manuscript.

Dewey, J. (1927) *The Public and its Problems*, London, George Allen and Unwin.

Diamond, L. (1992) 'Economic Development and Democracy Reconsidered', *American Behavioural Scientist*, vol. 35, no. 4–5, pp. 450–99.

Dimitrakopoulos, D. (2001) 'Incrementalism and Path Dependence: European Integration and Institutional Change in National Parliaments', *Journal of Common Market Studies*, vol. 39, no. 3, pp. 405–22.

Döring, H. (1995) (ed.) *Parliaments and Majority Rule in Western Europe*, Frankfurt, Campus Verlag.

Duff, A. (1997) *The Treaty of Amsterdam: Text and Commentary*, London, Federal Trust.

Dworkin, R. (1996) *Freedom's Law*, Cambridge, Mass., Harvard University Press.

Easton, D. (1957) 'An Approach to the Study of Political Systems', *World Politics*, vol. 9, no. 5, pp. 383–400.

Eijffinger, S. and De Haan, J. (1996) 'The Political Economy of Central Bank Independence', *Princeton Special Papers in International Economics*, no. 19.

Eleftheriadis, P. (1998) 'Begging the Constitutional Question', *Journal of Common Market Studies*, vol. 36, no. 2, pp. 255–72.

Elkins, Z. (2000) 'Gradations of Democracy. Empirical Tests of Alternative Conceptualisations', *American Journal of Political Science*, vol. 44, no. 2, pp. 293–300.

Elster, J. (ed.) (1998), *'Deliberative Democracy'*, Cambridge, Cambridge University Press.

Eriksen, E. and Fossum, J. (2000) 'Post-national integration' in E. Eriksen and J. Fossum (eds) *Democracy in the European Union: Integration Through Deliberation*, London, Routledge, pp. 1–28.

Eurobarometer: Public Opinion is the European Community (two issues per year). Brussels, Office for Official Publications of the European Communities.

Eurobarometer (1995) *Special Report on European Citizenship.*

European Central Bank (2001) *The Monetary Policy of the ECB*. Frankfurt Am Main, European Central Bank.

European Commission (1992) *The Treaty on European Union*. Luxembourg, European Commission.

European Commission (1995) *Openness and Transparency in the EU Institutions*. Brussels, European Commission.

European Commission (1997) *Evolution in Governance. What Lessons for the Commision? A First Assessment*. Working Paper compiled by Notis Lebessis and John Paterson. Brussels, European Commission.

European Commission (1999a) *Better Lawmaking 1998. A Shared Responsibility. Commission Report to the European Council*. Brussels, European Commission.

European Commission (1999b) *Adapting the Institutions to make a Success of Enlargement. Contribution by the European Commission to Preparations for the IGC on Institutional Issues*. Brussels, European Commission.

European Commission (1999c) *Code of Conduct for Commissioners*. Brussels, European Commission.

European Commission (2000a) *Reforming the Commission. Consultative Document. Communication from Mr Kinnock in agreement with the President and Ms Schreyer*. CG 3 (2000). Brussels, European Commission.

European Commission (2000b) *Strategic Objectives 2000–2005: Shaping the New Europe*. Com (2000). Brussels, European Commission.

European Commission (2000c) *Comparative Analysis of Member States' Legislation Concerning the Access to Documents*. Brussels, European Commission.

European Commission (2000d) *White Paper on Governance, 'Enhancing Democracy in the European Union' Work Document*. Brussels, European Commission.

European Commission (2001a) *Amended Proposal for a Regulation of the European Parliament and of the Council regarding public access to European Parliament, Council and Commission Documents*. Brussels, European Commission.

European Commission (2001b) *Perceptions of the European Union. A Qualitative Study of the Public's Attitudes to and Expectations of the European Union in the 15 Member States and the 9 Candidate Countries*. (The Optem Report) Brussels, European Commission.

European Commission (2001c) *White Paper on European Governance. Report of Working Group 'Consultation and Participation of Civil Society'*. Brussels, European Commission.

European Commission (2001d) *European Governance, A White Paper*. Brussels, European Commission.

European Commission (2001e) *Governance in the European Union ('Cahiers of the Forward Studies Unit')*. Brussels, European Commission.

European Commission (2001f) *Decentralisation, Better Involvement of Local and Regional Actors*. Brussels, European Commission.

European Commission (2002a) *Consultation Document: Towards a Reinforced Culture of Consultation and Dialogue – Proposals for General Principles and Minimum Standards for Consultation of Interested Parties by the Commission*. Brussels, European Commission.

European Convention (2002a) *The Role of National Parliaments in the European Architecture*. Brussels, Secretariat of the European Convention.

European Convention (2002b) *'Securing the Influence of National Parliaments, Use of Scrutiny Reserves in the Council*. Paper by Kimmo Kiljunen Member of the Convention, Brussels, Secretariat of the European Convention.

European Convention (2002c) *Various Notes on Plenary Meetings during 2002*. Brussels, Secretariat of the European Convention.

European Convention (2002d) *Working Group IV. Paper by Andrew Duff*. Brussels, Secretariat of the European Convention.

European Convention (2003a) *Various Notes on Plenary Meetings during 2003*. Brussels, Secretariat of the European Convention.

European Convention (2003b) *Summary of Discussions in the Contact Group with Regional and Local Authorities*. Brussels, Secretariat of the Convention.

European Convention (2003c) *Draft Constitution.* Brussels, Secretariat to the Convention.

European Council (1993) *Conclusions of the Presidency*, Copenhagen, 21–22 June 1993. Brussels, General Secretariat of the Council.

European Council (1999a) *Presidency Conclusions.* Cologne, 3–4 June 1999. Brussels, General Secretariat of the Council.

European Council (1999b) *Presidency Conclusions.* Tampere, 15–16 October 2001. Brussels, General Secretariat of the Council.

European Council (2001) *Presidency Conclusions*, Laeken, 14–15 December 2001. Brussels, General Secretariat of the Council.

European Liberal and Democratic Reform Group of the European Parliament (1999). Press Release, *Constitutive Agreement – Not a Political Coalition*, Brussels, 15 July 1999.

European Parliament (1997) *Report on Relations between the European Parliament and National Parliaments* (Neyts-Uytterbroeck). Brussels, European Parliament.

European Parliament (1998a) *Report on the Co-Decision Procedure After Amsterdam.* European Parliament, Brussels.

European Parliament (1998b) *Report on the Moderation of Procedures for the Exercise of Implementing Powers – Comitology* (Aglietta report). Brussels, European Parliament.

European Parliament (1998c) *Nominations to the Executive Board of the European Central Bank: European Parliament. Confirmation Hearings*, Brussels, 7–8 May.

European Parliament (1998d) *Resolution on Democratic Accountability in the Third Phase of EMU* (The Randzio-Plath Report), Brussels, European Parliament.

European Parliament [Maurer, A.] (1999a) *Co-Governing After Maastricht. The EP's Institutional Performance 1994–99.* Luxembourg, European Parliament D-G for Research.

European Parliament (1999b) *Report on the Proposal for a Council Decision Laying Down the Procedures for the Exercise of Implementing Powers Conferred on the Commission.* Brussels, European Parliament.

European Parliament (1999c) *On the Decision-Making Process in the Council in an Enlarged Europe* (Bourlanges report). Brussels, European Parliament.

European Parliament (1999d) See series of documents *Reply to Questionnaires in Preparation for Hearings with Commissioners designate.* Brussels, European Parliament.

European Parliament (1999e) See series of documents *Confirmation Hearings of Commissioners-designate.* Brussels, European Parliament.

European Parliament (1999f) *Hearing with Dr. Willem Duisenberg President of the European Central Bank Brussels, 18 January 1999.* Brussels, European Parliament.

European Parliament (1999g) *Background Information: Motions of Censure.* Brussels, European Parliament.

European Parliament (2000a) *Report on the European Parliament's Proposals for the Intergovernmental Conference* (Dimitrakopoulos–Leinen). Brussels, European Parliament.

European Parliament (2000b) *Report on Initiative Amending the Europol Convention* (Karamanou Report). Brussels, European Parliament.

European Parliament (2000c) *Report on the Progress Achieved in the Implementation of the Common Foreign and Security Policy* (Response to Council of Ministers report on CFSP during 1999) (Brok Report). Brussels, European Parliament.

European Parliament (2000d) *Report on the White Paper on reforming the Commission* (Lamassoure Report). Brussels, European Parliament.

European Parliament (2000e) *On the Draft General Budget for 2001* (European Parliament, Council) (Ferber Report). Brussels, European Parliament.

European Parliament (2001a) *On Progress in Establishing an Area of Freedom, Security and Justice (AFSJ) in the Year 2000* (Posselt Report). Brussels, European Parliament.

European Parliament (2001b) *Recommendation for Second Reading Amending Council on the use of the Financial System for Money Laundering*. Brussels, European Parliament.

European Parliament (2001c) *Report on initiative for a Council Decision on the Provisional Establishment of the European Police College* (Posselt Report). Brussels, European Parliament.

European Parliament (2001d) *Report on Proposal for a Regulation on the Protection of Individuals with regard to the Processing of Personal Data by the Institutions and Bodies of the Community* (Paciotti report). Brussels, European Parliament.

European Parliament (2001e) *Report on the Progress Achieved in the Implementation of the Common Foreign and Security Policy* (Response to Council of Ministers report on CFSP during 2000) (Brok Report). Brussels, European Parliament.

European Parliament (2001f) *Report on Relations between the European Parliament and the National Parliaments in European Integration* (Napolitano Report). Brussels, European Parliament.

European Parliament (2001g) *On the Financial Regulation Applicable to the General Budget of the European Communities* (Dell'Alba Report). Brussels, European Parliament.

European Parliament (2001h) *On the 1999 Discharge* (Blak Report). Brussels, European Parliament.

European Parliament (2001i) *On the Proposal for a European Parliament and Council Decision on the Mobilisation of the Flexibility Instrument* (Wynn Report). Brussels, European Parliament.

European Parliament (2002a) *On the Role of Regions in European Integration* (Napolitano Report). Brussels, European Parliament.

European Parliament (2003a) *On the Proposal for a Council Regulation Adapting the Provisions Relating to Committees which Assist the Commission in the Exercise of its Implementing Powers* (Frassoni Report). Brussels, European Parliament.

Farrell, H. and Héritier, A. (2002) 'Formal and Informal Institutions under Co-decision: Continuous Constitution Building in Europe', *Europe On-line Papers*, vol. 6, no. 3.

Ferry, J.-M. (2000) *La question de l'État Européen*, Paris, Gallimard.

Fischer, J. (2000) Vom Staatenverbund zur Föderation – Gedanken über die Finalität die europäischen Integration. Rede am 12 Mai 2000 in der Humboldt Universität in Berlin.

Fishkin, J., Luskin, R. and Jowell, R. (2000) 'Deliberative Opinion Polling and Public Consultation', *Parliamentary Affairs*, vol. 53, no. 4, pp. 657–66.

Fitzmaurice, J. (1996) 'National Parliamentary control of EU policy in the three new Member States', *West European Politics*, vol. 19, no. 1, pp. 88–96.

Folketinget (2002) *National Parliaments in the European Institutional Framework, Report by Ivor Hansen, Speaker of the Danish Folketing*. Copenhagen.

Føllesdal, A. (2001) *Union Citizenship: Unpacking the Beast of Burden.* ARENA Working Papers WP 01/9.

Forster, A. (1999) *Britain and the Maastricht Negotiations*, Basingstoke, Macmillan.

Fortescue, J. (1995) 'First Experiences in the Implementation of the Third Pillar Provisions' in R. Bieber and J. Monar (eds) *Justice and Home Affairs in the European Union: the Development of the Third Pillar.* Bruges, College of Europe, pp. 19–29.

Franchino, F. (2000) 'Control of the Commission's Executive Functions: Uncertainty, Conflict and Decision Rules', *European Union Politics*, vol. 1, no. 1, pp. 63–92.

Franchino, F. (2001) Delegating Powers in the European Community. Paper Presented at the Annual Meeting of the American Political Science Association, San Francisco, 30 August–2 September 2001.

Franklin, M. (2001) 'How Structural Factors Cause Turnout Variations at European Parliament Elections', *European Union Politics*, vol. 2, no. 3, pp. 309–29.

Franklin, M., Marsh, M. and McLaren, L. (1994) 'Uncorking the Bottle: Popular Opposition to European Unification in the wake of Maastricht', *Journal of Common Market Studies*, vol. 32, no. 4, pp. 455–72.

Freedom House (2002) *The Annual Survey of Press Freedom 2002,* New York, Freedom House.

Fukuyama, F. (1989) 'The End of History?', *The National Interest*, vol. 16, pp. 3–18.

Garcia, G. and Le Torrec, V. (2003) *L'Union Européenne et les Médias, Regards Croisés sur L'Information Européenne*, Paris, L' Harmattan.

Garrett, G. (1995) 'The Politics of Legal Integration in the European Union', *International Organisation*, vol. 49, no. 1, pp. 171–81.

Garrett, G., Tsebelis, G. and Corbett, R. (2001) Examining the EU Legislative Process: Academics vs. Practitioners – Round 2. *European Union Politics*, vol. 2, no. 3, pp. 353–67.

Gerstlé, J., Semetko, H., Schoenbach, K. and Villa, M. (2000) 'L'Européanisation défaillante des campagnes nationales' in P. Grünberg, P. Perrineau, and C. Ysmal, *Le Vote Des Quinze: Les elections européennes du 13 Juin 1999*, Paris, Presses De La Fondation Nationales des Sciences Politiques, pp. 95–120.

Giddens, A. (1984) *The Constitution of Society, Outline of the Theory of Structuration*, Cambridge, Polity Press.

Giddens, A. (2000) 'A Third Way for the European Union' in M. Leonard (ed.) *The Future Shape of the European Union*, London, Foreign Policy Centre, pp. 69–76.

Giddings, P. and Drewry, A. (1996) *Westminster and Europe. The Impact of the European Union on the Westminster Parliament*, Basingstoke, Macmillan.

Gray, M. and Stubb, A. (2001) 'Keynote Article: the Treaty of Nice – Negotiating a Poisoned Chalice?' in G. Edwards and G. Wiessala (eds) *The European Union: Annual Review of the EU 2000–2001.* Oxford, Blackwell, pp. 1–23.

Greenwood, J. (1997) *Representing Interests in the European Union*, Basingstoke, Macmillan.

Haan, J. de (1997) 'The European Central Bank: Independence, Accountability and Strategy: A review', *Public Choice*, vol. 93, pp. 395–426.

Haan, J. de and Eijffinger, S. (2000) 'The Democratic Accountability of the European Central Bank: A Comment on Two Fairy Tales', *Journal of Common Market Studies*, vol. 38, no. 3, pp. 393–407.

Habermas, J. (1989 [1962]) *The Structural Transformation of the Public Sphere*, Cambridge, Mass., Cambridge University Press.

Habermas, J. (1992) 'Citizenship and National Identity. Some Reflections on the Future of Europe', *Praxis International*, vol. 12, no. 1, pp. 1–19.
Habermas, J. (1996) *Between Facts and Norms*, Cambridge, Polity.
Habermas, J. (2001) 'Why Europe Needs a Constitution', *New Left Review*, vol. 11.
Hadenius, A. (1992) *Democracy and Development*, Cambridge, Cambridge University Press.
Hallstein, W. (1970) *L'Europe Inachevée*, Paris, Robert Laffont.
Hayes-Renshaw, F. and Wallace, H. (1997) *The Council of Ministers*, London, Macmillan.
Hegeland, H. and Neuhold, C. (2002) 'Parliamentary Participation in EU Affairs in Austria, Finland and Sweden: Newcomers with Different Approaches', *European On-Line Papers*, vol. 6, no. 10, pp. 1–18.
Held, D. (1996) *Models of Democracy*, 2nd edn, Cambridge, Polity.
Held, D. (1997) *Democracy and Globalization*, Max Planck Institut Working Paper 97/5.
Héritier, A. (1997) 'Policy-making by Subterfuge: Interest Accommodation, Innovation and Substitute Democratic Legitimation in Europe – Perspectives from Distinctive Policy Areas', *Journal of European Public Policy*, vol. 4, no. 2, pp. 171–89.
Hibbs, D. (1977) 'Political Parties and Macroeconomic Policy', *American Political Science Review*, no. 23, pp. 1467–88.
Hitzel-Cassagnes, T. (2000) *'Law versus Democracy? Democratic Constitutionalism and the Role of Judges in the European Union'*, Paper presented to ECPR Joint Sessions, Copenhagen April 2000.
Hix, S. (1995) *Political Parties in the European Union System: A 'Comparative Political Approach' to the Development of the European Party Federations*, unpublished PhD thesis. Florence, European University Institute.
Hix, S. (1999) *The Political System of the European Union*, London, Macmillan.
Hix, S. (2001) 'Legislative Behaviour and Party Competition in the EP', *Journal of Common Market Studies*, vol. 39, no. 4, pp. 663–89.
Hix, S. and Lord, C. (1996) 'The Making of a President: the European Parliament and the Confirmation of Jacques Santer as President of the Commission', *Government and Opposition*, vol. 31, no. 1, pp. 62–76.
Hix, S. and Lord, C. (1997) *Political Parties in the European Union*, London, Macmillan.
Hix, S. and Raunio, T. (2000) 'Backbenchers Learn to Fight Back: European Integration and Parliamentary Government', *West European Politics*, vol. 23, no. 4, pp. 142–68.
Hix, S., Raunio T. and Scully, R. (1999) *An Institutional Theory of Behaviour in the European Parliament*, European Parliament Research Group (EPRG) Working Paper 1.
Holmberg, S. (2001) *Swedish Voting Behaviour*. Göteborg, Swedish Electoral Studies Programme.
House of Lords (1996) *27th Report on the Scrutiny of European Business*. Select Committee on European Legislation. London, HMSO.
Jansen, T. (1996) *Die Entstehung eines Europäischen Partei: Vorgeschichte, Gründung und Entwicklung der EVP*, Bonn, Europa Union Verlag.
Joerges, C. and Neyer, J. (1997) 'Transforming strategic interaction into deliberative problem-solving: European comitology in the foodstuffs sector', *Journal of European Public Policy*, vol. 4, no. 4, pp. 609–25.

Johansson, K-M. (1997) *Transational Party Alliances, Analysing the Hard-Won Alliance between the Conservatives and Christian Democrats in the European Parliament*, Lund, Lund University Press.

Johansson, K.-M. (1999) 'Tracing the Employment Title in the Amsterdam Treaty. Uncovering Transnational Coalitions', *Journal of European Public Policy*, vol. 6, no. 1, pp. 85–101.

Johansson K.-M. and Raunio, T. (2001) 'Partisan Responses to Europe. Comparing Finnish and Swedish Political Parties', *European Journal of Political Research*, vol. 39, no. 2, pp. 225–49.

Judge, D. and Earnshaw, D. (2003) *The European Parliament*, Basingstoke, Palgrave.

Kahnemann, D., Slovik, P. and Tversky, A. (eds) (1982) *Judgement under Uncertainty*, London, Cambridge University Press.

Karlsson, C. (2001) *Democracy, Legitimacy and the European Union*, Uppsala, University of Uppsala.

Kassim, H. and Menon, A. (2003) 'The Principal–Agent Approach and the study of the European Union', *Journal of European Public Policy*, vol. 10, no. 1, pp. 121–39.

Katz, R. (2001) 'Models of Democracy: Elite Attitudes and the Democratic Deficit', *European Union Politics*, vol. 2, no. 1, pp. 53–80.

Katz, R. and Mair, P. (1995) 'Changing Models of Party Organisation and Party Democracy: the Emergence of the Cartel Party', *Party Politics*, vol. 1, no. 1, pp. 5–28.

Keohane, R. (2001) 'Governance in a Partially Globalised World', *American Political Science Review*, vol. 95, no. 1, pp. 1–13.

Kohl, H. (1992) *Bilanzen und Perspektiven. Regierungspolitik 1989–1991*, Bonn, Presse und Informationsamt der Bundesregierung.

Kohler-Koch, B. (1996) 'Catching up with Change: the Transformation of Governance in the European Union', *Journal of European Public Policy*, vol. 3, no. 3, pp. 359–80.

Krehbiel, K. (1991) *Information and Legislative Organisation*, Ann Arbor, University of Michigan Press.

Kreppel, A. (2000) 'Rules, Ideology and Coalition Formation in the European Parliament: Past, Present and Future', *European Union Politics*, vol. 1, no. 3, pp. 340–62.

Kux, S. and Sverdrup, U. (2000) 'Fuzzy Borders and Adaptive Outsiders: Norway, Switzerland and the EU', *European Integration*, vol. 29, no. 1, pp. 1–34.

Kydland, F. and Prescott, E. (1977) 'Rules Rather than Discretion: the Inconsistency of Optimal Plans', *Journal of Political Economy*, vol. 85, no. 1, pp. 137–60.

Laffan, B. (1997) *The Finances of the European Union*, London, Macmillan.

Laffan, B. (1999) 'Democracy and the European Union' in L. Cram, D. Dinan and N. Nugent (eds), *Developments in the European Union*, London, Macmillan.

Laver, M. and Shepsle, K. (1996) *Making and Breaking Governments: Cabinets and Legislatures in Parliamentary Democracies*, Cambridge, Cambridge University Press.

Lequesne, C. and Rivaud, P. (2001) 'Les comités d'experts independents: l'expertise au service d'une démocratie supranationale', *Revue Française de Science Politique*, vol. 51, no. 6, pp. 867–81.

Levitt, M. and Lord, C. (2000) *The Political Economy of Monetary Union*, Basingstoke, Macmillan.

Lewis, J. (1998) *The Institutional Problem-Solving Capacities of the Council: The Committee of Permanent Representatives and the Methods of Community*. Köln, Max–Planck–Institut, Discussion Paper 98/1.
Lewis, J. (2002) 'National Interests: Coreper' in J. Peterson and M. Shackleton (eds) *The Institutions of the European Union*, Oxford, Oxford University Press.
Lijphart. A. (1979) 'Consociational Democracy', *World Politics*, vol. 32, pp. 207–25.
Lijphart, A. (1984) *Democracies: Patterns of Majoritarian and Consensus Government in Twenty-One Countries*, New Haven, Yale University Press.
Lijphart, A. (1997) 'The Puzzle of Indian Democracy: A Consociational Interpretation', *American Political Science Review*, vol. 90, no. 2, pp. 258–68.
Lipset, S. M. (1959) 'Some Social Requisites of Democracy', *American Journal of Political Science*, vol. 53.
Lohmann, S. (1992) 'Optimal Commitment in Monetary Policy: Credibility Versus Flexibility', *American Economic Review*, vol. 82, pp. 273–86.
Lohmann, S. (1998) 'Federalism and Central Bank Independence: The Politics of German Monetary Policy 1957–92', *World Politics*, vol. 50, no. 3, pp. 401–46.
Lord, C. (1998a) *Democracy in the European Union*, Sheffield, Sheffield University Press.
Lord, C. (1998b) 'The Untidy Right in the European Parliament' in D. Bell and C. Lord (eds) *Transnational Parties in the European Union*, Aldershot, Ashgate.
Lord, C. (2000) 'Le Nouveau Parlement Européen' in G. Grünberg, P. Perrineau and C. Ysmal (eds) *Le Vote Des Quinze*, Paris, Presses de la Fondation Nationale Des Sciences Politques, pp. 317–40.
Lord, C. (2001a) 'Assessing Democracy in a Contested Polity', *Journal of Common Market Studies*, vol. 39, no. 4, pp. 641–61.
Lord, C. (2001b) 'Les partis politiques au niveau européen: quel type de concurrence imparfaite' in P. Delwit, E. Külachi and C. van de Walle (eds) *Les fédérations européennes de partis. Organisation et influence*, Brussels, Université Libre de Bruxelles, pp. 39–56.
Lord, C. (2002) 'What role for Parties in EU Politics?' *Journal of European Integration*, vol. 24, no. 1, pp. 39–52.
Lord, C. (2003) 'The European Parliament in the Economic Governance of the European Union', *Journal of Common Market Studies*.
Lord, C. (2003) 'The European Parliament, Not a very European Parliament?', *Intégration Européenne*, no. 9, pp. 30–49.
Lord, C. and Beetham, D. (2001) 'Legitimizing the EU: Is there a "Post-parliamentary Basis" for its Legitimation', *Journal of Common Market Studies*, vol. 39, no. 3, pp. 443–62.
Lord, C. and Magnette, P. (2004) 'E Pluribus Unum? Creative Disagreement about Legitimacy in the EU', forthcoming in *Journal of Common Market Studies*.
Lucas, R. (1981) 'Expectations and the Neutrality of Money' in R. Lucas (ed.) *Studies in Business Cycle Theory*, Oxford, Blackwell.
Lukes, S. (1974) *Power, A Radical View*, London, Macmillan.
MacIntyre, A. (1981) *After virtue: a study in moral theory*, London, Duckworth.
Magnette, P. (1999) 'L'Union européenne: Un régime semi parlementaire' in P. Delwit, J.- M. DeWaele, and P. Magnette (eds) *À quoi sert le Parlement européen?* Bruxelles, Éditions Complexes.

Magnette, P. (2000a) *L'Europe L'État et la Démocratie*, Bruxelles, Editions Complexes.

Magnette, P. (2000b) 'Le principe démocratique au-delà de la représentation' in P. Magnette (ed.) *La constitution de l'Europe*, Bruxelles, Editions de l'Université de Bruxelles.

Magnette, P. (2001) 'Entre contrôle parlementaire et "État de droit"; le rôle politique du médiateur dans l'Union européenne', *Revue Française de Science Politique*, vol. 51, no. 6, pp. 933–48.

Magnette, P. (2003a) *Contrôler l'Europe. Pouvoirs et Responsabilité dans l'Union Européenne*, Brussels, Éditions de l'Université de Bruxelles.

Magnette, P. (2003b) '*In the Name of Simplification. Constitutional Rhetoric in the Convention on the Future of Europe*', Paper presented to CIDEL Workshop 2, Deliberative Constitutional Politics in the EU, Albarracín 20–21 June 2003.

Mair, P. (2000) '*Populist Democracy vs Party Democracy*'. Paper presented to ECPR Workshop on Competing Conceptions of Democracy, Copenhagen April 2000.

Majone, G. (1996) 'The European Commission as regulator' in G. Majone (ed.) *Regulating Europe*, London, Routledge, pp. 61–79.

Majone, G. (2001) 'Two Logics of Delegation: Agency and Fiduciary Relations in EU Governance', *European Union Politics*, vol. 2, no. 1, pp. 103–21.

Majone, G. and Everson, M. (2001) 'Institutional Reform, Independent Agencies, Oversight, Coordination and Procedural Control' in O. De Schutter, N. Lebessis and J. Paterson (eds) *Governance in the European Union*, Brussels, European Commission.

Manin, B. (1997) *The Principles of Representative Government*, Cambridge, Cambridge University Press.

March, J. and Olsen, J. (1995) *Democratic Governance*, New York, Free Press.

Mattila, M. (2003) 'Why Bother? Determinants of Turnout in European Elections', *Electoral Studies*, vol. 22, no. 3, pp. 449–68.

Mattila, M. and Lane, J.-E. (2001) Why Unanimity in the Council? A Roll-Call Analysis of Council Voting, *European Union Politics*, vol. 2, no. 1.

Maurer, A. (2001) *National Parliaments after Amsterdam: Adaptation, Recalibration and Europeanisation by Process*. Paper for Working Group Meeting, XXIVth COSAC, 8–9 April 2001.

Maurer, A. (2003a) *Auf dem Weg zur Staatenkammer, Die Reform des Ministerrats der EU*, Berlin, Deutsches Institut für Internationale Politik und Sicherheit.

Maurer, A. (2003b) 'The Legislative Powers and Impact of the European Parliament', *Journal of Common Market Studies*, vol. 41, no. 2, pp. 227–47.

Maurer, A. (2003c) '*The Convention Method for Enhancing EU Democracy*'. Paper presented to CIDEL Workshop 2, Deliberative Constitutional Politics in the EU, Albarracín 20–21 June 2003.

Maurer, A. and Wessels, W. (2001) 'National Parliaments after Amsterdam: From Slow Adapters to National Players' in A. Maurer and W. Wessels (eds) *National Parliaments on their ways to Europe: Losers or Latecomers?* Baden-Baden, Nomos Verlag, pp. 425–76.

Mazey, S. and Richardson, J. (1996) 'Policy Framing: Interest Groups and the lead up to 1996 Intergovernmental Conference', *West European Politics*, vol. 20, no. 3, pp. 111–33.

McKelvey, R. (1976) 'Intransitivities in Multidimensional Voting Models and Some Implications for Agenda Control', *Journal of Economic Theory*, vol. 12, no. 3, pp. 472–82.

Mény, Y. (2002) '*De la démocratie en Europe*: Old Concepts and New Challenges', *Journal of Common Market Studies*, vol. 41, no. 1, pp. 1–13.

Miller, D. (1993) 'Deliberative Democracy and Social Choice' in D. Held (ed.) *Prospects for Democracy. North, South, East, West*, Cambridge, Polity.

Mill, J. S. (1972 [1861]) *Utilitarianism, On Liberty and Considerations on Representative Government*, London, Dent.

Moberg, A. (2002) 'The Nice Treaty and Voting Rules in the Council', *Journal of Common Market Studies*, vol. 40, no. 2, pp. 259–82.

Moore, M. (1995) Democracy and Development in Cross-National Perspective: A New Look at the Statistics', *Democratization*, vol. 2, no. 2.

Moravcsik, A. (1998) *The Choice for Europe. Social Purpose and State Power from Messina to Maastricht*, London, UCL Press.

Moravcsik, A. (2002) 'In Defence of the Democratic Deficit: Reassessing Legitimacy in the European Union', *Journal of Common Market Studies*, vol. 40, no. 3, pp. 603–24.

Moser, P., Mulder, D. and Trout, J. (1998) *The Theory of Knowledge, A Thematic Introduction*, Oxford, Oxford University Press.

Neuhold, C. (2001) 'The "Legislative Backbone" keeping the institution upright. The role of European Parliament committees in the EU policy-making process', *European Integration On-line Papers*, vol. 5, no. 10.

Niedermayer, O. (1990) 'Turn-Out in European Elections', *Election Studies*, 9, pp. 45–50.

Niedermayer, O. (1995) 'Trust and Sense of Community' in O. Niedermayer. and R. Sinnott (eds) *Public Opinion and Internationalized Governance*, Oxford, Oxford University Press, pp. 227–46.

Nordhaus, W. (1975) 'The Political Business Cycle', *Review of Economic Studies*, vol. 42, pp. 169–90.

Nugent, N. (2001) *The European Commission*, Basingstoke, Palgrave.

Offe, C. (1999) 'How Can we Trust our Fellow Citizens?' in M. Warren (ed.) *Democracy and Trust*, Cambridge, Cambridge University Press.

Olson, M. (1965) *The Logic of Collective Action*, Cambridge, Harvard University Press.

Ostrom, E. (1998) 'A Behavioural Approach to the Rational Choice Theory of Collective Action: Presidential Address APSA 1997', *American Political Science Review*, vol. 92, no. 1, pp. 69–93.

Page, E. and Wouters, L. (1994) 'Bureaucratic Politics and Political Leadership in Brussels', *Public Administration*, vol. 72, no. 3, pp. 445–59.

Pennings, P. (2000) 'Parliamentary Control of the Executive in 47 Democracies'. Paper presented to ECPR Joint Sessions April 2000.

Peters, B. G. (1999) *Institutional Theory in Political Science. The 'New Institutionalism'*, London, Pinter.

Peterson, J. (1995a) 'Decision-Making in the European Union: Towards a Framework for Analysis', *Journal of European Public Policy*, vol. 2, no. 1, pp. 69–93.

Peterson, J. (1995b) 'Playing the Transparency Game: Consultation and Policy-Making in the European Community', *Public Administration*, vol. 73, no. 4, pp. 473–92.

Pettit, P. (1997) *Republicanism: A Theory of Freedom and Government*, Oxford, Oxford University Press.

Pierson, P. (2000) 'Increasing Returns, Path Dependence, and the Study of Politics', *American Political Science Review*, vol. 94, no. 2, pp. 251–67.

Plamenatz, J. (1973) *Democracy and Illusion, An Examination of Certain Aspects of Modern Democratic Theory*, London, Longman.

Pollack, M. (1997a) 'Delegation, Agency and Agenda Setting in the European Community', *International Organisation*, vol. 51, no. 1, pp. 99–134.

Pollack, M. (1997b) 'Representing Diffuse Interests in EC Policy-Making', *Journal of European Public Policy*, vol. 4, no. 4, pp. 572–90.

Pollack, M. (1998) 'The Engines of Integration? Supranational Autonomy and Influence in the European Union' in W. Sandholtz and A. Stone Sweet (eds) *European Integration and Supranational Governance*, Oxford, Oxford University Press, pp. 217–50.

Popper, K. (1959) *The Logic of Scientific Discovery*, London, Hutchinson.

Powell, G. B. (1989) 'Constitutional Design and Electoral Control', *Journal of Theoretical Politics*, vol. 1, no. 2, pp. 107–30.

Powell, G. B. (2000) *Elections as Instruments of Democracy: Majoritarian and Proportional Visions*, New Haven, CT, Yale University Press.

Puchala, D. (1972) 'Of Blind Men, Elephants and European Integration', *Journal of Common Market Studies*, vol. 10, no. 2, pp. 267–84.

Putnam, R. (1993) *Making Democracy Work. Civic Traditions in Modern Italy*, Princeton NJ, Princeton University Press.

Quermonne, J.-L. (1994) *La Système Politique de l'Union Européenne*, Paris, Montchrétien.

Radaelli, C. (1999) *Technocracy in the European Union*, London, Longman.

Ranney, A. (1962) *The Doctrine of Responsible Party Government*, Urbana, University of Illinois Press.

Raunio, T. (1999) 'Always One Step Behind? National Legislatures and the European Union', *Government and Opposition*, vol. 34, no. 2, pp. 180–202.

Raunio, T. (2002) in B. Steunenberg and J. Thomassen (eds) *The European Parliament. Moving Towards Democracy in the EU*, Lanham, Maryland, Rowman & Littlefield.

Raunio, T. & Wiberg, M. (2000). 'Does Support Lead to Ignorance? National Parliaments and the Legitimacy of EU Governance', *Acta Politica*, vol. 35, no. 2, pp. 146–68.

Rawls, J. (1993) *Political Liberalism*, New York, Columbia University Press.

Reif, K. and Schmitt, H. (1980) 'Nine Second-Order National Elections: A Conceptual Framework for the Analysis of European Election Results', *European Journal of Political Research*, vol. 8, no. 1, pp. 3–45.

Rinsche, G. and Welle, K. (1999) *Mehrheit für die Mitte: Muß das Europäische Parlament socialitistisch sein?* Bonn, Konrad Adenauer Stiftung, 1999.

Rogoff, K. (1985) 'The Optimal Degree of Commitment to an Intermediate Monetary Target', *Quarterly Journal of Economics*, vol. 100, pp. 169–90.

Rozenberg, O. (2002) *Une Européanisation pas comme les autres. Les variables explicatives de l'examen des affaires européannes par les parlements nationaux.*

Paper presented to the 7th Congress of the French Political Science Association, Lille, 18–21 September 2002.

Ruben, D.-H. (1998) 'The Philosopy of the Social Sciences' in A. Grayling (ed.) *Philosophy 2*, Oxford, Oxford University Press, pp. 420–69.

Ryan, A. (1998) 'Political Philosophy' in A. Grayling (ed.) *Philosophy 2*, Oxford, Oxford University Press, pp. 351–419.

Scharpf, F. (1996) Democratic Policy in Europe, *European Law Journal*, vol. 2, no. 2, pp. 136–55.

Scharpf, F. (1999) *Governing in Europe: Effective and Democratic?*, Oxford, Oxford University Press.

Scharpf, F. (2001) *'European Governance. Common Concerns vs. the Challenge of Diversity'*. MPIFG Working Paper 01/6. Bonn, Max Planck Institut.

Scharpf, F. (2003) *'Problem Solving Effectiveness and Democratic Accountability in the EU'*, MPIFG Working Paper 03/01. Bonn, Max Planck Institut.

Schattsneider, E. (1960) *The Semi-Sovereign People, A Realist's View of Democracy in America*, New York, Holt.

Schmitt, H. and Thomassen, T. (2000) 'Dynamic Representation: the Case of European Integration', *European Union Politics*, vol. 1, no. 3, pp. 340–63.

Schmitter, P. (1992) 'Representation and the Future Euro-Polity', *Staatswissenschaften und Staatspraxis*, vol. 3, no. 3, pp. 379–405.

Schmitter, P. (2000) *How to Democratise the European Union and Why Bother?* Lanham MD, Rowman and Littlefield.

Schmitter, P. (2001) 'What is there to legitimise in the European Union and how might this be accomplished?' *Jean Monnet Working Paper No. 6/01, Symposium: Responses to the European Commission's White Paper on Governance*, Harvard.

Schmitter, P. and Karl, T. (1992) 'The Types of Democracy Emerging in Southern and Eastern Europe and in South and Central America' in P. Volten (ed.) *Bound to Change: Consolidating Democracy in East Central Europe*, New York, Institute for East-West Studies.

Schmitter, P. and Torreblanco, J. (2001) *'Old "Foundations" and New "Rules" for an Enlarged European Union'*, Paper presented to 'Europe – Le Grand Débat', European Commission, Brussels, 15–16 October 2001.

Schönlau, J. (2001) *The EU Charter of Fundamental Rights: Legitimation through Deliberation*, University of Reading. Unpublished PhD thesis.

Schumpeter, J. (1943) *Capitalism, Socialism and Democracy*, London, George Allen & Unwin.

Scully, R. and Farrell, D. (2003) 'MEPs as Representatives: Individual and Institutional Roles', *Journal of Common Market Studies*, vol. 41, no. 2, pp. 269–88.

Shackleton, M. (1998) 'The European Parliament's New Committees of Inquiry: Tiger or Paper Tiger?', *Journal of Common Market Studies*, vol. 36, no. 1, pp. 115–30.

Shaw, J. (1999) 'Postnational Constitutionalism in the European Union', *Journal of European Public Policy*, vol. 6, no. 4, pp. 579–98.

Shepsle, K. and Bonchek, M. (1997) *Analysing Politics: Rationality, Behaviour and Institutions*, New York, W.W. Norton.

Sousa, de P. (2001) 'Independent and Accountable Central Banks and the European Central Bank', *European Integration on-ligne Papers*, vol. 5, no. 9.

SPD (Sozialdemokratische partei Deutschland) (2001). *Keynote Proposal: Responsibility for Europe*.

Spiro, H. (1969) *Responsibility in Government: Theory and Practice*, New York, Van Nostrand Rheinhold Co.

Stone Sweet, A. (2000) *Governing with Judges: Constitutional Politics in Europe*, Oxford, Oxford University Press.

Stone Sweet, A. and Brunell, T. (1998) 'The European Court and National Courts: a Statistical Analysis of Preliminary References 1961–95', *Journal of European Public Policy*, vol. 5, no. 1, pp. 66–97.

Stone Sweet, A. and Caporaso, J. (1998) 'European Court and Integration' in W. Sandholtz and A. Stone Sweet (eds) *European Integration and Supranational Governance*, Oxford, Oxford University Press, pp. 92–133.

Stuart, G., Knowles, V. and Pottebohm, S. (2003) 'Zwischen Legitimät und Effizienz: Ergebnisse der Arbeitsgruppen "Einzelstaatliche Parlamente" und "Verteidigung" im Konvent'. *Integration* 1/03, pp. 10–17.

Sverdrup, U. (2002) 'An Institutional Perspective on Treaty Reform: Contextualising the Amsterdam and Nice Treaties', *Journal of European Public Policy*, vol. 9, no. 1, pp. 120–40.

Sveriges Riksdag (2001) *Synthesis of answers to questionnaire to European Union Affairs Committees*.

Trondal, J. (2001) *Administrative Integration Across Levels of Governance. Integration Through Participation in EU Committees*. Oslo, ARENA Report No. 7/2001.

Trondal, J. (2002) 'Beyond the EU Membership-non-membership Dichotomy? Supranational Identities among National EU Decision-makers', *Journal of European Public Policy*, vol. 9, no. 3, pp. 468–87.

Tsebelis, G. (1994) 'The Power of the European Parliament as a Conditional Agenda-Setter', *American Political Science Review*, vol. 88, no. 1, pp. 128–42.

Tsebelis, G. and Garrett, G. (2000) 'Legislative Politics in the European Union', *European Union Politics*, vol. 1, no. 1, pp. 9–36.

Tsebelis, G. and Kalandrakis, A. (2002) 'The European Parliament and Environmental Legislation' in B. Steunenberg and J. Thomassen (eds) *The European Parliament. Moving Towards Democracy in the EU*, Lanham, Maryland, Rowman & Littlefield.

Tsebelis, G. and Yataganas, X. (2002) 'Veto Players and Decision-Making in the EU After Nice: Policy Stability and Bureaucratic/Judicial Discretion', *Journal of Common Market Studies*, vol. 40, no. 2, pp. 283–307.

UK Government (2000) Prime Minister's Speech to the Polish Stock Exchange 6 October 2000. Available at www.pm.gov.uk/speeches.

UK Government (2002) 'A Clear Course for Europe', Prime Minister's Speech in Cardiff 28 November 2002. Available at www.pm.gov.uk/speeches.

Vreese, C. de (2001) ' "Europe in the News", A Cross-National Comparative Study of the News Coverage of Key EU Events', *European Union Politics*, vol. 2, no. 3, pp. 283–307.

Wallace, H. and Hayes-Renshaw, F. (1997) *The Council of Ministers*, Basingstoke, Macmillan.

Walsh, C. (1995) 'Optimal Contracts for Central Bankers', *American Economic Review*, vol. 85, pp. 150–67.

Warleigh, A. (2001) ' "Europeanizing" Civil Society', *Journal of Common Market Studies*, vol. 39, no. 1, pp. 619–41.

Weale, A. (1999) *Democracy*, London, Macmillan.

Weiler, J. (1997a) 'The European Union Belongs to the Citizens: Three Immodest Proposals', *European Law Review*, vol. 4, no. 4, pp. 495–519.

Weiler, J. (1997b) 'Legitimacy and Democracy of Union Governance' in G. Edwards, and A. Pijpers, (eds) *The Politics of European Union Treaty Reform*, London, Pinter.

Weiler, J., Haltern, U. and Mayer, F. (1995) 'European Democracy and its Critique', *West European Politics*, vol. 18, no. 3, pp. 4–39.

Weiler, J. (1999) *'The Constitution of Europe. "Do the New Clothes have an Emperor?" and Other Essays on European Integration'*, London, Cambridge University Press.

Weiler, J. (2002) 'A Constitution for Europe? Some Hard Choices', *Journal of Common Market Studies*, vol. 40, no. 4, pp. 563–80.

Weir, S. and Beetham, D. (1999) *Political Power and Democratic Control in Britain: The Democratic Audit of the United Kingdom*, London, Routledge.

Wessels, B. (1995) 'Development of Support. Difussion or Democratic Replacement?' in O. Niedermayer and R. Sinnott (eds) *'Public Opinion and Internationalized Governance'*, Oxford, Oxford University Press, pp. 105–137.

Wessels, W. (1997) 'Comitology: fusion in action. Politico–Administrative trends in the EU system', *Journal of European Public Policy*, vol. 5, no. 2, pp. 209–34.

Wessels, W. (2001) 'Nice Results: the Milennium IGC in the EU's Evolution', *Journal of Common Market Studies*, vol. 39, no. 2, pp. 197–219.

Westlake, M. (1997) 'Mad Cows and Englishmen: The Institutional Consequence of the BSE Crisis', *Journal of Common Market Studies*, vol. 35, Annual Review, pp. 11–37.

Wiberg, M. and Raunio, T. (1996) 'Strong Parliament of a Small EU Member State: the Finnish Parliament's Adaptation to the EU', *Journal of Legislative Studies*, vol. 2, no. 4, pp. 302–21.

Wiener, A. and Della Salla, V. (1997) 'Constitution Building and Citizenship Practice: Bridging the Democracy Gap in the EU', *Journal of Common Market Studies*, vol. 35, no. 4, pp. 595–614.

Yataganas, X. (2001) 'The Treaty of Nice: The Sharing of Power and Institutional Balance in the European Union – A Continental Perspective', *European Law Journal*, vol. 7, no. 3, pp. 239–88.

Zanger, S. (2000) 'Good Governance and European Aid: The Impact of Conditionality', *European Union Politics*, vol. 1, no. 3, pp. 293–318.

Zweifel, T. (2002) 'Who is without sin cast the first stone: the EU's democratic deficit in comparison', *Journal of European Public Policy*, vol. 9, no. 5, pp. 812–40.

Index